CHAOS · GAIA · EROS

Chaos · Gaia · Eros

A CHAOS PIONEER UNCOVERS
THE THREE GREAT STREAMS OF HISTORY

Ralph H. Abraham

HarperSanFrancisco
A Division of HarperCollinsPublishers

A Catalyst Book of the General Evolution Research Group.

Book design by Janet Bollow.

FIRST EDITION

Library of Congress Cataloging-in-Publication Data
Abraham, Ralph.
Chaos, gaia, eros : a chaos pioneer uncovers the three great streams of history / Ralph H. Abraham. —1st ed.
p.   cm.
Includes index.
ISBN 0–06–250013–9 (pbk. : alk. paper)
I. Title
BF1999.A224   1994
191—dc20
                                                                94–2820
                                                                CIP

94 95 96 97 98 RRD(H) 10 9 8 7 6 5 4 3 2 1
This edition is printed on acid-free paper that meets the American National Standards Institute Z39.48 Standard.

Dedicated to Hypatia,

A.D. 370–415

Redrawn from the only known rendering of Hypatia

This book is devoted to the Orphic tradition, and to its recovery from the suppressions of the past six thousand years. In this partnership tradition, mathematics and philosophy were united, providing the basis for religion and for daily life. The brilliant mathematician and philosopher Hypatia, a charismatic and popular teacher at the great university of Alexandria, was a wise adviser to individuals and governments. She epitomized this wisdom tradition, and was brutally murdered during its suppression, by a Christian mob. Ironically, after her martyrdom, she was canonized in the Christian hierarchy as Saint Catherine of the Wheel, whose cult began in the ninth century at Mount Sinai.

Drawing by Diane Rigoli, after Charles Kingsley, 1853 A.D.

Caravaggio, *Saint Catherine of Alexandria*. Fondazione Schloss Rohoncz, Lugano. Photo: Alinari/Art Resource, New York.

Saint Catherine of the Wheel

CONTENTS

CONTENTS

ILLUSTRATIONS

_____

FIGURES

_____

ILLUSTRATIONS

TABLES

ACKNOWLEDGMENTS

I am deeply grateful to my mother, Constance Baumann Abraham, who taught me to love math and books; and to my pal, Paul A. Lee, who has given me support, encouragement, pointers to the literature, extensive editorial guidance, and hours and hours of help over these past six years, for which I give great thanks.

I am particularly thankful to the following for their extensive feedback on early drafts of this work: Constance Abraham, Fred Abraham, Walker Abel, Robert Artigiani, Harry Burnham, Warren Burt, Ed Dolph, Ron Eglash, Riane Eisler, Melissa Goodman, Lillien Greeley, Marvin Greenberg, Oliver Haskard, Tanya Haskard, Buffie Johnson, David Loye, Mavrett McClellan, Deena Metzger, Bill Orr, Tim Poston, Suzi Shedd, Ray Gwyn Smith, and William Irwin Thompson.

For inspiration in the 1970s, I am indebted to Fred Abraham, Harry Burnham, and Russell Spring, in Vermont; to S. D. Batish and his family, Emilia Hazelip, the late Erich Jantsch, Terence McKenna, and the late Russell Schofield, in California; to Bill Levy, Jack Moore, Judith Schavrien, and Simon Vinkenoog, in Amsterdam; to René Thom and Christopher Zeeman of the international mathematics community; and to the late Neem Karoli Baba of Uttar Pradesh and his community at Kainchi.

During the 1980s I received valuable support and encouragement from my neighbors and visitors in California, including: Fred Abraham, Andra Akers, José Argüelles, Bob Artigiani, Frank Barr, Chris Berendes, Morris Berman, Linda Blitz, Peter Broadwell, Allyn Brodsky, Norman O. Brown, Nick Burgogne, Fritjof Capra, Ellis Cooper, Jack Corliss, Jim Crutchfield, Larry Cuba, David Dunn, Riane Eisler, Doyne Farmer, Jean Ferreux, Arthur Fischer, Marsha King, Marilyn Ferguson, Alan Garfinkel, Joan Halifax, Stu Hameroff, Donna Haraway, Oscar Hechter, Hazel Henderson, Nick Herbert, Moe Hirsch, Judith Hooper, Arthur Iberall, John Jacobus, Mara Keller, Al Kelley, Kevin Kreitman, Bob Langs, Ervin Laszlo, Tom Levinson, Chris Loye, David Loye, Jim Lovelock, Nancy Kaye Lunney, John Lynch, Terence McKenna, Will McWhinney, Gottfried Mayer-Kress, Deena Metzger, Bill Moore, Gene Moriarty, Charles Muses, Norman Packard, Tim Poston, Jill Purse, Peter Rosencrantz, Otto Rossler, Evan Schaffer, Chris Shaw, Rob Shaw, Barbara Rose Schuler, Bob Schwartz, Rusty Schweickart, Katie Scott, Rupert Sheldrake, David Shire, Steve Smale, Barbara T. Smith, Elaine Smith, Elin Smith, Page Smith, Ray Gwyn Smith, Dorothy Spencer, Bruce Stewart, Brother John Sullivan, Jeremy Taylor, David Thiermann, Jurgen Voigt, Lori Williams, Douglas Wolf, and Connie Zweig.

During the 1990s my family of editors have greatly improved the manuscript: Paul Lee (*immer wieder*), Mark Salzwedel, Tom Grady, Caroline Pincus, and especially, Ralph Melcher.

For assistance with the research, many thanks to Paul Kramerson and Nina Graboi. For vital emotional support, I am grateful to the members of the International Synergy Institute, the General Evolution Research Group, the Lindisfarne Fellowship, and the Institute of Ecotechnics. For material contributions to this work, it is a pleasure to thank the Brookhaven National Laboratory, the Esalen Institute, the Ojai Foundation, the Institut des Hautes Études Scientifiques, the University of California, the villages of Nainital and Dinapani in India, and the cities of Firenze, Siena, and Bologna in Italy.

The University of California at Santa Cruz has been a wonderful home for this project. Here I have met and learned from people such as Gregory Bateson, Norman O. Brown, Paul Lee, and Page Smith. I have had access to 5 million books through MELVYL, the computerized catalog of the California state library system, to superb word processing support from our campus UNIX system, and to redwoods and deer. Also, I have been able to teach this material to wonderful groups of students in my course on the history of mathematics. I am grateful to the staff of the McHenry Library and for the assistance of Diane Rigoli, artist, and Lindsay Kefauver, photo researcher. We are all deeply indebted to our bionic copyeditor, Naomi Lucks.

Grateful acknowledgment is made for permission to quote from the following: Robert Artigiani, A. N. Athanassakis, Gregory Bateson, Morris Berman, Frank Cross, Mary Daly, the *Dartmouth Bible,* Riane Eisler, Jane Ellen Harrison, Alexander Heidel, E. O. James, David Loye, Martin P. Nilsson, Nicolas Rashevsky, Emmet Robbins, A. H. Sayce, Merlin Stone, William Irwin Thompson, E. C. Tolman, and Burton Watson; and from my own articles previously published in *Reality Club 2; International Synergy Journal; Journal of World Futures; Annals of Earth; ReVision; Journal of Biological and Social Structures; ICIS Forum; Physis,* by M. Ceruti and E. Laszlo; *Cognitive Maps,* by Robert Artigiani, Ignazio Masulli, Vilmos Csanyi, and Ervin Laszlo; *Dharma/Gaia,* by Allan Hunt-Badiner; *Qualitative Models,* by Paul A. Fishwick; and *Cooperation,* by Allan Combs.

TO THE READER

When my agent, John Brockman, first saw the manuscript for this book in December 1990, he exclaimed: "Oh, what a chaotic manuscript!"

Indeed, this is not a normal narrative book. If it were, it would run to many volumes, like Toynbee's or Voegelin's. I do not have time to write them, and you would not have time to read them. Instead, I have tried to compact a large amount of historical information in such a way that my view of the data is communicated to you by a kind of resonance, like poetry. By means of a chaotic collage of ideas, data, graphics, rhyming sentence fragments, and telepathic communion, I hope to evoke a *metapattern* of history. Furthermore, a book on the Orphic trinity *should* be chaotic, Gaianic, and erotic!

This book collects evidence for a theory. Rather than expand this collage of information into a pretense of normal narrative, for you to recondense in your own mind, I have kept it in condensed form. The information is not in linear (one-dimensional) order. Its natural order is multidimensional: one-dimensional time, two-dimensional space, plus many-dimensional ideas. Thus the same theme may be traced through time, over space, or through an evolution of ideas or myths. Wittgenstein wrote in the Preface to his *Philosophical Investigations,* "The very nature of the investigation . . . compels us to travel over a wide field of thought criss-cross in every direction. Thus this book is really only an album."

This project has provided me with many wonderful hours in the library. Its best function may be to lead you to some good books. I have included a large number of pointers to the literature. If you want to pursue a topic, endnote numbers in the text lead to the Notes section at the back of the book, which refers to books listed in the Bibliography, which leads in turn to your local library or bookstore.

The library has its dark side also. While some of the newer books contain awareness of the urgent issues of bias (of gender, race, and so on) emerging at present, older ones naturally do not. It is impossible to revise all of the older material according to this new awareness. As I have relied heavily on the library for the substance of this book, it contains unwanted biases I am unable to dispel.

CHAOS • GAIA • EROS

————————

The Orphic Revival

Since 1960, I've been working in the area of dynamical systems theory, a classical branch of mathematics created by Isaac Newton in the seventeenth century. In the midst of the cultural upheavals of the 1960s, great inroads were made in the field of dynamical systems, due in part to the computer revolution. Dynamical systems theory deals with moving systems, such as the solar system, and the patterns they trace in space and time. Newton discovered mathematical laws that such systems obey, and constructed mathematical models that are abstract analogues of their space-time patterns. His discovery has been credited as one of the greatest intellectual contributions ever made by a single person.

About a century ago, dynamical systems theory was revolutionized by Henri Poincaré, the great French mathematician, when he discovered models for highly complex motions (which later came to be called *strange attractors*).[1] By the late 1960s, numerous examples of strange attractors had been discovered in computer simulations.

In 1972 I traveled to the Institut des Hautes Études Scientifiques, in France, to visit with René Thom. In his book on *morphogenesis,* the study of pattern formation, Thom introduced a new language for the application of dynamical systems theory, which included the terms *attractor, basin of attraction,* and *catastrophe.* I was interested in pursuing these ideas with him, but when I arrived, Thom was onto something new. He showed me a book of photographs by Hans Jenny, an amateur scientist from Basel. The photographs showed forms created by sound vibrations in sand, powder, and water. They were suggestive of galaxies, plants, brain waves, memories, hallucinations, and abstract works of art. A theory of morphogenesis, in which the mysteries of creation were seemingly revealed, was projected wordlessly by the book. My mind reeled with new possibilities for the application of dynamical systems theory to nature and society.

That summer I went to India on holiday and soon found myself living in a cave in the jungle of the Himalayas, a mile above sea level. The cave had been inhabited for centuries by jungle yogis, and in it I experienced a number of illuminations on the concepts of vibration in Hindu philosophy,

---

One of the main goals of this book is to introduce the concept of dynamical historiography, *the application of the mathematical theory of dynamical systems, chaos, and bifurcations to the patterns of history. It is hoped that from the future development of this mode of inquiry we may evolve a better understanding of ourselves and our evolutionary challenges.*

and on harmony and resonance concepts in mathematics, music, and mysticism.

When I returned to California in 1974, I began a program of research and teaching on vibrations, chaos, computation, and computer graphics, delving deeply into the histories of these subjects, going ever backward—to the Baroque, to the Renaissance, to ancient Greece, and beyond. Soon after my return, I found other people who shared these interests, including Terence McKenna and the late Erich Jantsch. Erich was a missionary of *general evolution theory,* a whole systems theory evolving from the work of a number of twentieth-century scientists interested in conceptualizing a science of the all-and-everything. The theory offered a strategy by which to understand the structure of history through the kind of mathematical model introduced by René Thom. Here, my Himalayan cave illuminations could be abstracted and applied to society, to the history of consciousness (and unconsciousness), and therefore to the future.

I've spent the last twenty years exploring a broad range of applications for these concepts, on which this book is a meditation. It offers a conceptual model for history, constructed from the mathematical tools conceived by René Thom and applied in the style of Erich Jantsch. Such a model may be crucial for understanding our history and as an aid in creating our future.

The Chaos Revolution, Gaia Hypothesis, and Erodynamics

During the 1970s paradigm shifts within the sciences began to emerge into public view. Around 1973 new dynamical models were applied to turbulent fluid motions (for example, boiling water[2]

and a dripping faucet[3]), but it was not until 1975 that these models were connected with the word *chaos.*[4] The terms *strange attractor* and *dynamical systems theory* were replaced by *chaotic attractor* and *chaos theory.* The new theory swept through the sciences in a wave of renewal. The Chaos Revolution was underway.

Journalists began calling me to ask: "What is chaos theory? Does it have anything to do with chaos in ordinary life? What is the theory good for? Why are scientists so excited about it?"

These questions, which I could not easily answer, drove me deeply into the literature of myths and cultural history. I found that the word *Chaos* first appeared in a book called *Theogony,* by Hesiod, one of the early Greek poets. His poem is a creation myth telling stories of the origins of the gods. Here the word *chaos* does not mean disorder. Instead, it represents an abstract cosmic principle referring to the source of all creation. It also appears in connection with the two other fundamental concepts: *Gaia* (the created universe) and *Eros* (the creative impulse).

I was amazed to realize that this same trinity, which preceded the creation of the gods and goddesses of the usual pantheon of early Greek paganism (also called *Orphism*), is also associated with three revolutionary movements underway in the sciences:

- The Chaos Revolution was named in 1975 for a new branch of mathematics that provides models for many intrinsically irregular natural processes.
- The Gaia Hypothesis, named in 1973, proposes a self-regulation capability of the complex system composed of earth, ocean, atmosphere, and the living ecosystems of our

---

Chaos does not mean disorder. . . . It represents an abstract
cosmic principle referring to the source of all creation.

planet. According to Gaia theory, which views Earth as a living system, the biosphere acts to create and maintain favorable conditions for life.

• Erodynamics, named in 1989, applies dynamical systems theory to human social phenomena.

What strange synchronicity, I wondered, led to three different recent innovations in the sciences, in apparently independent developments, sharing a common mathematical basis, bearing names (Chaos, Gaia, Eros) that are associated in Hesiod's trinity almost three thousand years ago?

An Orphic Theory: Three Conjectures

One discovery led to another. As my trail traversed the boundaries of many disciplines, a picture or metapattern gradually emerged. I saw the residue of suppressed themes of great antiquity emerging from the collective unconscious and forcing their way into science, the dominant religion of modern times. I call it an Orphic theory, with three conjectures.

CONJECTURE 1: THREE PHASES

The meanderings of human history and prehistory during these past 25,000 years reveal a persistent pattern of cyclic recurrence in three phases, associated with the three root concepts of the Orphic trinity (Chaos, Gaia, and Eros). This pattern is recognizable today in the context of the new mathematics of space-time patterns called chaos theory.

The importance of this conjecture, if true, is that it enables us to better understand our own place in time and in the natural dynamics of history. With this enhanced understanding of our past and our future, we may better face our evolutionary challenges.

CONJECTURE 2: THE ORPHIC TRADITION

The three concepts of the Orphic trinity (Chaos, Gaia, and Eros) belong to a continuous tradition flowing

from the Paleolithic past to the present. Occasionally, one or more has been suppressed, only to surface again. The meanings of these three abstract concepts (and the names, images, genders, and other aspects of their cultural representations) have undergone gradual, and occasionally sudden, changes over the past 25,000 years.

I call this irrepressible theme in our cultural history the *Orphic tradition,* or the *long line of Orphism.* Although the word *Orphism* usually refers to the male-centered religion of ancient Crete, Mycenae, and Greece founded by Orpheus, it has its origins in the worship of a Divine Mother and her Divine Son or Lover. What I call the *Orphic revival* is the spontaneous upwelling of this old current after its long cultural repression.

The characteristic features of this tradition are the trinity:

• Chaos, the creative void, source of all form
• Gaia, the physical existence and living spirit of the created world
• Eros, the spiritual medium connecting Chaos and Gaia; the creative impulse

Some secondary characteristics of this tradition include:

• a regard for all life as sacred (sometimes manifest as vegetarianism)
• a high priority for peace and security
• the avoidance of violence
• rituals and myths focused on love
• sexual laxity
• a special regard for music and math

The importance of this conjecture, if true, is that it allows us to utilize the upwelling force of this cultural current to help us create a future society that is peaceful, maintainable, and beautiful— in fact, an Orphic utopia. I believe this kind of utopian vision is a fundamental human activity essential for our evolution.

CONJECTURE 3: OUR TRANSFORMATION

The Chaos Revolution currently underway in the sciences, and the related paradigm shifts associated with the names Gaia and Eros, signal a major phase shift in history.

The importance of this conjecture, if it is true, is that it gives us an opportunity to end entirely the harmful repression of chaos, which may be crucial for our understanding of, and harmonious coexistence with, nature and the development of a peaceful global society.

How This Book Is Organized

This book presents the evidence I've uncovered to support my case for the Orphic theory. It's organized into three parts, corresponding to the three conjectures presented above. Each part is divided into two triads, for a total of six chapters per part.

PART 1: THE ORPHIC TRINITY IN HISTORY

Part 1 presents the case for the first conjecture: that our prehistory and history over the past 25,000 years falls naturally into three phases, or epochs, associated with the abstract cosmic principles of the Orphic trinity, Chaos, Gaia, and Eros.

I use the word *history* usually in reference to the written records of human affairs. Occasionally, it occurs in place of *prehistory,* for the unwritten record revealed through archaeology. I use the word *myth* for the written records of oral literature, whether religious or secular, ancient or recent. *Metahistory* refers to the overall pattern of prehistory and history as seen by prehistorians and historians.

Chapters 1, 2, and 3 introduce simple concepts from the mathematical theory of dynamical systems—attractors and bifurcations—providing a framework for viewing metahistory. Chapters 4, 5, and 6 develop the idea that history (and prehistory) can be seen in a cycle of three phases, associated with the concepts of the Orphic trinity.

The Gaian Epoch began with agriculture, 12,000 years ago; the Eros phase began with the wheel, six thousand years ago; and the Chaos stage is beginning now. For reasons related to the mathematical concepts, I also call these three phases the *Static, Periodic,* and *Chaotic Epochs,* respectively. Their spans:

- Static/Gaia: 10,000–4000 B.C. (agriculture and partnership)
- Periodic/Eros: 4000 B.C.–A.D. 1962 (the wheel, patriarchy, and science)
- Chaotic: after 1962 (neopagan and postmodern).

Transitions between these epochs, which I call *bifurcations* (for reasons that will become clear in the text), are the Neolithic Revolution (ca. 10,000 B.C.); the arrival of the wheel, patriarchal dominance, and science (ca. 4000 B.C.); and the Chaos Revolution (beginning around 1962 and ongoing), with its paradigm shifts associated with the Gaia Hypothesis and erodynamics.

PART 2: THE ORPHIC TRINITY IN MYTH

Part 2 explores the roots of the three dynamical revolutions that arose in the 1960s, digging deep into the matriarchal past. Thanks to the feminist scholarship of the last several decades, in which the maternal roots of our culture have been excavated from patriarchal oblivion, the dynamical pattern of our evolution can be seen emerging from mystery. I present evidence for our second conjecture, tracing the Orphic trinity of Chaos, Gaia, and Eros backward through time—from Hesiod in

---

The Chaos Revolution currently underway in the sciences, and the related paradigm shifts associated with the names Gaia and Eros, signal a major phase shift in history.

ancient Greece, to the dawn of history in Sumer, and on back into prehistory—seeking the ultimate meaning of our current social transformation.

In chapters 7, 8, and 9, we move through time in a fast-forward collage: from Cro-Magnon caves to Anatolian farms to the city-states of Sumer, Babylon, Assyria, Ugarit, Canaan, Egypt, Crete, Mycenae, Greece, and the Roman Empire. Along the way we see the trinity of the goddess passing through the Orphic phase and turning into the patriarchal trinity of Christianity, with Jesus replacing Orpheus as the Shepherd of Being. Most of the fundamental concepts of the original trinity are lost or degraded in the transition.

Chapters 10, 11, and 12 look at the meanings assigned to these concepts in the myths of early cultures. This evolution is an example of a dynamical process I call *mythogenesis,* the process of historical development of the religious fundament in a culture—its rituals, myths, paradigms, social customs, cognitive maps, beliefs, and so on, as seen from an evolutionary perspective. In the process of historical scholarship, we find that most of this information is encoded for us in the mythology of the culture.

PART 3: THE ORPHIC TRINITY IN SCIENCE

Part 3 is devoted to three scientific revolutions occasioned by the emergence of dynamics concepts, showing that they constitute an Orphic revival. These chapters make a case for the third conjecture of our theory, which interprets current events in the physical, biological, and social sciences (Chaos Revolution, Gaia Hypothesis, and Erodynamics) as an Orphic revival and as an onset of the Chaotic Epoch.

Chapters 13, 14, and 15 set the stage for our consideration of current events by reviewing the repression of the chaos concept within the sciences. This story spans the Eros Epoch, from around 4000 B.C. to 1962. It opens with the over-running of the partnership (goddess) culture by patriarchal dominators, who portrayed chaos as

evil. Their fundamental m[...] the slaying of the (female [...] male war god. Subsequent [...] as early Christianity, late [...] dors, the Cathars, the Ren[...] were violently suppressed. [...] given to the period around 1[...] Newton and the emergence of scientism as the dominator religion.

Chapters 16, 17, and 18 illustrate the three major shifts underway in the sciences today. I've chosen a few of many possible examples to illustrate the impact of the Orphic trinity on science.

- The *Chaos Revolution* began in the physical sciences. Our example is the science of celestial dynamics, the newly acknowledged chaotic motions of the planets and comets in our solar system. The truth is that virtually all areas of the physical sciences have been affected by the Chaos Revolution.
- The *Gaia Hypothesis,* which began in the biological sciences, affirms the intelligence of the whole life system of our planet in creating and regulating the physical conditions optimal for the emergence and maintenance of life. The history of the temperature and climate of Earth, with its regulation by the biosphere and its irregularities (ice ages) caused by chaos in the solar system, is used to illustrate Gaian theory. Biogeography, ocean biology, the origin of life, and many other areas of biological science have been transformed by the Gaia Hypothesis.
- *Erodynamics,* which began in the social sciences, is the current research frontier of applied chaos theory. It provides the basis for understanding the symbiosis of human populations and the biosphere, and explores dynamic models for the world economy and the global environment in tightly coupled interaction. Psychology, social theory, management science, and anthropology have all been transformed by erodynamics.

...ive today in the midst of a major cultural transformation that echoes similar events throughout our history. Our choice to nurture this historical imperative, rather than pursuing yet another suppression, may determine our future, and even whether our species has a future.

We are now at a hinge in history, not an apocalypse. Our own participation in the creation of the future may be improved in quality and power by mathematically illuminated images of space-time patterns in our history that are in harmony and resonance with similar rhythms of the universe and Earth. We can choose to participate optimistically in the present metamorphosis, trying to bias the outcome toward a new social organization with a healthy future. We may reclaim the best features of the old traditions—pagan, Orphic, and archaic—as well as those of the modern world.

Most especially, we may use mathematics in its sacred role, midway between heaven and earth, to restore our spiritual connection to the divine patterns that have successfully guided our evolution through the challenges and metamorphoses we've met in our long line of genesis.

Here, I rest my case.

We live today in the midst of a major cultural transformation that echoes similar events throughout our history. Our choice to nurture this historical imperative, rather than pursuing yet another suppression, may determine our future, and even whether our species has a future.

PART ONE

Dynamics and the Orphic Trinity in History

Dynamic concepts have always been crucial to our history and our survival as a species. For example, the dynamic concepts of time, manifest in the clock and the calendar, led to the Agricultural Revolution. The dynamic concept of cyclic behavior, which materialized as the wheel, led to the Urban Revolution. Understanding these concepts gives us a new and perhaps startling perspective on history, and allows us to see the metapattern that weaves together many strands.

For example, the three parts of this book, a trinity, are relatively independent. Part 2 presents the Orphic trinity in myth, and part 3 explores the Orphic trinity in science; together they express the breadth and depth of the current Orphic revival. Recently, however, the Orphic trinity of myth has appeared in science, and this is an especially noteworthy event—a major paradigm shift, or bifurcation, in history itself. This understanding is based on a new view of history, a view conditioned by developments in the mathematical theory of dynamical systems, chaos, and bifurcations. Here, in part 1, we present a compact introduction to this new view of history, called *dynamical historiography*.

Understanding the dynamics of history may be of greater importance now than ever before. By failing to surmount the evolutionary challenges of population explosion and ecological catastrophe, our own culture—perhaps even our species—may be facing extinction. Without the lessons of history, we may have no future.

UNDERSTANDING THE DYNAMICS OF HISTORY

Dynamics is a branch of mathematics that provides models for processes and their transformations, called *bifurcations*. The application of dynamic concepts to the process of history had already occurred to Newton in the 1660s. For about a century, the theory of dynamical systems has been extensively applied in all of the sciences, primarily to *periodic processes*, such as tides and daylight. The application of this

Without the lessons of history, we may have no future.

theory to history has led to an appreciation of historical cycles. Since the beginning of the Chaos Revolution of the 1970s, dynamical systems theory has provided models for *chaotic processes* and their bifurcations, thus improving our chances for understanding history—which certainly seems chaotic.

In order to connect dynamics and history, we must think about the history of history. We have dynamical metaphors appropriate to the description of cultural history, including evolution, cycles, progress, transformation, and selection. On another level, we may apply these concepts to the evolution of our image of history. First we must acknowledge the arbitrariness of our understanding of history. Although the past differs from the future in having happened already, our knowledge of the past (at least the distant past) is almost as uncertain as our knowledge of the future. There are different views of the past, just as there are different views of the future in science fiction and fantasy literature. Our views of the past are based on a cul-

tural image, paradigm, or filter—or, as we will call it in this part, a *cognitive map*. Thus our view of the past radiates from the present, just as our view of the future does.

Our images of both past and future are evolving in the present. When we experience a shift of paradigm in the present, we revise our view of history. At some prior shifts, the older histories were actually burned and replaced with the revisions. Now, however, we have a rapid accumulation of parallel histories. *Historiography*, comprising the history of history, the theory of history, and the philosophy of history, has become an active scholarly pursuit. By *dynamical historiography*, then, we mean the application of dynamical systems concepts and models to history.

According to dynamical historiography, social evolution is a dynamic process: cultures are born in profusion, develop variously, submit to selection processes, and die. Gods, rituals, and myths appear on the screen of history, diffuse and transform, and disappear in a process

---

Our view of the past radiates from the present.

called *mythogenesis*. With the aid of process metaphors, we try to understand cultural evolution, and through this understanding surmount the challenges that natural selection applies to the mutations of cultures.

We begin our introduction to dynamical historiography with a look at some topics that belong to historiography: hermeneutics, cognitive maps, and a survey of early steps toward the dynamics of history, including a survey of various theories of cycles in history. Part 1 culminates with a theory of the history of consciousness based on the dynamical concepts of attractors and bifurcations. One type of attractor is the *chaotic attractor:* a new model for chaos provided by the mathematical theory of dynamical systems. It empowers the Chaos Revolution now underway in the sciences. The new mathematical knowledge of this attractor and its bifur-cations gives us hope for a new understanding of history, a revolution in dynamical historiography. A consideration of this possibility, and its application to the mythic layer of history, are among the goals of this book.

THE CONJECTURE

Part 1 explores the following conjecture, which was fully outlined in the Introduction: *The meanderings of human history and prehistory, during these past 25,000 years, reveal a pattern of cyclic recurrence in three phases, associated with the three root concepts of the Orphic trinity.* The first six chapters of this book, then, will clarify the relationships between (1) the three kinds of attractors in the mathematical theory of dynamical systems; (2) the three epochs of history and prehistory; and (3) the three cosmic principles of the Orphic trinity.

Social evolution is a dynamic process. . . . Gods, rituals, and myths appear on the screen of history, diffuse and transform, and disappear in a process called mythogenesis.

DYNAMICAL VIEWS OF HISTORY

The World According to Grok

CHAPTER 1

In spring 1985 Gene Moriarty came to my office to introduce himself. A professor at California State University, San Jose, and my neighbor in Santa Cruz, he had written a paper on Lewis Frye Richardson's arms race model. Although I had heard of Richardson through Gregory Bateson, I knew little about him. Gene gave me his own excellent paper, which summarized Richardson's biography and ideas, and described hermeneutics as well. But I had never heard of hermeneutics, so I went to Paul Lee, my friend and neighbor, a philosopher. He gave me an impromptu mini-lecture on Wilhelm Dilthey, Paul Ricoeur, Hans Georg Gadamer, Jürgen Habermas, and Jacques Derrida, and an enormous burden of books. As I kept stumbling over the word *hermeneutics*, I took inspiration from my former neighbor, Robert Heinlein, and replaced it with the word *grok*.

The Grok Circle

We grok something (an archaeological find, artifact, art work, text, poem, letter, natural process, and so on) by a cycle of observing, thinking, poking, and once again observing. This is not the same as explaining it, representing it, or translating it.

The word grok . . . *is a translation of the technical term* Verstehen, *meaning "to understand."*

We grok something (an archaeological find, artifact, artwork, text, poem, letter, natural process, and so on) by a cycle of observing, thinking, poking, and once again observing. This is not the same as explaining it, representing it, or translating it.

Robert Heinlein introduced the word *grok* in his science fiction classic of 1961, *Stranger in a Strange Land.*[1] It's a translation into English of the technical term *Verstehen,* which was introduced by Wilhelm Dilthey into the literature of hermeneutics. *Verstehen* (from the German verb *zu verstehen,* meaning to understand) refers, not unlike the word *hermeneutics* (which comes from a Greek root meaning "to interpret"), to a special form of sympathetic, experiential, and intuitive understanding.[2]

What I call the *grok circle* is similar to the dialectical process of thesis, antithesis, and synthesis, and it constitutes the basic process in hermeneutical thought, called the *hermeneutical circle*. Some think of it as a spiral—the turning of this circle or spiral being the motor for the growth of our understanding. The evolution of science, of Old Testament scholarship, or of Cretan archaeology, for example, may be regarded as a hermeneutical spiral.[3] Understanding this spiral may be crucial for our own evolution, as we struggle with the challenges of postmodern planetary society.[4]

Historical Bifurcations

Despite their seeming differences, the discovery of the wheel around 4000 B.C. and the Chaos Revolution that began in the 1970s are related and significant events in history. Dynamical historiography calls them *bifurcations*, after the mathematical events in which *attractors* (representing the stable regimes of history) appear, disappear, or undergo radical transformations. For example, the development of agriculture accompanied a social transformation in which a stable form of society—hunting and gathering—destabilized, dissolved, shifted shape, and reformed into a new stable structure. This metamorphosis is a canonical example of a bifurcation in history.[5]

After the advent of the wheel, around 4000 B.C., and the related Urban Revolution, natural philosophy began a process of disintegration into numerous specialities. This disintegration could be understood as a sequence of bifurcations, in which one discipline divided into two, as in biological cell division. Social structures became increasingly hierarchical. A bifurcation in social structure created two distinct castes: the sacred and the secular. Math (including calendrics and astronomy) became the specialty of the priestly elite. Commoners participated in rituals. As we will see later, the Indo-European New Year festivals—featuring the sacred marriage, the annual return of the goddess from the underworld, and the domination of Chaos by Order—may be seen as a cultural response to this bifurcation between the sacred and the secular. In the festival, the priests obtained the blessing of the goddess for the common welfare.

The History of Consciousness

The Greek word *physis* means "what grows." The word *nature*, in ancient times, referred to the materials, the characteristics, the properties, and the spirits of things.[6] The history of natural philosophy, or *physiology*, as it was called by Thales (one of the first Greek philosophers), is all about Mother Nature.

✸

This philosophical tradition may be traced back to Cro-Magnon times, 25,000 B.C., in which the late Paleolithic cave paintings have mathematical, as well as astronomical and mythological, significance. Further, they include symbols that may be among the roots of the Old European alphabet.[7] We will be satisfied here with the written historical records of the European tradition, especially:

- *the ancient Greek literature,* from Homer and Hesiod around 800 B.C. to the end of the Eleusinian mysteries and the destruction of the Alexandrian Library in 641 A.D.;[8]
- *the Alexandrian Hermetic Corpus,* with its devious transmission through the Dark Ages and arrival in Italy in 1456, after the fall of Byzantium and the flight of the Greeks; and
- *the Neoplatonic writings* (Plotinus, Porphyry, Iamblichus) surviving in the early Christian, Gnostic, Sufi, and Kabbalist communities, propelled toward Italy along with the expulsion of the Jews and Moors from Spain in 1492.

Throughout this voyage, physiology maintained its integrity as the unified science of mind and nature, although there were some losses of essential branches. This is shown as the trunk of the tree of perennial philosophy, in figure 1.1, in the style of the Catalan mystic and poet, Ramon Llull.

Llull was a natural philosopher in the Middle Ages, when the Jewish, Christian, and Moslem societies were harmoniously intermixed. He had an important influence on the Renaissance Neoplatonists, and on the seventeenth-century German philosopher and mathematician Gottfried Wilhelm Leibniz. Llull's tree of knowledge is shown in figure 1.2.[9]

THE PHYSICALIST/VITALIST SPLIT

Following the Renaissance, physiology disintegrated into distinct specialities. First came the basic split between matter and spirit marked by the departure of John Dee from England (ending his leadership of its intellectual life) in 1583, the burning of Giordano Bruno in 1600, the death of Queen Elizabeth I in 1603, the crucial dream of René Descartes in 1617, and the efforts of Marin Mersenne around 1623 to separate science from magic.[10] This split, culminating in the debates of Newton and Leibniz in 1716, still dominates the growth of science.[11]

Then came the branching of physicalism and vitalism with the synthesis of urea in 1828.[12] The physicalists believed that matter was dead, and the chemical synthesis of urea, an organic chemical previously produced only by living bodies, seemed to

The physicalists believed that matter was dead. . . . The vitalists maintained that life was maintained by a nonphysical life force, or soul.

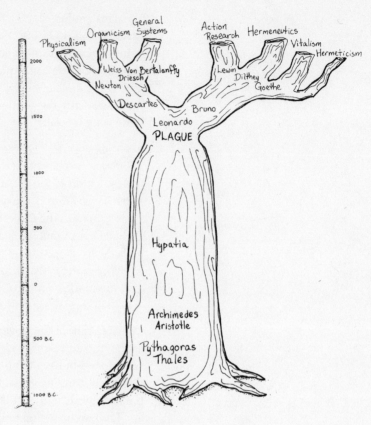

FIGURE 1.1
The Tree of Perennial Philosophy

Drawing by Diane Rigoli, © Ralph H. Abraham.

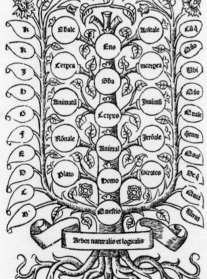

FIGURE 1.2
The Tree of Ramon Llull

From Ramon Llull, 1512.

validate their view. The vitalists maintained that life was maintained by a nonphysical life force, or soul. Soon after this branching, hermeticism (the magical Alexandrian heritage fundamental to the Renaissance, which included magic, astrology, and alchemy) departed from vitalism, and virtually died.[13]

Then came the birth of organicism from physicalism, an attempt to regain the advantages of vitalism without its life force. And from organicism came holism, general systems theory, and recently, general evolution theory.[14]

Meanwhile, after Goethe, and after biology was converted to physicalism,[15] hermeneutics split off from vitalism, trying to keep the spirit present within the social sciences. Social psychologist Kurt Lewin's contact with the hermeneutical tradition of

✿ DYNAMICS AND THE ORPHIC TRINITY IN HISTORY

Dilthey in Berlin led to his development of social psychology and action research, which branched from hermeneutics, courageously carrying out the hermeneutic program in the practical context of social psychology.[16] As we see in figure 1.1, these two inner branches, general systems theory and action research, may soon rejoin in an attempt to repair the physicalist/vitalist split, and they may then reenchant the world.[17] This is the goal of *erodynamics,* which will be discussed later in this book.

COGNITIVE RESONANCE:
VIBRATING TOGETHER

We may regard the evolution of consciousness, and the growth of this tree, as a manifestation of *morphic resonance* (or, in this context, *cognitive resonance*).[18] The process of the grok circle, in the mind of an individual scholar, takes the form of an oscillation (perhaps with a relatively long temporal period). Thus a group (circle, school, community) of scholars may be modeled as a *vibratory field,* that is, a group of oscillators with some degree of mutual influence or interaction.[19]

Further, we may extend the resonance concept to a field of *chaotic systems,* as it is known that regular patterns emerge from these fields of chaos.[20] This provides an even better model for a group of scholars, who are notorious for their disorderly conduct. With mutual coupling of these oscillators through written or spoken communications, the vibratory field evolves toward some kind of coherent, cooperative behavior, or self-resonance. Adjacent schools (for example, English and Continental schools of the philosophy of science) may then resonate with each other, as do adjacent piano strings. In this way the mechanics of resonance may function in a grok circle, supporting the understanding of the history of consciousness and the evolution of culture.

Patterns in Consciousness

Cultural evolution may thus be envisioned, in the spirit of general evolution theory, as an *autopoetic* (self-organizing, pattern-formation) process in a vibratory field. This evolution-theoretic view of the advance of consciousness makes space for everyone in the pattern-formation process of history, or *morphogenesis.* It's not a question of a few intellectual leaders inventing new thoughts, musical styles, scientific theories, and technological gadgets. All who wish to participate may do so, just by paying attention and interacting.

We may think of three similar processes of morphogenesis:

- Geological forms evolve in the geosphere of earth, ocean, and air.
- Life forms evolve in the biosphere of all living matter.

- Thought forms evolve in the noosphere of all conscious minds.

The harmony of these spheres, interacting in resonance, constitutes a model for the planetary mind, which may itself be a resonance phenomenon in which *noogenesis* is directed by nature herself.[21] It may even *be* nature herself.

Grokking in Science

The grok circle or spiral, applied to the history of science, is the basis of one of the main branches of the philosophy of science.[22] In fact, Kurt Lewin, the father of social psychology, turned the grok circle into a scientific method, called *action research*. Lewin put it as simply as possible in 1945: "Action research consists of analysis, fact-finding or evaluation; and then a repetition of this whole circle of activities; indeed, a spiral of such circles."[23]

This spiral of circles may be interpreted as observation/ analysis, experiment/theory, intervene/explain, or participate/ model. Each arc of the cycle is very complex, and has an extensive literature.

MODELS AND OBSERVATIONS

The concept of *model* varies through an enormous spectrum of meanings. Some similar words found in the literature of the philosophy of science include: paradigm, homology, simile, analogy, figure, metaphor, explanation, theory, catachresis, artifact, and exemplar.[24] Here we are dealing with attempts to circumscribe *mimesis*, or cognitive strategies of representation, in a spectrum from larger to smaller representations.

The word *observation* similarly has its own spectrum of meanings. These range from detached observer totally isolated from the target system, to the diary of a lover: the spectrum of participation or involvement.

BACK TO THE GROK CIRCLE

It is implicit in grok theory that *the model and the observation are linked* within the grok circle, as shown in figure 1.3.

Observation is done in the ambience of a model, while the model is created in the context of an observation strategy. The rotation of this cycle advances the adequacy of the model and the quality of our observations, and hence our understanding of the world around us.

For example, the text may be read under the sway of a theory of interpretation, or model. Then the model may be modified according to the understanding of the text. The text may then be reread according to the new model, and so on. In this way we have evolution in understanding, which comprises grokking.

The model and the observation are linked within the grok circle. . . . Major shifts in the model, called paradigm shifts, are experienced as revolutions in archaeology, the sciences, the arts, in social organization, as revisions of history, and so on.

Major shifts in the model, called *paradigm shifts,* are experienced as revolutions in archaeology, the sciences, the arts, in social organization, as revisions of history, and so on.

SCIENTISM

In the dogma of scientism, a particular model becomes identified with its target system in nature. This sin is particularly prominent in the physical sciences, in which the fancier mathematical models of simple, physical processes are thought *to be* the actual processes. These models, ironically, are made from the mathematical tools introduced by Newton, a grok hermeticist throughout his life.[25] According to grok, mathematical models (although elegant and abstract) are just another way of grokking. That is, the cycle of model and target system, as they evolve in our collective consciousness, comprise grokking. Mathematical models have no other meaning. But to the disciple of scientism, the models become reality.

Scientism is the antithesis of a grok view of the history of science. . . . To the disciple of scientism, the models become reality.

Summary

The conflict between the pragmatic approach of hermeneutics/ vitalism and the dogmatic stance of scientism/logicism/physicalism is a fundamental force in the history of science.[26] What we may learn of its intrinsic action from a study of the Scientific Revolution may be applied to help us to surmount our difficulties in the present time. For example, many social and cultural problems derive from the dominator paradigm adopted by cultures and maintained by the myths and rituals of our primary religion, scientism. An understanding of mythogenesis as the hermeneutics of our own existence may guide us back to the partnership structures of earlier, pagan times. In the next chapter, we will turn to mythogenesis.

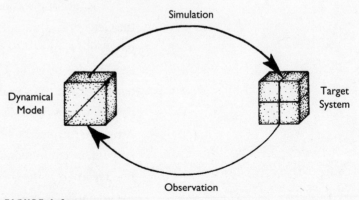

FIGURE 1.3
The Grok Circle

Drawing by Diane Rigoli, © Ralph H. Abraham.

Cognitive Maps and Mythogenesis

CHAPTER 2

In May 1985 I was working in my office at the University of California at Santa Cruz. Social psychologist Dave Loye called from Carmel, a small city about fifty miles away. He introduced himself as a social scientist familiar with my work, and the partner of Riane Eisler, author of *The Chalice and the Blade*. He said that general systems philosopher Ervin Laszlo was coming from Italy for a visit, and that the three of them would like to meet me. We made a date for lunch the following week at the Whole Earth, a restaurant on the UCSC campus with a wonderful view of the Pacific. On the morning of our appointment, I was absorbed in writing. It was late when I remembered lunch, and rushed to the restaurant. There they were, pacing and worried, but we immediately fell into a close friendship and partnership that persists to this day.

This meeting was one of the key steps in the founding of the General Evolution Research Group (GERG) and its journal, *World Futures: The Journal of General Evolution*. Stimulated by this meeting, I began a series of short papers on dynamics and the social sciences, which culminate in the last chapter of this book. Dave, Riane, and Ervin, along with Bob Artigiani, the historian and fellow GERGian, were particularly interested in modeling social transformations. Through Bob I learned of the theory of cognitive maps, and many of the references and ideas in this chapter came from him.

In May 1989 the University of Bologna in Italy, the oldest surviving European university, sponsored a GERG symposium in celebration of its nine-hundredth birthday. Under Bob Artigiani's influence, along with Vilmos Csanyi, another GERGian, the cognitive map concept was chosen as the theme of the symposium. This chapter grew out of Bob's visit to UCSC in February 1989, and my participation in his symposium.[1]

Grok Evolution

Chapter 1 described the hermeneutical circle as the motor of understanding and the fuel for the evolution of consciousness. Later we will expand this understanding to include textual interpretation, and eventually history itself. The fundamental process is the effort to understand one's sensory experience of the external universe. Here we arrive at cognitive psychology and the sociology of knowledge, subjects that attempt to grok grokking!

History and Myth

"History is how a society explains itself to itself."

Myth and history are different approaches to our understanding of ourselves. Historian Robert Artigiani says: "History is how a society explains itself to itself." And according to historian William Irwin Thompson, "History, by definition, is a civilized, literary record of events; it is a conscious self-image of a society projected by an elite. . . . Myth is the mirror-opposite of history. Myth is not the story of the ego of a civilization but the story of the soul."[2]

Cognitive Maps

Both history and myth are seen through an image, paradigm, theory, or cognitive process. The result of this self-imaging process is called a *cognitive map*.[3] The images created are partly cultural, partly individual, and the cultural image evolves along with its parent culture. As a result, history appears somewhat arbitrary. Although we like to think of history as an account of truth or fact, it is actually uncertain and vague, a reconstruction from fragmentary data, filtered through largely unconscious processes. The deeper the past, the more vague is our understanding of it.

A theory of cognitive maps attempts to learn the imaging process through the disciplines of anthropology, sociology, and psychology—the social sciences. One of the uses of this theory is in the reconstruction of history. This application provides an opportunity for the mathematical theory of dynamical systems to enter the hermeneutical circle, as we will see in a later chapter.

Gestalt theory began in Germany in 1912 with a paper by Max Wertheimer. *Gestalt,* in German, means whole, and Gestalt theory may be regarded as a form of holism, a theory of whole systems, in contrast to reductionism, which tries to understand the whole system through a study of its parts. Gestalt is also related to vitalism, a view of nature in which a vital spirit or field infuses all matter.

Wolfgang Kohler's book about his experiments on perception and problem-solving with apes (1913–17) appeared in 1917, and Kurt Koffka's book on the mind was published in 1924. The English translations of these two books appeared in 1925 and 1924, respectively, and had a substantial impact on the development of psychology in the United States.[4] The Gestalt movement was influenced by Dilthey and the hermeneutical tradition, as were Freud and Kurt Lewin. Concepts of holism and vitalism were embedded within it, as well as those of phenomenology.[5] Lewin's social field theory is an outgrowth of the Gestalt movement, which is particularly relevant to our present subject.[6] His idea of life space is roughly equivalent to the cognitive map, as a sort of psychological field, or cognitive structure, extending over a group of animals.[7] The current burgeoning interest in maps and myths can be seen as a renaissance of the Gestalt movement.[8]

TWO SMART RATS

Universities have their branches, such as psychology, and the branches have branches, such as rat psychology. Rat psychologists perform studies on rats trying to find food at the end of one of the many tunnels of a maze (see figure 2.1). In the early days of rat psych, it was thought that rats memorized the local instructions: left, right, left, and so on, leading to the food. This form of memory is called a *strip map.*

One day in the 1920s, K. S. Lashley, the pioneer rat man, saw two of his subjects, after having learned the maze, pushing back the cover near the starting box, climbing out, and running directly across the top to the goal box, where they climbed down into the box again and ate.[9] His conclusion was that smart rats can integrate strip maps into a wider spatial map.[10] Later rat men, such as E. C. Tolman and coworkers in 1946, confirmed this skill of Lashley's rats with more sophisticated mazes.[11]

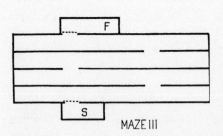

FIGURE 2.1
Maze 3, of Lashley's Smart Rats
Drawing by Diane Rigoli, after Lashley (1964).

My argument will be brief, cavalier, and dogmatic. I am not myself a clinician or a social psychologist. What I am going to say must be considered, therefore, simply as in the nature of a rat psychologist's ratiocinations offered free.[12]

After this modest disclaimer, Tolman concluded a 1948 lecture, entitled "Cognitive Maps in Rats and Men," with three applications of the cognitive map concept to human psychology. They illustrate a proposed mechanism in which strong motivation or frustration produces an unwanted narrowing of the individual's cognitive map. Later generations of rat people have elaborated the cognitive mapping function and physiology, locating the actual map in the hippocampus.[13]

SAILING CANOES

Further applications to human psychology have been proposed. An outstanding example, corresponding well with Lashley's rat team, was told to me by Bob Artigiani. It involves the navigators of traditional sailing canoes in the islands of the South Pacific. The culture of these people was explored in the pioneering work of the Polish anthropologist Bronislaw Malinowski (1884–1942).[14]

The islanders liked to go sailing for fun, even at night after a party, to a neighboring island about a hundred miles distant. At first it was thought that they navigated by dead reckoning, like Tolman's rats, or by a strip map. This is only partially true. Thomas Gladwin, in 1970, showed that they had also integrated the strip maps into global spatial maps of the South Pacific and the celestial sphere.[15]

The Concept of Culture

The next phase in the hermeneutical exegesis of our human cultural history is the extension of the cognitive map concept from a single cognitive process, such as spatial cognition, to the entire knowledge base of an individual. In other words, this means expanding it to the concept of culture, as it evolved in the early history of anthropology.

MALINOWSKI, 1922

Bronislaw Malinowski, a social anthropologist teaching at the London School of Economics and Political Science, worked with the Trobriand Islanders and became widely known and influential after publication of his classic, *Argonauts of the Western Pacific,* in 1922.[16] Along with the structural anthropologist A. R. Radcliffe-Brown, he introduced the word *culture* in the sense of "the systematic body of learned behavior which is transmitted from parents to children."[17]

In her bestselling text *Patterns of Culture,* written in 1934, Ruth Benedict (1887–1948) made the culture concept more widely known. She emphasized the diversity of cultures in a Nietzschean typology of Apollonian and Dionysian cultures. Nietzsche, in his studies of Greek tragedy, described the Dionysian disposition as "annihilation of the ordinary bounds and limits of existence," while the Apollonian distrusts and outlaws this. For example, Benedict described the Southwest Pueblo cultures as Apollonian, in contrast to the surrounding Native Americans, who she described as Dionysian.[18] Later, she introduced the term *social synergy,* a measure for the integrity of a cognitive map.[19]

Another early step in the extension of the cognitive map concept to cultures was taken by Gregory Bateson, an anthropologist influenced by Malinowski. In 1935, in an article called "Cultural Contact and Schismogenesis," Bateson advocated Malinowski's holistic view of culture, and introduced a dynamical process of cultural evolution, which he called *schismogenesis.*[20] This is a kind of bifurcation event in a social system, in which a schism—for example, racism—develops in the society. Later, in his classic book *Naven,* recounting his fieldwork with the Iatmul people of New Guinea, he adapted Ruth Benedict's concept of ethos to encompass "the expression of a culturally standardized system of organization of the instincts and emotions of the individual."[21]

In 1939 Bateson learned of the work of Lewis Frye Richardson (1881–1953), the founder of arms race models and politicometrics,[22] and in 1949 he connected these concepts into a dynamically evolving picture of ethos.[23] In 1972 his essays on this subject were collected into a volume, *Steps to an Ecology of Mind,* the classic of general systems theory and cybernetics as applied to anthropology.[24]

A derivative of nineteenth-century hermeneutics and vitalism, in the line of Dilthey (as described in chapter 1), *general systems theory* was developed in Canada by Ludwig von Bertalanffy in the 1940s.[25] *Cybernetics* is a similar theory of systems, which emerged in the context of engineering and technology at about the same time.

Complex dynamical systems theory (CDS theory) is an extension of the mathematical theory of dynamical systems, in the spirit of Henri Poincaré. It is based on general systems theory and cybernetics, revised and extended by the new theories of chaos and bifurcation. It provides the modeling strategy for a new understanding of complex systems, of social systems, and of history. The application of this modeling strategy to the social sciences is the basis for new developments, including mathematical anthropology, mathematical sociology, mathematical psychology, and so on.[26]

Collectively, we call these new developments *erodynamics*, referring to the study of social behavior using dynamical models. We will explore the meaning and reasons for this term in the last chapter of this book.

BOULDING, 1956

Bateson attended seminars of Malinowski in London as a graduate student at Oxford, and later he attended the Macy conferences at which the cybernetic revolution got under way. Kenneth Boulding (b. 1910) was also a participant in these meetings, and became one of the founding fathers of general systems theory.

During a year in retreat at the Center for Advanced Study in the Behavioral Sciences at Stanford, California (1954–55), he produced a monograph called "The Image," which, as he says, was "dictated in uninterrupted composition" and published in 1956. This is a visionary synthesis of general systems theory and the social sciences: economical, political, social, and historical. Its basic concepts are the image, which is the cognitive map, or knowledge structure, of the individual, and the message, which produces a change in the image. He speaks explicitly of the image of man, the image of the history of the universe, and of public images, shared by a society. The evolution of society and the public image under the influence of messages is described hermeneutically: "The image not only makes society, society continually remakes the image."[27] Culture is the exfoliation of an image as germ, the unfolding of a cognitive map in its role as seed of society.

"The image not only makes society, society continually remakes the image."

ARTIGIANI, 1987

Recently, Robert Artigiani has updated cultural evolution theory by connecting the cognitive map, or public image, to general evolution theory. Using CDS theory, he presents a complex dynamical model for a network of grok circles of multiple environments and cognitive maps, coupled through messages. Using the bifurcation concept of the mathematical theory of dynamical systems, he proposes a complex dynamical model for social transformations such as the Scientific Revolution, and for political revolutions as well.[28] Further, he advances to another level, in envisioning the evolution of history in terms of self-replicating social organisms in a milieu of natural selection. To Artigiani,

> Cognitive maps are sets of symbols representing physical phenomena, people, and procedures that group sequences of facts and ideas governing particular behavior sets around values, with each behavior set playing the role of a cultural gene. The symbols in cognitive maps originate in experience and are tested against their environment. These symbols are communicated more-or-less completely to all members of a society and, through the emotive effect of values, they guide action. Through media like language, myth, tools, art, ritual, and simple imitation, cognitive maps communicate the information characterizing a particular human group between individuals and generations. Thus, as each new generation is educated in the meanings of a culture's cognitive map, it acquires the traditions of its society and learns to behave in manners largely undistinguishable from those of its ancestors.[29]

The Hermeneutic Circle, Again

This brings us to the present, and yet another view of our history.[30]

MYTHOGRAPHY

Mythography is a way of looking at the past as if it were unrelated to the present. For example, a mythographer might go through the whole of Greek literature, from Homer and Hesiod up until the last stroke of ancient Greece in 641, and whenever he comes across the name of an ancient god or goddess or mythical place like the River Styx, he writes it down on an index card. When done, he sorts these index cards into piles, one for Orpheus, one for Pluto, and so on. He then takes each of these piles and writes a story about it. Each story the mythographer calls a "myth." A splendid book, written in this style of mythography, is *The Greek Myths,* by Robert Graves.[31] All the piles (myths) are there, and after every myth he gives all the sources—every single Greek author, place, page, and line. However, if you read about one of the characters in several different piles, you find there are many inconsistencies, because the references come from different times and places.

Another style of analysis was used by Jane Ellen Harrison, a classical scholar at the turn of the century in England. She preferred to follow an idea—the abstract concept of Orpheus, for example—through the whole of history, even when it radically changed its name.[32] Diodorus of Sicily gave an example of this when he said that Orpheus was Osiris translated from Egypt to Greece, along with the rituals and myths of Osiris, Isis, and Horus. Here, in 50 B.C., the idea of the myth evolving within a culture and leaping the boundaries from one culture to another was already apparently present.

Myths are always changing. There is no static myth of Orpheus. There is an evolving, never-ending tradition with long roots, which continues to this day, in consciousness or in unconsciousness. Recently, this approach, called *mythogenesis,* has become popular as a way of looking at the history of myth. The great master of this view, of course, is the late Joseph Campbell.[33]

We continually interpret and reinterpret the past. . . . We do the same with the future, projecting forward our fantasies and eventually receiving feedback in the form of certainties or uncertainties in the present.

HERMENEUTICS

As we have said, the hermeneutic circle, in which target system and model are connected into a cycle—a kind of commodious vicus of recirculation—provides the motor for the evolution of consciousness. One application of this hermeneutic circle is to our understanding of the past. As we read history through our current paradigm in the present, we revise history without changing its data, filtering it through a new image. We continually interpret and reinterpret the past. Just as we interpret the Bible, a historical text, or an archaeological site, we reinterpret our own memories, our records, libraries, the detritus of preceding cultural maps, according to our image of the present. We do the same with the future, projecting forward our fantasies and eventually receiving feedback in the form of certainties or uncertainties in the present. We can thus think of a second hermeneutic circle between our present dialogue and our future.

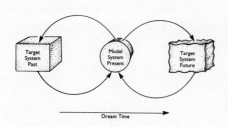

FIGURE 2.2
The Double Cycle of a Cognitive Map in Dream-Time

Drawing by Diane Rigoli, © Ralph H. Abraham.

THE GYRE

Figure 2.2 is a graphic for an individual cognitive map, or ICM. This map is evolving, so our cognitive map in the present moment has grown from some germ in the past, which may be represented as a point. We have this double ice cream cone figure as a model for the ICM and its history, shown in figure 2.3.

At some point in time, when many individuals are sharing the same map, a *collective cognitive map,* or *cultural cognitive map,* or CCM, may begin, which repeats the same process from a new germ.

In figure 2.4 we have, in one figure, the ICM and the CCM. Clock time, or real time, is represented as motion to the right in the figure. But we also have time in another, orthogonal direction, which is fictitious time in the present, which we might call dream time. This figure already exists in the literature, under the name Gyre, in "The Vision," by William Butler Yeats. This is a slightly different but equivalent figure, revealed to Yeats by his wife through automatic writing.

Summary

We apply the grok circle idea to the efforts of our species to understand itself and its place in the universe. The concept of cognitive map emerges within a hierarchy of models for consciousness. In any given culture, cognitive maps, both individual and collective, are in a continual process of evolution. Cultural history and myth are aspects of the evolving collective cognitive map. Social transformations or bifurcations, in the dynamical theory of Robert Artigiani, are sudden jumps (catastrophes, paradigm shifts) in this process of evolution. In the cybernetic view of Gregory Bateson and Kenneth Boulding, or the general systems approach of Ludwig von Bertalanffy, this model provides a new theory of history. In the next chapter, we will survey the history of history.

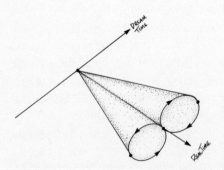

FIGURE 2.3
The Gyre of a Cognitive Map in Its Real-Time Evolution

Drawing by Diane Rigoli, © Ralph H. Abraham.

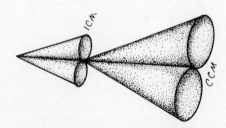

FIGURE 2.4
Evolution of a CCM from an ICM

Drawing by Diane Rigoli, © Ralph H. Abraham.

The History of History

CHAPTER 3

In high school in the 1950s, I got tuberculosis and was confined to bed for two years. My mother kept me well supplied with historical novels, and I thought the history they told was true. During the 1960s my Vermont pals Harry Burnham and Russ Spring introduced me to Chinese literature, which showed me that there seemed to be alternative histories. Then, with the hippies, the New Age, and our own pagan revival in the 1970s, history came to be entirely mythical to me. Lately, in the 1980s, thanks to the General Evolution Research Group (GERG) and other influences, I have tried to trace back the mythical history of history itself. Is there a dynamical evolution of historical maps or images, the lenses through which we view history?

Images of History

The history of history may be summarized as a list of maps, or images, that have each given way in major shifts. . . . History itself is radically revised after each of these paradigm shifts.

This chapter offers a compact collage of maps and images that provide, in fast forward, a context in which to see dynamical historiography. Tables 3.1 and 3.2 provide biographical data for the historians of this chapter.

The study of historical literature throughout the ages reveals a pattern in which plateaus of gradual change are punctuated by jumps, or catastrophes, as seen with the origin of species in paleontology (see figure 3.1). Thus the history of history may be summarized as a list of maps, or images, that have each given way in major shifts. In fact, as Voegelin has said, "the order of history emerges from the history of order."[1] History itself is radically revised after each of these paradigm shifts. A recent example of paradigm shift in science is provided by plate tectonics, a

TABLE 3.1
Historians 100–1800

Dateline	100	300	500	700	900	1100	1300	1500	1800
Origin (Alexandria)	▬								
Augustine (Africa)		▬							
Albiruni (Asia)						▬			
Joachim (Italy)						▬			
Ibn-Khaldûn (Spain)							▬		
Cusanus (Italy)							▬		
More (England)								▬	
Bodin (France)									▬
Leibniz (Prussia)									▬
Vico (Italy)									▬
Voltaire (France)									▬

TABLE 3.2
Historians 1700–2000

Dateline	1700	1750	1800	1850	1900	1950	2000
Rousseau (France)	▬▬▬						
Turgot (France)	▬▬▬						
Herder (Germany)		▬▬▬					
Hegel (Germany)		▬▬▬					
Comte (France)			▬▬▬				
Burckhardt (Switzerland)				▬▬▬			
Marx (Germany)				▬▬▬			
Engels (Germany)				▬▬▬			
Spencer (England)				▬▬▬			
Gage (America)				▬▬▬			
Tylor (England)				▬▬▬			

TABLE 3.2 *(continued)*
Historians 1700–2000

Dateline	1700	1750	1800	1850	1900	1950	2000
Dilthey (Germany)			▬▬▬▬▬▬▬▬				
Petrie (England)				▬▬▬▬▬▬▬			
Aurobindo (India)				▬▬▬▬▬▬▬			
Lovejoy (America)				▬▬▬▬▬▬▬▬			
Beard (America)				▬▬▬▬▬▬▬			
Spengler (Germany)				▬▬▬▬▬			
Richardson (England)				▬▬▬▬▬▬▬▬			
Tillich (America)				▬▬▬▬▬▬▬			
Rosenstock-Huessy (America)				▬▬▬▬▬▬▬▬			
Radhakrishnan (India)				▬▬▬▬▬▬▬▬			
Sorokin (America)				▬▬▬▬▬▬▬▬			
Rashevsky (America)				▬▬▬▬▬▬▬			
Toynbee (England)				▬▬▬▬▬▬▬			
Voegelin (America)				▬▬▬▬▬▬▬▬			
Von Bertalanffy (America)				▬▬▬▬▬▬▬			
Eliade (Romania)				▬▬▬▬▬▬▬▬			
Gebser (Spain)				▬▬▬▬▬▬▬			

new theory of the motion of continents.[2] Another impressive case is the discovery of *deep time*.[3] There are many smaller shifts within this story, such as the radical discoveries brought about by the archaeological spade, or the revision of carbon14 dates by the study of tree rings, or the feminist revision of history and prehistory. Then, of course, there is the leap into space, which globalized our vision of Earth and humankind. Each of these examples has led to a radical revision of our image of history.

Cultural Evolution

Some images of history are dynamical. *Cultural evolution* is a convenient phrase for an evolutionary type of historical image that contains the dynamical concepts of the birth, development, and death of cultures. What follows is a survey of such paradigms, and their champions.

OLD TESTAMENT, 1200 B.C.

We begin our survey with the Old Testament. This early and fundamental sacred literature of our European tradition has been credited by many historians with the origins of historicity itself. According to their theories, the history of a tribe was not part of its self-image before the Old Testament.[4]

EARLY HISTORIES

The epics of Hesiod, circa 800 B.C., contain a simple idea of cultural history and evolution, which we will describe in the next chapter. History and geography, as we know them, may be said to begin with Hecateus of Miletus (born around 550 B.C.). Better known are Herodotus (484–420 B.C., who claimed that Egyptian history had three ages: of gods, of heroes, and of men)[5] and Thucydides (b. ca. 460 B.C.).[6]

PLATO, 385 B.C.

In the *Republic,* dated sometime after the opening of the Academy around 385 B.C., Plato (427–347 B.C.) expresses a theory of social evolution:

> And, moreover, said I, the state, if it once starts well, proceeds as it were in a cycle of growth. I mean that a sound nurture and education if kept up creates good natures in the state, and sound natures in turn receiving an education of this sort develop into better men than their predecessors both for other purposes and for the production of offspring as among animals also.[7]

Plato believed that the course of history repeats itself every 72,000 years.

Plato believed that the course of history repeats itself every 72,000 years. Thus he began the European tradition of the cyclical theory of history.[8]

DIODORUS SICULUS, 50 B.C.

Diodorus of Sicily (80–20 B.C.) wrote: "It is fitting that all men should ever accord great gratitude to those writers who have composed universal histories, since they have aspired to help by their individual labours human society as a whole."[9] Diodorus himself wrote a comprehensive history of the world in twelve volumes, weaving together previously existing bits into a continuous narrative that is an enormously detailed and accurate report of the Greco-Roman world up to 60 B.C.

The most astonishing part of this story is the first volume, on prehistory. While conflicting in some details with the results of recent archaeology, the broad outlines are very convincing, beginning with a Big Bang in Egypt, an evolutionary scenario of flora and fauna culminating in human civilization, and a diffusion/transformation of mythology in which Osiris becomes Dionysos, Isis becomes Gaia and Demeter, and Horus becomes Apollo. Here is an important example of the migration of a triad: trinitarian transformation. While a historiographical theory of civilization is lacking in Diodorus, a basis for one is provided.

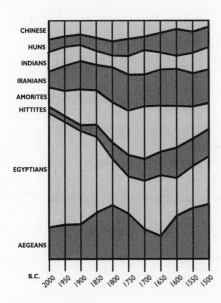

FIGURE 3.1
A Map of Empires

Drawing by Diane Rigoli, after Sparks (1931).

In response to the sack of Rome in 410 A.D. by Alaric the Visigoth, Saint Augustine (354–430) wrote *The City of God*, comprising twenty-two books on the church and containing a philosophy of history. This work lays the foundation for medieval civilization and our tradition of historical interpretation.[10] In the eleventh book Augustine refutes the pagan theory of eternal recurrence.[11] History is modeled as a single grand cycle, what Christian culture calls the *Epic*,[12] leading from Eden to the Fall, the Redemption, the Millennium, the Last Judgment, and the Return of Paradise. This Great Week of the human journey proceeds in eight stages:

1. Adam to Noah and the Flood
2. Noah to Abraham
3. Abraham to David
4. David to the Exile
5. Exile to the birth of Christ
6. The current Age of the Church
7. The Redemption yet to come (the Sabbath of the Great Week)
8. The Lord's day, the eschaton at the end of time, the end without end, eternity in the City of God or the City of Satan[13]

As an aside, Augustine, in his *Confessions*, invented autobiographical history as well.

Abu-Raihan Muhammad ben Ahmad Albiruni of Khwarizm (973–1048) lived in Central Asia. Around the turn of the first millennium, he compiled and published his classic, *Athar al-Baqiyah,* or *Vestiges of the Past,* known in English as *The Chronology of Ancient Nations.* This was probably the model for Sir Isaac Newton's *The Chronology of Ancient Kingdoms Amended.*

While residing in Hyrcania on the southern shores of the Caspian Sea, Albiruni collected traditions from various religious sects and nations: Persian, Zoroastrian, Muslim, Jewish, and so on. His great contribution was a mathematically careful exposition of the calendars of these traditions, and their synthesis into a chronology of ancient history presented in a set of tables, with columns of dates according to various calendars, emphasizing eras and cycles.

JOACHIM, 1197

Joachim de Fiora (1132–1202) was a Cistercian monk with the gift of prophesy. After retiring as the Abbot of Sambucina around 1170, he devoted himself to his writings, which had extensive influence on European society.

His eschatological interpretations and predictions, published in a great trilogy, contained a model of world history in three *status,* or stages of spiritual growth: the first age coinciding with the Old Testament, the second beginning with the coming of Christ and the New Testament, the third beginning around 1260. Joachim associated these three status with the Holy Trinity: the Father, the Son, and the Holy Spirit. According to this scheme, we are now in the Age of the Holy Spirit. Joachim predicted that this would be the most Holy Age, although it would deteriorate at the end. The sequence ends at the Apocalypse. From the first book of his trilogy, *Liber Concordie Novi et Veteris Testamenti,* in 1197:

> The First Age of the world began with Adam, flowered with Abraham, and was consummated with Christ. The Second began with Oziah, flowered from Zachary, the father of John the Baptist, and will receive its consummation in these times. The Third Age, beginning from St. Benedict, began to bring forth fruit in the twenty-second generation and it is to be consummated in the consummation of the world.[14]

The consummation of the world is called the *eschaton,* depicted in the Apocalypse of Saint John.

Each status lasts about 1,260 years (forty generations), and the transitions are characterized by the appearance of chaos and antichrists. Some of the triplets of Joachim's concordance are given in table 3.3.

TABLE 3.3
Cosmogonical Principles

Father	Son	Spirit
Law	Grace	Love
Laymen	Clergy	Monks
Winter	Spring	Summer
Knowledge	Wisdom	Intelligence

In the second work of his trilogy, *Expositio in Apocalypsim,* Joachim explores the apocalyptic symbols in the Old and New Testaments. In the third, *Psalterium Decem Chordarum,* he draws an analogy between the three-phase model of history, the Holy Trinity, and the musical trinity of the psalter, its songs, and its musical structure.

This model of history is dynamic (a series of ages), progressive, and apocalyptic. Joachim was influenced by Greek philosophy and by Origen, and in turn had an enormous influence on later European thinkers, including Dante, Vico, and Marx.

IBN-KHALDÛN, 1377

Ibn-Khaldûn (1332–1406) was an original and isolated historical genius, living in Spain and North Africa.[15] His Yemenite ancestors fled Spain during the thirteenth-century Christian advance. Of his work Toynbee wrote: "He has conceived and formulated a philosophy of history which is undoubtedly the greatest work of its kind that has ever yet been created by any mind in any time or place."[16]

His lifework, *Kitâb al-'Ibar,* or *World History,* completed in 1377, begins with the *Muqaddimah* (introduction and book one), running to three volumes in English translation.[17] Here the general principles of historiography are given, which he calls *social science.* As far as we know, this is the first attempt by a historian to discover a pattern of growth and decline in the evolution of human societies. This takes a step beyond the cycle of the ancients, applying a pattern to the whole of history. In this fundamental *Muqaddimah,* Ibn-Khaldûn introduces a universal cycle of rising and falling development for a state or dynasty, and a universal force, called *asabiyah,* which drives the cycle. This force is a cultural field, the evolutionary lifeblood of the society. The cyclical pattern of cultural development, analogous to human development, is called the *dynastic cycle,* occurring in three, four, or five stages, lasting altogether 120 years.[18]

CUSANUS, 1452

Nicholas Cusanus (1401–64) was a Christian Neoplatonist and monk of great importance to the Florentine Renaissance. With a theory of time in his work *Idiota,* published in 1452, he lay the groundwork for Johannes Kepler (who calls him "the divine Cusanus") and Leibniz, for modern mathematics and physics, and for a new theory of history. Cusanus proposed that the human mind creates time to order the multiplicity of perceived phenomena, and creates history by a process of explication, or unfolding, itself.[19]

Merging distinct strands of idealistic literature, especially the ideal city of the Greeks and the Judeo-Christian heaven, Thomas More (1478–1535) created a new type of literature with his fantasy, *De Optimo Reipublicae Statu deque Nova Insula Utopia Libellus Vere Aureus,* published in 1516. In his title, he combined the Greek *ou* (a general negative) and *topos* (place or region) to create the neologism *Utopia* (nowhere), the name of his ideal island society. This tremendously successful novel gave birth to a new genre of literary works, called *utopias,* of which there are now thousands, written by utopographers of every land. Here are a few milestones of utopology:

- 1595: Philip Sydney ranked poetry and utopia above philosophy and history in usefulness.
- 1600: John Donne gave birth to the adjective *utopian* (ideal), which also gained the meaning of *dystopian* (chimerical, wild, or foolish).
- 1808: Charles Fourier published his doctrine of passionate attraction, in which the utopian concept was enlarged from an enclosed island or city into an international movement that would spread into an ideal planetary society covering the globe, *the universal utopia.*
- 1840: Louis Reybaud published the first study of the *social utopia,* and utopian literature became a social science.
- 1918: Ernst Bloch began the propagation of a utopian revival, aimed at the transition from the possible to the actual, the fulfillment of a universal utopian vision in an actual planetary society.
- 1951: Paul Tillich connected the kingdom of God, as a utopian model actualizing in time, with the course of history, giving birth to *utopian theology.*
- 1959: Teilhard de Chardin published *The Phenomenon of Man,* closing the utopian genre (and history itself) into a circle, in which humanity arrives in the kingdom of God at the omega point, at the end of history.[20]
- 1980: The utopian genre appeared to decline during the 1960s, while utopian communities appeared all over the world. But as these Blochian realizations failed, the fantasies resumed.

Jean Bodin (1530–96) was the first philosopher of history in France. In his *Historic Method,* published in 1557, he described history as a progressive evolution. In the seventh chapter, he refuted the Hindu moral devolution model of four declining ages, from gold to iron.[21] Bodin was the intellectual master of the sixteenth century. One should note, however, that he was also its demon. In 1580 he sparked the witch craze of the seventeenth century, with his book *De la Demonomanie des Sorciers.*[22]

Gottfried Wilhelm von Leibniz (1646–1716) is known primarily for his mathematical work, which overlapped that of Newton. He was also a philosopher who was influenced by missionaries returning from China, and who, in turn, influenced Immanuel Kant. While employed as a professional historian by the Duke of Brunswick, he introduced the evolution concept explicitly into historiography, perhaps as early as 1697.[23] He wrote in *Nouveaux Essais,* published in 1765:

> Nothing happens all at once, and nature never makes jumps. I call that the law of continuity. In starting from ourselves and going down to the lowest, it is a descent by very small steps, a continuous series of things which differ very little—fishes with wings, animals very like vegetables, and again animals which seem to have as much reason as some men.[24]

He emphasized a universal history of civilization, including geography, philology, literature, arts and sciences, laws, and religions.[25]

Giambattista Vico (1668–1744) was another isolated genius, contemporary with Newton and Leibniz. Like Ibn-Khaldûn, of whom he was unaware but whose theory his resembles, he called his work *a new science.*[26] The first systems theorist, he proposed a universal pattern, or ideal history, for the rise, progress, maturity, decline, and fall of nations. He wrote, "First the forests, then the huts, then the villages, then the cities, and finally the academies."[27]

Vico was influenced by Joachim, Spinoza, Descartes, Francis Bacon, and Jean Bodin.[28] His proposed pattern was a cycle of cultural rise and fall, like Ibn-Khaldûn's dynastic cycle (see figure 3.2). It was the pattern of a wheel divided into three phases, analogous to human development.[29] He called these phases the

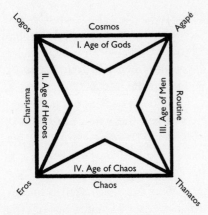

FIGURE 3.2
Vico's Quarternity

Drawing from Thompson (1985), figure 7. Courtesy of William Irwin Thompson. Reprinted with permission.

Age of the Gods (childhood), the Age of the Heroes (adolescence), and the Age of Men (maturity). In addition, there is a fourth phase between the end of one cycle and the start of another, called the Age of Chaos.[30]

Vico was influenced by Herodotus, who ascribed this pattern to the ancient Egyptians. He sent a copy of his work to Newton, who did not reply.[31]

Vico, in turn, had an important influence on Goethe, Johann Gottfried von Herder, Wilhelm Dilthey, Benedetto Croce, Ernst Cassirer, R. G. Collingwood, and Erich Auerbach, who figure in our story, and on Joseph Schumpeter, the economist who founded the theory of business cycles.[32] He also influenced the English intellectual scene, beginning with James Joyce, who read Vico's *New Science* in Italian around 1905.[33] The first English translation of *New Science* appeared in 1948. As the creator of hermeneutics, Vico's influence is still felt.[34]

TURGOT, 1750

On July 3, 1750, the twenty-three-year-old prior Anne Robert Jacques Turgot, Baron de l'Aulne (1727–81), delivered two lectures at the Sorbonne, in which he introduced the modern concept of progress. On this day, it can be said, the European mind switched from religious to earthly morality.[35]

VOLTAIRE, 1756

François Voltaire (1694–1778) published his *Essai sur les moers* in 1756. According to Fernand Braudel, the history of civilization begins with this work.[36]

ROUSSEAU, 1762

Jean-Jacques Rousseau (1712–78), a self-taught philosopher, championed the evolutionary paradigm in political philosophy with his controversial work *The Social Contract,* written in Geneva and published in 1762. In it he claimed that war was a law of cultural nature, and founded the study of sociology, anticipating August Comte.

HERDER, 1774

Johann Gottfried von Herder (1744–1803) wrote thirty-three volumes on history, politics, language, culture, progress, and a multitude of other subjects. He was a German cultural idol who, along with Goethe, belonged to the *Storm and Stress* group,[37] and was regarded as the founder of the philosophy of history.[38] He converted the classical tradition of the Great Chain of Being into a sequence of cultural stages.

Herder was apparently familiar with Vico's ideas.[39] Both Vico and Herder were translated into French at about the same time,

DYNAMICS AND THE ORPHIC TRINITY IN HISTORY

and both had a major influence on the prevailing French view of a linear progress to history, to which they introduced the cyclical view of the rise and fall of nations. Herder maintained that while nations are born and die, culture itself only progresses.[40]

HEGEL, 1822

The German philosopher Georg Wilhelm Friedrich Hegel (1770–1831) began teaching at the University of Berlin in 1818. Every other year from 1822 to 1831, he devoted his lectures to the philosophy of history. Five sets of lecture notes taken by auditors were edited by Professor Eduard Gans, after Hegel's death, and published in 1837 as the *Philosophy of History*. A second edition, edited by Karl Hegel with the addition of material from G. W. F. Hegel's own notes, appeared in 1840, and was published in English in 1857.[41] An Introduction to the lectures, originally written by G. W. F. Hegel himself in 1822, and edited for the fourth time by Johannes Hoffmeister, was published in 1955 as *Lectures on the Philosophy of World History, Introduction: Reason in History,* and appeared in English in 1975.[42]

Hegel's one-cycle theory is based on the dialectical thesis-antithesis pattern. A spiral progress of development from lower to higher levels, in phases of thesis and antithesis, unrolls in the historical process of the entire world, which falls into four stages:

- absolute emperorship (Asia)
- adolescence of the Spirit (Greece)
- manhood of Spirit (Rome)
- the old age of the Spirit (Germany)

To Hegel, history is the concrete manifestation of the life of the Spirit.[43] He believed that the evolution of human thought, in a dynamic process of progressive development, was a manifestation of God.[44] This view of history—the whole of human history seen as a single evolutionary process—came to an end with the development of liberal democracy, according to historian Francis Fukuyama.[45]

COMTE, 1839

Auguste Comte (1798–1857), along with Claude-Henri de Rouvroy Saint-Simon, founded the positivist school of philosophy with the publication of *Cours de Philosophie Positive,* in six volumes, in 1830–42, and *Systeme de Politique Positive,* in four volumes, in 1851–54. The last three volumes of the *Cours,* of 1839, 1841, and 1842, present his historical philosophy. The first of these, volume 4, includes his *Social Physics.* Comte claimed to be the true founder of sociology (see Rousseau), which he divided in two parts, *Social Statics* and *Social Dynamics,* the latter being a philosophy of history. The Appendix of this volume contains essays published previously. In one of these, first published in 1822, is found the *law of three stages,* which Comte regarded as his greatest discovery.[46]

MARX, 1845

The German socialist Karl Marx (1818–83) was contemporary with Herbert Spencer and Jacob Burckhardt, and likewise under the influence of Herder. His philosophy of history appears in *The German Ideology,* written in 1845 with Friedrich Engels, and in a letter written December 28, 1846. These refer to and criticize Hegel, from a socialist perspective.[47] In a newspaper article of November 11, 1847, he presents a theory of stages of historical development.[48]

SPENCER, 1855

Herbert Spencer (1820–1903) wrote extensively on the process of social evolution. Although largely dismissed today, he was highly regarded in his time. The originator of a philosophy of universal evolution, his influence was acknowledged by the pioneers of evolutionary theory, Alfred Wallace Russell and Charles Darwin. In this theory evolution is a series of different stages of development, in which each stage is the antithesis of its preceding stage, and is produced by intentional revolution. Thus humans participate in history, rather than passively viewing it from outside.[49]

Spencer wrote voluminously, and his theory of universal evolution first appeared in the first of three volumes of *The Principles of Sociology,* in 1855. This was four years before the publication of Darwin's *The Origin of Species.* In fact, Spencer preceded Darwin in the use of the word *evolution,*[50] and first coined the phrase *the survival of the fittest.*[51] His five-volume *First Principles,* published in 1862, is a veritable manifesto for general evolution theory, elaborated with numerous examples showing the generality of Spencer's view. Social evolution was particularly prominent in Spencer's writing after 1857:

> The advance from the simple to the complex, through a process of successive differentiations, is seen alike in the earliest changes of the Universe to which we can reason our way back; and in the earliest changes which we can inductively establish; it is seen in the geologic and climatic evolution of Earth, and of every single organism on its surface; it is seen in the evolution of Humanity, whether contemplated in the civilized individual, or in the aggre-

gation of races; it is seen in the evolution of Society in respect alike of its political, its religious, and its economical organization; and it is seen in the evolution of all . . . [the] endless concrete and abstract products of human activity.[52]

And later, in 1898: "Evolution is a change from a state of relatively indefinite, incoherent, homogeneity to a state of relatively definite, coherent, heterogeneity."[53] It appears that Spencer viewed evolution as a universal process of linear progression in the evolution of form; in other words, morphogenesis.[54]

BURCKHARDT, 1860

Jacob Burckhardt (1818–97) was one of the greatest historians of modern times. He championed the idea that the Italian Renaissance was a sudden, catastrophic event in history. This claim led to a debate that gave rise to historiography as it is known today. His idea of sudden jumps in social evolution was the first step toward the current trend of modern cultural history, in which mathematical dynamics, especially *bifurcation theory,* is used to model social transformations. We will return to this trend later on.[55]

TYLOR, 1871

Edward Burnett Tylor (1832–1917) published *Primitive Culture* in 1871, thus founding modern anthropology. Since that time, cultural anthropology has joined history, sociology, and philosophy in the hermeneutics of cultural evolution and change. On the first page of this fundamental work, Tylor defined culture as "that complex whole which includes knowledge, belief, art, morals, law, custom, and any other capabilities and habits acquired by man as a member of society."
Further, he wrote, following Leibniz,

> The condition of culture among the various societies of mankind . . . is a subject apt for the study of laws of human thought and action. On the one hand, the uniformity which so largely pervades civilization may be ascribed, in great measure, to the uniform action of uniform causes: while on the other hand its various grades may be regarded as stages of development of evolution, each the outcome of previous history and about to do its proper part in shaping the history of the future.[56]

GAGE, 1893

Matilda Joslyn Gage (1826–98) was a radical feminist theoretician in New York, and published her major work, *Women, Church and State,* in 1893. She was among the first, apparently, to write about the connection between the male suppression of prehistoric matriarchies and goddess religions and our modern social problems.[57]

DILTHEY, 1905

Wilhelm Dilthey (1833–1911) was one of the founders of the grok concept. His applications of hermeneutics to history were outlined in a series of papers in the period 1905–10, called *Studies Towards the Foundations of the Human Studies.* These were revised and extended from his notes posthumously in 1926, and published in English translation in 1961.[58]

PETRIE, 1911

William Matthew Flinders Petrie (1853–1942) was the archaeologist who dug up ancient Egypt. Inspired in 1866 by Piazzi Smyth's book on Cheops's pyramid, he sailed for Egypt, arriving at the pyramid a few days before Christmas, in 1880.[59]

After excavating three thousand years of continuous history and discovering eight distinct cycles of civilization, he realized that he had the first actual data for prehistorical cultural theory, leading him to the development of historiography as an observational science. This resulted in a little book called *The Revolutions of Civilization,* which he wrote in 1911, comparing eight periods of Egyptian (see figure 3.3) and six periods of European (see figure 3.4) civilization, and proposing a universal pattern for the progress of civilizations (see figure 3.3).

Like the ancients, Petrie used the analogy of the seasons of a year, in which each civilization advances through a cycle of seasons of great innovation in sculpture, painting, literature, mechanics, science, and wealth, in that order.[60] The average length of a period, in the histories Petrie studied, is 1,330 years. Climatic cycles were proposed as a possible cause of this period-

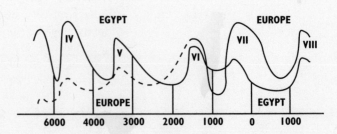

FIGURE 3.3 **Waves of Art in Egypt and Europe**
Drawing from Petrie (1911/1922).

❋ DYNAMICS AND THE ORPHIC TRINITY IN HISTORY

icity. In the spirit of Heraclitus and anticipating Toynbee, he proposed a theory of advance through strife, in explanation of the rising, falling, and renewing phases of civilization. [61]

LEWIS FRYE RICHARDSON, 1917

Around the time of World War II, an important creative leap took place within the sciences. Identified variously with operations research, mathematical modeling and computer simulation, game theory, holism, information theory, cybernetics, and cognitive science, it renewed the old vitalist roots of natural philosophy and physiology, and promoted a new synthesis of the

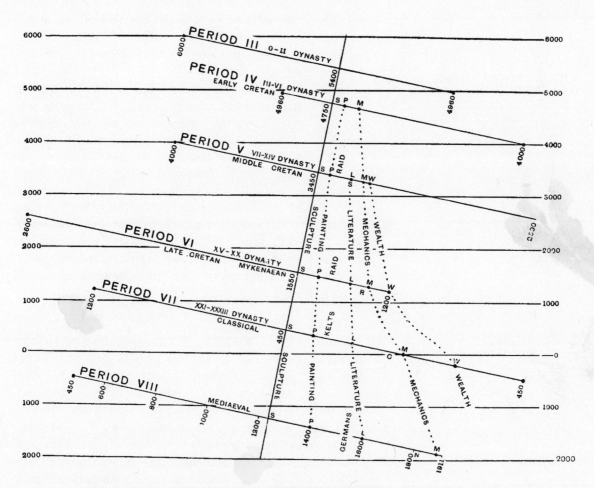

FIGURE 3.4 **The Periods and Phases of Mediterranean Civilization**
Drawing from Petrie (1911/1922).

sciences.[62] This event, located on the tree of knowledge in figure 1.1, leads to the vigorous development of what we now call *erodynamics,* which was created by Lewis Frye Richardson (1881–1953) in 1917, and which we will explore in chapter 18.

SPENGLER, 1917

Oswald Spengler (1880–1936) was the first of the great cycle historiographers of the twentieth century. Following Ibn-Khaldûn, Vico, and Petrie, he envisioned a cyclical pattern in the evolution of cultures. In *The Decline of the West: Outline of a Morphology of World History,* published in 1917, he attempted to establish a cycle of the four seasons for cultures, analogous to phases of human development: spring (childhood), summer (adolescence), fall (maturity), and winter (senility). Each of his seasons lasts about one thousand years, and a Great Year lasts about four thousand ordinary years. The development of a culture unfolds under the guidance of its *Destiny-idea,* or cognitive map.[63]

RADHAKRISHNAN, 1924

Sarvepalli Radhakrishnan (1888–1975) was knowledgeable in the history of philosophy of Europe as well as India. In his early writings, he proposed a one-cycle model for history, as opposed to the usual Hindu multicycle model. He gave the *Taittiriya Upanishad* (800 B.C.) as the source of his model.[64]

LOVEJOY, 1933

Arthur O. Lovejoy (1873–1962) founded the History of Ideas Club at Johns Hopkins University, in Baltimore, Maryland, one of the earliest of the great American universities.[65] His program to organize the history of ideas by following the adventures of a single dominant idea throughout its entire lifetime was epitomized in his Harvard lectures on the Great Chain of Being in 1933.

TOYNBEE, 1934

Arnold Toynbee (1889–1972), in *A Study of History,* ten volumes published in 1934–37, presented a cyclical pattern in the rise and fall of great civilizations in four phases, which he called: Challenge and Response, Growth, Breakdown, and Disintegration.[66] Toynbee endorsed Saint Augustine's theory of Providence, combining a cyclic pattern with a slower linear advance into a spiral approach to the City of God.[67] He partitioned history into an evolutionary series of twenty-one civilizations.[68] The idea of a chaotic transformation between stable structures, common to the Egyptian and Vichian models, appears in Toynbee as well.[69]

SOROKIN, 1937

Sorokin (1889–1968), in his four-volume *Social and Cultural Dynamics,* presented a cultural development cycle in three phases: the ideational, the idealistic, and the sensate. Humanity is described as a superorganism in an endless, linear progression of historical necessity, punctuated by stages or epochs similar to the growth phases of a plant.[70]

ROSENSTOCK-HUESSY, 1938

Eugen Rosenstock-Huessy (1888–1973) was inspired, while in the trenches of Verdun in World War I, to create a theory of European history based on the key role of the wars of revolution in Russia, France, England, Germany, and the United States. In his eight-hundred-page classic, *Out of Revolution,* first published in 1938, he revised nine hundred years of European history in the light of this inspiration. Here we find a universal paradigm of social revolution, parallel to those of Vico and Petrie.[71]

BEARD, 1946

Mary Ritter Beard (1876–1958), an American historian and activist for women's suffrage, campaigned for the recognition of women's contributions to society. In *Woman as Force in History: A Study in Traditions and Realities,* published in 1946, she challenged the idea that women are a subject sex. She worked for years to collect an archive of forgotten documents in support of this thesis, and for the commemoration of women's achievements. Ironically, she overlooked Matilda Joslyn Gage, who had independently discovered important parts of this legacy half a century earlier.

GEBSER, 1949

Jean Gebser (1905–73), a Polish expatriate, was pushed around Europe throughout his life by wars and persecution. In Spain, in 1932, he received a flash of inspiration on the structure of consciousness, which he eventually described in *The Ever-Present Origin,* published in 1949. His theory is essentially dynamical, describing human consciousness as an evolutionary sequence, which he calls *the unfolding of consciousness,* with critical bifurcations in five stages: the archaic, the magical, the mythical, the mental/rational, and the integral (or aperspectival). He traced this sequence in the histories of physics, mathematics, biology, sociology, philosophy, law, and the arts.[72]

ELIADE, 1949

Mircea Eliade (1907–86) was a creative scholar who approached historiography from the viewpoint of myth and religion. In 1949, while a professor at the Sorbonne, he published *The Myth of the Eternal Return: Archetypes and Repetition*. This book appeared in English in 1954 with the subtitle *Cosmos and History*, a title originally chosen by the author for the first draft of the French edition. While concerned explicitly with the mythology of New Year rituals in the ancient Near East, and cyclical myths of history such as those of India, it proceeds on the assumption that myths evolve from history. Hence the author had also considered the subtitle *Introduction to a Philosophy of History*. Many of the ideas developed later (and described below) by Voegelin, Fukuyama, and others (including part 2 of this book) first appeared in Eliade.

AUROBINDO, 1952

Sri Aurobindo Ghose (1872–1950) was an intellectual who became a great yogi and teacher. In *The Problem of Rebirth*, published in 1952, he presented a personal version of the Hindu Tantric theory of history, in which there is a single cycle: a fall from the Infinite into matter, and a divine return. In contrast to the usual Hindu multicycle models, this one-cycle model is similar to those of Augustine and Radhakrishnan.[73]

VOEGELIN, 1956

Eric Voegelin (1901–85), in his three-volume *Order and History* published in 1956 and 1957, deals with order and pattern in history on a grand scale.[74] He suggests that the emergence of order and pattern, and thus meaning in history, is a spontaneous process of self-organization. He contrasts the *Israelite conception of history*, with its linear time, to the cyclic patterns of Spengler and Toynbee, even though both models feature the great epochs of history.[75] This agrees with the spirit of the general systems and cybernetic views of history, and with the emerging models of complex dynamical systems, general evolution, and erodynamic theories, based on the bifurcation concept. These theories will be explained further in chapter 18.[76]

TILLICH, 1963

Paul Tillich (1886–1965), the Christian theologian, presented an analysis of the dynamics of history in the third volume of his *Systematic Theology*, published in 1963. While praising the metahistories of Hegel and Toynbee, he pointed out the arbitrariness of the divisions into great epochs, and of the concepts of progress.[77]

DYNAMICS AND THE ORPHIC TRINITY IN HISTORY

VON BERTALANFFY, 1968

An important component in the development we are tracing was the biological philosophy of Ludwig von Bertalanffy (1901–72), and the *general systems theory* outlined in his *Modern Theories of Development,* published in 1933. The application of general systems theory to the social sciences, and eventually to history itself, soon followed. In *General Systems Theory: Foundations, Development, Applications,* published in 1968, he proposed a systems theory of history, and described the theories of Vico, Hegel, Marx, Spengler, Toynbee, Sorokin, and Kroeber as serious first attempts.[78]

RASHEVSKY, 1968

Nicholas Rashevsky (1895–1964) escaped from the Russian Revolution to become the indefatigable pioneer of mathematical biology at the University of Chicago.[79] In 1939 he published an early erodynamic paper applying the methods of mathematical biology to sociology, and published a book on this subject in 1947. He edited the writings of Lewis Frye Richardson, the founder of erodynamics, for posthumous publication in 1960. In his *Looking at History through Mathematics,* published in 1968, he offers steps toward a mathematical model for Toynbee's theory of history. To explain revolutions, a tentative prevision of catastrophe theory is included:

> Whenever we have threshold phenomena, whether in physical, biological, or social systems, the configuration of the system *at the moment when the threshold is reached* becomes unstable and the slightest, even infinitesimal, displacement of the configuration in a proper direction leads eventually to a finite change in the configuration of the system. Therefore a change in the behavior of a single individual, no matter how small, may precipitate in an unstable social configuration, a process that leads to a finite, sometimes radical, change.[80]

An explicit recognition of the hermeneutic circle is presented in the Preface of this book, as part of an extensive defense of mathematical modeling.

RECENT WORK

The first model for history that significantly transcends that of the ancients is a fractal model presented by Dennis and Terence McKenna in 1975, in their pathfinding book, *The Invisible Landscape.*[81] In this model a peculiar curve called the time wave is constructed from the King Wen order of the hexagrams in the *I Ching,* a Chinese classic of divination. This curve is multiplied and compressed repeatedly, making a fractal curve, which is then fitted to the *novelty* manifest in recorded history.

Summary

In this chapter we have shown the gradual development of a general theory of social evolution, or historiography, until 1975. Since then, we've seen the development of dynamical historiography, in which the concepts of dynamical systems theory are applied to history. The models for the arms race, conflict resolution, codependence, and cooperation, described in part 3 under the name erodynamics, are part of this new development. Many steps in the story of this evolution have been necessarily omitted from this brief account, which aims to put dynamical historiography, including erodynamics, into its own historical context.

The theories explored in this chapter are devoted primarily to *local evolution,* the rise and fall of a single nation or social organism. In the next chapter, we consider *global evolution,* the progress of history as one nation succeeds another, and as the network of nations evolves in a process of morphogenesis. In recent years there has been a veritable explosion in this field.[82] This exploration prepares the ground for an erodynamical model of the emerging planetary society.

BIFURCATIONS OF CONSCIOUSNESS

The Ages of the World

CHAPTER 4

In June 1972, I jumped on a plane to India on impulse.

In June 1972, when classes came to an end at the University of Amsterdam, where I was teaching catastrophe theory, I jumped on a plane to India on impulse. I was happy to leave the academic world of books and scholarship behind me. On arrival in Delhi, fate led me to unexpected destinations: first to a cave in the Himalayan jungle, then to an ashram nearby. No sooner had I happened into this strange place, when the guru of the place, Neem Karoli Baba, yelled out in Hindi, "Where is that professor from California?" It appeared that he was expecting me, and had plans all ready! Soon I was set up in a village house, with an incredible library of Sanskrit classics in English translation. From these books and local teachings, I learned of ancient creation myths, a cyclical theory of history, and a mathematical model for vibrations and pattern formation in the physical, mental, and spiritual worlds. After about six months, I returned to California, transformed.

Mythical Ages of the World

Not only do most cultures have creation myths, they have mythical histories as well. The oral traditions of a cultural group seem to coalesce into a consensual reality, or mythical record, filling in the period from creation until the dawn of recorded history in the recent past. The play of the gods and mythical heroes, their family trees and wanderings, are committed to memory by successive generations in the form of epic poems and dramas. In broadest outline, these oral histories are divided into mythical *ages of the world,* and in this chapter we outline a few of these chronologies. We have selected those that illustrate the development of dynamical concepts, such as linear progression, eternal recurrence, and development from birth to death.

A combined form, the spiral of cycles plus the notion of progress, may have been known in the sixth millennium B.C.[1] One of the most evolved (and best known) mythical chronologies is the Hindu doctrine of cycles, called days of Brahma, or *maha yugas,* each lasting 4,320,000 (= 360 × 12,000) years.[2] Each cycle is divided into four *yugas,* called *krta, treta, dvapara,* and *kali.*

Two features are shared by most fully developed chronologies: it is cyclic, renewing creation after each catastrophic annihilation; and each cycle is declining in virtue.

This scheme illustrates two features shared by most fully developed chronologies: it is *cyclic,* renewing creation after each catastrophic annihilation; and each cycle is *declining* in virtue. In the Hindu system, the length of each yuga is proportional to its virtue. Thus, *krta* has 4800 × 360 years, *treta* has 3600 × 360, *dvapara* has 2400 × 360, and *kali yuga* has 1200 × 360, for a total of 12,000 × 360 years. In each succeeding age, virtue declines according to the proportions: 4, 3, 2, and 1.[3] In another reckoning the *maha yuga* of 4,320,000 is divided into about seventy-one periods, each subdivided into four yugas. The dates of the yugas according to this calendar are those shown in table 4.1.[4]

Next we consider the Babylonian system, probably the source for many later doctrines of this type. Its cycles and ages were modeled on the astrological zodiac, or path of the sun. The Babylonian zodiacal cycle is divided into twelve signs in four quarters, belonging to Marduk-Jupiter (spring equinox), Ninib-Mars (summer solstice), Nebo-Mercury (fall equinox), and Nergal-Saturn (winter solstice). These represent at once seasons in time, directions in space, planets of the solar system, and gods of the holy trinity (the rulers of the zodiac: Sun, Moon, Venus). The Moon (the star of the upper world) and the Sun (star of the lower world) are combatants in the Babylonian system. Due to the precession of the equinoxes, an astronomical phenomenon, the zodiacal constellation of Marduk's equinox changes every 2,200 years or so. The cycle begins in the sign of the Twins, thus the period from about 5000 B.C. to 2800 B.C. is called the Age of the Twins. This is followed by the Age of the Bull and the Age of the Ram. (The first three signs of the zodiac: Ram, Bull, and Twins, are also called Aries, Taurus, and Gemini.) In this progression virtue decays from perfection in the first Golden Age, toward destruction at the end of the 12 × 2200 = 26,400-year

TABLE 4.1
Hindu Ages

Dawn of Krta Yuga	58,042 B.C.
Beginning of Krta Yuga	56,026 B.C.
Beginning of Twilight	35,864 B.C.
Dawn of Treta Yuga	33,848 B.C.
Beginning of Treta Yuga	32,336 B.C.
Beginning of Twilight	17,215 B.C.
Dawn of Dvapara Yuga	15,703 B.C.
Beginning of Dvapara Yuga	14,695 B.C.
Beginning of Twilight	4614 B.C.
Dawn of Kali Yuga	3606 B.C.
Kali Yuga	3102 B.C.
Middle of Kali Yuga	582 B.C.
Beginning of Twilight	A.D. 1939
End of Twilight of Kali Yuga	A.D. 2442

Daniélou, 1985.

cycle. There are many complications due to the frequent calendric reforms made for political reasons by Babylonian rulers.[5]

EGYPT

In ancient Egypt history was divided into four great ages, of Gods, Heroes, Men, and Chaos. These are identical to the ages of Vico, as he himself noted (see chapter 1).[6]

GREEK

For the early Greeks, this scheme apparently matured into the four declining ages of Golden, Silver, Bronze, and Iron, corresponding roughly to the Hindu *yugas* in quality, if not length. According to another Greek tradition, a Heroic Age of the gods preceded our own. Hesiod blended these together in his *Works and Days.* This section, called *The Myth of Ages,* begins,

> In the beginning, the immortals
> who have their homes on Olympos
> created the golden generation of mortal people.
> These lived in Kronos' time, when he

was the king in heaven.
They lived as if they were gods,
their hearts free from all sorrow,
by themselves, and without hard work or pain;
no miserable
old age came their way; their hands, their feet,
did not alter.[7]

In this scheme there are five ages: Golden, Silver, Bronze, Heroic, and Iron.[8] The Hesiodic chronology continued its evolution well into our own medieval history.[9] Both Plato and Empedocles accepted this doctrine of the ages of history, which they learned from the Orphic writings. According to another Orphic tradition, there were three ages: the Golden under Phanes, the Silver under Kronos, and the Titanic under Zeus.[10] Historical evidence points to the ancient Orphic tradition as a source for the cyclic theory of history.

Modern Chronologies

Throughout the Middle Ages, a biblical cosmogony prevailed in which the world was created about six thousand years ago. Nowadays, we take for granted the concept of *deep time,* studied in various university departments, which includes millions of years of biological evolution.[11] This idea makes room for *paleontology,* the branch of geology dealing with prehistoric forms of life and fossils, *archaeology,* the scientific study of the life and culture of ancient peoples as revealed by the spade, and *prehistory,* a branch of archaeology dealing with the history of the world before written history.[12]

SCIENTISM

Although this scientific version of the ages of the world is firmly established for understanding the recent past, it becomes increasingly fictive and theoretical as we go deeper into time.

Our modern chronology, based on paleontology, archaeology, astrophysics, historical scholarship, and radiological dating technology, is not so different from the more traditional versions.[13] Although this scientific version of the ages of the world is firmly established for understanding the recent past, it becomes increasingly fictive and theoretical as we go deeper into time. The modern creation theory favored by astrophysicists, that of the Big Bang, may be regarded as a creation myth derivative of the Babylonian cosmogony.[14] This account depends on *evolutionism,* a theory in conflict with the declining virtue aspect of traditional theories of the ages. Intrinsic to Christianity,[15] it developed explicitly since Spencer and Darwin,[16] a century ago, along with paleontology.[17]

TABLE 4.2
500 Million Years of Gaian Evolution

Era or Group	Years	Period or System	Fauna	
CAINOZOIC	1 m	TERTIARY	Quaternary with *man*	MAMMALS BECOMING ABUNDANT
	30 m		First *apes*	
			First *lemurs*	
	58 m		First *placentals*	
MESOZOIC		CRETACEOUS	Angiosperms becoming frequent	
			Large dinosaurs	
	127 m	JURASSIC	First birds	
			Flying reptiles	
	152 m		Ammonites	
		TRIASSIC	First non-placental mammals	
			Conifers and seed ferns	
	182 m			
PALEOZOIC	203 m	PERMIAN		
		CARBONIFEROUS	First *reptiles* (Theromorpha)	
			Insects	
	255 m		Land spiders	
		DEVONIAN	First *amphibia*	
			First bony fishes (*Crossopterygians*)	
			First trees	
	313 m	SILURIAN	Scorpions	
			Trilobites	
	350 m		First land plants	
		ORDOVICIAN	First jawless fishes	
			Corals	
			Sea-urchins	
	430 m	CAMBRIAN	Foraminifera, starfishes, brachiopods, crustacea, marine 'spiders' (Merostomata)	
	500 m			
PROTEROZOIC			First *worms*	

TABLE 4.3
Twenty-five Million Years of Human Evolution

Tentative Time-Scale in Years	Period	Climatic Phase	Man and His Ancestors
15 000	HOLOCENE	POSTGLACIAL	*Homo sapiens*
100 000 150 000	UPPER PLEISTOCENE	LAST GLACIATION	Neanderthal Man
		LAST INTERGLACIAL	Fontéchevade Man
250 000	MIDDLE PLEISTOCENE	PENULTIMATE GLACIATION	
		GREAT INTERGLACIAL	Swanscombe Man
	LOWER PLEISTOCENE	ANTEPENULTIMATE GLACIATION	Heidelberg Man
500 000		ANTEPENULTIMATE INTERGLACIAL	Pithecanthropus Sinanthropus
		EARLY GLACIATION	
600 000		VILLAFRANCHIAN	*Australopithecus* (age conjectural) *Dryopithecus*
c 12 million	PLIOCENE		
c 25 million	MIOCENE		*Proconsul, Dryopithecus*

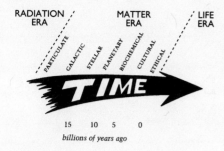

FIGURE 4.1

A Modern Chronology in Three Eras

Drawing by Lola Judith Chaisson, with additions.
Courtesy of the artist. Reprinted with permission.

The modern chronology is divided into ages, epochs, eras, and eons, in many different increments, depending on which branch of science is doing the dividing. One interesting division into four eras, by astronomer Eric Chaisson, is shown in figure 4.1.

Another division, basic to paleontology, is shown in table 4.2.[18] The divisions of deep time used by archaeologists provide another useful system, shown in table 4.3.[19]

Note that the ages of archaeology have dates depending on location. Thus they reveal a space-time pattern of progressing waves of transformation. The use of gardens, wheels, bronze, iron, and so on, sweeps across the map in a perplexing pattern, yet to be understood.[20]

Physicalism

Physicalism is a point of view developed in Vienna by the circle around philosopher Rudolf Carnap. It espoused the reduction of all entities to their physical and chemical forces (the physicalist oath formulated by Ernst Wilhelm von Brucke and Emil Dubois-Reymond), the elimination of metaphysics, and a theory of verification based on the empirical results of experimental laboratory procedures.[21]

Summary

In this chapter we've collected various traditional and modern schemes for the grokking of deep time. The space-time pattern of history depends on your cognitive map, and in fact, *it is a cognitive map*. The evolution of this map is now in rapid transformation. Yet another system for the division of space-time into ages is provided by the new perspective of dynamical systems theory, to which we turn in the next chapter.

The Three Dynamical Epochs

CHAPTER 5

During my year at the University of Amsterdam (1971–72), Christopher Zeeman came to visit. Then head of the Math Research Centre at the University of Warwick, Chris was one of the mathematicians closest to me in the world of ideas. He gave a lecture at the Math Institute of Amsterdam on a model for memory based on an array of oscillators. After his talk we retired to the cafeteria for tea. It was there that I first heard from him a theory of the evolution of human understanding by quantum jumps, like the sudden appearance of new species in biological evolution, based on catastrophe theory. Chris went on to important developments in catastrophe theory and its applications,[1] while I went on with his model for memory.[2]

The History of Dynamics

As Halley's comet approached Earth on a collision course in the seventeenth century, the question of the stability of the solar system took on a new urgency. Sir Edmund Halley himself challenged Newton with this question in the corridors of the newly formed Royal Society. Newton responded with his development of the calculus, described by historians as the greatest contribution to knowledge ever made by one man (more details are given in chapter 15). A century ago Poincaré, returning again to this question of the stability of the solar system, created dynamical systems theory (more about this in chapter 16), which now contains the theories of chaotic attractors and their bifurcations, as well as complex dynamical systems. All of these provide an extensive strategy for building models of complex systems and processes.

Complex Systems

A complex system is one with lots of parts. Previous attempts at modeling complex systems using Newtonian structures were abandoned when the models developed chaotic behavior. But under the new paradigm evolved from Poincaré, chaotic models are advantageous, for most complex systems do behave chaotically. The basic dynamical concepts of the new theory of complex systems are attractors, basins, and bifurcations. One of the most complex processes to which this strategy has been applied is the process of history itself, including the evolution of human consciousness.[3] This application, which we call erodynamics, is described in chapter 18.

Dynamical Models

In modern mathematics and science, several words are nearly synonymous with *dynamics,* the physics of forces and motions of discrete or continuous mass systems. We may distinguish *mechanics* (the art of making models, especially mathematical models for dynamical processes), *kinematics* (the abstract description of motion exclusive of mass and forces), and *kinetics* (the study of motion, including dynamics and kinematics). All these subjects are classical, with important contributions made by Archimedes, Galileo, and Newton.

Since Poincaré, however, dynamics and *dynamical systems theory* have come into standard use among mathematicians in place of kinematics. Here we will speak of dynamics in the mathematical sense, meaning the abstract mathematical theory of motion, without reference to mass, force, or any other physical property of the moving system. A *dynamical model* is an abstract mathematical model for a dynamical process. For example, a circle might model a cyclically recurring process. In this sense there are dynamical models for many systems, such as social systems or communication networks, which have no physical forces. These models, together with their simulation on digital computers with color graphics, comprise a new style in the traditional art of mechanics.

MODELING

The modeling process consists of four phases:

- an observation phase, in which data are collected from the target system (for example, historical data)
- a construction phase, in which a dynamical model is built from the data, and the collection of available model

structures (for example, a set of differential equations in the style of Newton)
- a simulation phase, in which the model is run to produce simulated data (usually as a computer program)
- a comparison phase, in which the simulated data and the observed data are compared (computer graphics are useful in this phase)

In the ideal world of mathematics, the evolution of a dynamical model is precisely determined forever. This aspect of Newtonian models was particularly emphasized by the French mathematician Pierre-Simon Laplace (1749–1827), when he resumed Newton's work on the stability of the solar system. According to this mathematical ideal, called *Laplacian determinism,* if the positions and velocities of all the planets and comets in the dynamical model for the solar system *are known exactly,* then they can be predicted exactly for all time. In practice, this is a mighty big *if.* Even if the chaotic behavior discovered by Poincaré in this model did not occur, the ideal would probably be unattainable.

Attractors and Bifurcations

From the viewpoint of dynamics, history falls into stages described by special forms of dynamical behavior called *attractors* and connected by particular kinds of transformations called *bifurcations.* The simple forms called attractors are observed as representations of the stable (or observable) states of a system. In the theory there are three types of attractors: *static, periodic,* and *chaotic.*

ATTRACTORS

Static attractors (also called point attractors) are just points, to which nearby points are dynamically attracted. They represent the system at rest, as they model its stationary states. Periodic attractors consist of a cycle of states, repeated again and again, always in the same period of time. They represent the system in oscillation. Chaotic attractors consist of fractal (infinitely folded) sets of states, over which the model system moves, occupying different states in a sequence called a *trajectory,* or time series. This trajectory, while appearing irregular or random, actually progresses in a deterministic manner. Chaotic attractors display, at once, features of chaos and features of order. They represent systems in states of agitation, as in the case of turbulence.[4]

These three mathematical objects—the static, periodic, and chaotic attractors—were not discovered all at once. The point attractor emerged first, soon after Newton developed the basic mathematics for dynamical systems (the branch of mathematics now known as *ordinary differential equations*) about 1665. The periodic attractor came into general use around 1850, spawning a new branch of mathematics known as *nonlinear oscillation theory*.[5] The chaotic attractor, although known in one form to Poincaré in 1899 (the so-called *homoclinic tangle*),[6] emerged into scientific consciousness only around 1961.[7] These three dates, 1665, 1850, and 1963, mark great leaps in our mathematical understanding of dynamical processes.

How can we convey an ordinary understanding of these three kinds of dynamical behavior: the static, the periodic, and the chaotic? Certainly, the point and the cycle are very simple, basic, and familiar mathematical objects, even if the chaotic attractor is not. The point represents the system at rest, the cycle represents the system in oscillation, and the chaotic attractor models a state that is disorderly, but ordered to a degree, and unpredictable, but predictable to a degree. This limited predictability replaces Laplacian determinism in the new theory of chaotic dynamics.

The important map provided by dynamical systems theory to a scientist, or to anyone trying to understand a process in nature, is the *response diagram*. This is a map of the attractors moving about, as external conditions are changed. While moving around, the attractors occasionally disappear, explode, or change their type. These distinct changes in the map are called *bifurcations,* and dynamical systems theory provides a partial encyclopedia of them.[8] To someone trained in this encyclopedia, the response diagram of a dynamical model provides a map of the behavior of a process modeled, such as the solar system in motion or the critical moments of history.

Mathematics and Evolution

According to a "folk theory" circulating among mathematicians, a mathematical object will emerge into the collective consciousness of a group somewhat after the complexity of the group mind evolves to the necessary minimum level to support the cognition of that object.[9] That is, the brain and mind evolve, consciousness evolves, mathematical skills evolve, language evolves, all of these

According to a "folk theory" circulating among mathematicians, a mathematical object will emerge into the collective consciousness of a group somewhat after the complexity of the group mind evolves to the necessary minimum level to support the cognition of that object.

coevolve. According to this theory, mathematical objects are "discovered" as soon as a people are able to understand them. Different cultures, in this way, evolve different views of mathematical reality, and thus, via the grok circle, different views of ordinary reality. Extrapolating this evolutionary view to the grand scale of the history of consciousness itself, we may transcend the level of mathematical model, and look for the emergence of the dynamical concepts themselves as a simple division of history into three historical ages corresponding to the three dynamical models: the Static Age, the Periodic Age, and the Chaotic Age.

Referring to Eric Chaisson's chronology depicted in chapter 4, figure 4.1, we will consider now only the period since the human mind evolved to the level of the conscious awareness of static forms. Let us begin, for practical purposes, with the important development of language, although the beginning of this period may precede the development of language, which could have emerged with early *Homo sapiens* about 50,000 years ago, or much earlier, with *Homo erectus,* for example. We know little about our parent species, so we will restrict our attention to the past 50,000 years.[10]

THE STATIC AGE, 9000 B.C.

The first event in this hypothetical series of cultural transformations, or bifurcations, is the emergence of the static concept into awareness. This might coincide with the development of linguistic structures such as the command to *stand still.* The first material manifestation of this bifurcation might be the development of agriculture, the *Neolithic Revolution,* around 9000 B.C.[11] The domestication of plants and animals defeated the chaos of nature by stabilizing the wanderers in homeostasis, a static state. Thus we mark the onset of the Static Age with the beginnings of agriculture in the Fertile Crescent, around 9000 B.C.[12]

THE PERIODIC AGE, 3500 B.C.

The Periodic transformation, like the Static, proceeded in waves of diffusion. Periodic processes, such as the cycle of seasons, the menstrual cycle, the phases of the moon, and the daily solar cycle, were understood, even essential, long before the Periodic Revolution, as evidenced in artistic representations of the phases of the Moon done by the Cro-Magnon people, around 25,000 B.C.[13] The conceptualization of this dynamical archetype has been identified with the dawn of mathematics.[14] An understanding of the cycle of the seasons, necessary for successful hunting and gathering, was in place long before the materialization of the static concept in the agricultural revolution. The material manifestation (or realization) of the cyclic idea comes much later, however, in the invention of the wheel, around 3500 B.C. This marks the beginning of the Periodic Age.[15]

THE CHAOTIC AGE, A.D. 1961

The chaotic process emerged into awareness in remote antiquity, when it was represented by symbols such as serpents, sea monsters, and the goddesses Inanna, Ishtar, and Tiamat.

The chaotic process emerged into awareness in remote antiquity, when it was represented by symbols such as serpents, sea monsters, and the goddesses Inanna, Ishtar, and Tiamat. In various ancient cultures, chaos plays an integral part in art, architecture, and daily life (see figure 5.1). The chaotic concept did not fare well in the history of Indo-European consciousness, perhaps because of its suppression by dominator figures like Marduk, Zeus, Yahweh, and Saint Michael.

Many concepts emerge on the mathematical level before appearing in the material record as artifacts of human society. One example is the cycle concept, as described above. As a mathematical object, the chaos concept was known to Poincaré, the French mathematician, a century ago. However, its modern realization, and materialization, is in the computer models observed by Yoshisuke Ueda in November 1961, and by Edward Lorenz, in 1963. The Chaotic Age began with these simulations.[16]

THE THREE-AGE CYCLE

The entire span of these three ages is about 10,000 or 12,000 years thus far, a dynamical epoch analogous to the *maha yuga* of the Hindu theory of four ages,[17] and corresponding roughly to the Holocene Interglacial period. Interglacials are the relatively

FIGURE 5.1
Fractal Architecture in Africa: Mali Rabizanga

Photo George Gerster/Compage. Courtesy of Comstock. Reprinted with permission.

rare periods between ice ages, during which the temperate zone is widespread. James Lovelock calls them *Gaian fevers*.[18] The Holocene Interglacial is the fever in which we now live. If we suppose that:

- the recognition of chaotic processes functioned normally in the human conscious system before the Neolithic (agricultural) Revolution
- the development of agriculture marked the beginning of the Static Age, after which chaotic recognition was demoted to the unconscious system
- the development of the material wheel marked the beginning of the Periodic Age (characterized by the further suppression of chaos)
- the recent bifurcation in 1961 marks the beginning of a new Chaotic Age

then we are now at the renewal of a cycle of three ages, beginning with the Chaotic, Static, Periodic, and so on. We do not know the duration of the current Chaotic Age (nor the preceding one, for that matter), therefore we cannot guess the span of a complete cycle.

The Ice Ages, Patriarchy, and the Wheel

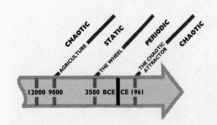

FIGURE 5.2
A Dynamical Chronology in Cycles[22]

Drawing by Diane Rigoli, © Ralph H. Abraham.

Dates of the most recent ice ages have been accurately determined, and we may speculate that Neolithic revolutions (and thus static ages) may have occurred in previous interglacial periods. (We have no concrete evidence of this.) If we accept the possibility that *Homo erectus* was an intelligent species (they did successfully navigate ships to all continents), and interpret freely the findings at Terra Amata (300,000-year-old dwellings discovered in downtown Nice, in France) and Shanidar (100,000-year-old dwellings, recently excavated in Iraq), the likelihood of agriculture in an earlier interglacial is not negligible.[19]

There have been attempts to identify the glaciations with a periodic process, but recently it has been suggested that they occur chaotically.[20] We might look for a three-age cycle in every interglacial, but the motions of the sun within the solar system, which strongly influence our global climate (particularly ice ages), are chaotic, not periodic. We should not necessarily expect history to follow periodic cycles either.[21] Conceivably, a new Static Age could occur again after the next glaciation recedes. Thus the dynamical cycle of three ages might be recurring chaotically in the future, giving realization to the ancient theories of the ages of the world, as shown in figure 5.2.

PATRIARCHY AND THE WHEEL

Comparing this chronology with those described above, we see that our traditional creation myths begin in the middle Neolithic period, around 4000 B.C., the time of the first wave of Kurgan people from the northern steppes. Along with this invasion came patriarchal domination over the culture of the Great Goddess, the introduction of the wheel, and the onset of the Periodic Era.[23] The domination of Chaos by Cosmos (order) on the mythic plane, characteristic of Enuma Elish and Genesis, coincides with the onset of the Periodic Era on the material plane.

Summary

Our current world is troubled by global problems, largely caused by our growing human population. Many of us have looked for an evolutionary leap in human consciousness and social organization that will bring us to a new plateau, on which these problems may have solutions.[24] The transformation to a Golden Age may indeed be underway, with the rediscovery of chaos by modern science being one of its first signs. This event may mark the beginning of a transition from the Life Era into the Conscious Era, in Chaisson's chronology, as well as the bifurcation from the Periodic to the Chaotic Age, in our dynamical chronology.

The conquest of chaos (always associated with creativity and evolution) by the forces of law and order (meaning fixed or periodic processes, according to dynamics) is a basic feature of the dominator society. To achieve the transformation to a Golden Age or Conscious Era, we must learn to see the good side of chaos, to understand the shadow side of order, and to recognize how we participate in the repression of Chaos and creativity by Cosmos (order) in our daily lives.

The Evolution of Consciousness

CHAPTER 6

In 1983 I was surprised by an invitation to Provence from the Institute for Ecotechnics, for their Cosmos Conference. I had never heard of the Institute, but I accepted. In November, on a farm in Provence in the south of France, I met an extraordinary group of people, and listened to some of the best lectures on science I have ever heard. There the idea was born for a new field, biospherics, and this led to a later conference on this subject near Tucson, Arizona.

In Tucson I met Jim Lovelock and watched his video simulating the stabilization of Earth's climate. I was introduced to biogeography for the first time, and imagined an application of Cellular Dynamical Systems Theory to this field. Later, under the influence of GERG, I extended this modeling idea to include social phenomena, and the close interaction of the sociosphere and the biosphere.

An Encyclopedia of Bifurcations

Suppose that a natural process evolves in time. A model for that process might depend on parameters that also change over time. Dynamical models appropriate for this task are called *dynamical schemes,* and the significant changes in their behavior are known as *bifurcations.* As we have a growing encyclopedia of generic bifurcations in the annals of dynamical systems theory, we should expect to be able to use them to model special events in the evolution of a natural process.[1]

This expectation is reasonable, even exciting, and has been vindicated with important applications in the physical sciences, such as the science of fluid flow. Moreover, we should be able to use the encyclopedia of bifurcations to make models in general evolution theory. Not much has yet been achieved in this context, as here we must contend with highly complex, hierarchically structured systems. The extension of dynamical systems theory to the traditional territory of general systems theory and cybernetics, known as holarchic (or complex) dynamics, has just begun.

This chapter is devoted to the bare outline of two main themes: general evolution theory and holarchic dynamical models. To grasp the concepts, one must go to the sources given in the bibliography, or better, to the original sources, which include J. B. Lamarck, Alfred Lotka, Jan Smuts, L. L. Whyte, Joseph Needham, Teilhard de Chardin, Erwin Schrodinger, and Albert Szent-Gyorgyi. An excellent bibliography was given by Arthur Koestler.[2]

General Evolution Theory

General evolution theory begins with Jean Baptiste Lamarck (1744–1829), who dealt with the origin of mind in his classic of 1809, *Zoological Philosophy,* which introduced the concept of *biosphere.*[3] Around the turn of the century, the subject was taken up by Hans Driesch and Henri Bergson. The terms *lithosphere* and *atmosphere* were introduced around 1875, apparently by Eduard Suess (1831–1914). Another early version of general evolution theory was given by Alfred James Lotka, in 1925.[4] He tried to describe the evolution of the geosphere and the biosphere, and the origin of consciousness, seeking a general theory of evolution equally applicable to all three envelopes.

Teilhard de Chardin extended these theories, increasing the distinction between individual and social consciousness by coining the term *noosphere* in 1925.[5] In parallel with the *geogenesis* and *biogenesis* of the denser envelopes of the planet, he made extensive use of the terms *noogenesis* and *psychogenesis* to refer to the emergence of planetary consciousness.[6] The following year Jan Smuts introduced the concept of *holism.*[7] The full scientific implications of the holist system of the spheres was envisioned by Vladimir Vernadsky in his book *Problems of Biogeochemistry,* first published in 1929.[8]

BIOSPHERICS

Recently, in a similar attempt to discern overall patterns in evolution, Arthur Koestler introduced the concept of *holarchy* to refer to structures of cooperative, yet autonomous, individuals, which he called *holons.*[9] Since then, there is a growing literature on general evolution theory.[10] According to the modern theory, the geosphere has component envelopes, including the solid core, liquid core, lower mantle, transition zone, asthenosphere, lithosphere, and crust. The hydrosphere has layers as well. Our atmosphere includes the troposphere, mesosphere, thermo-sphere, and exosphere. The terms ionosphere and stratosphere are also used.[11]

SOCIOGENESIS

The biosphere has its subspheres as well, mostly unnamed. Of these subspheres, we single out for attention the stratum of human affairs, the *sociosphere*. Here is the crux of world problems. Its evolution—*cultural evolution,* or *sociogenesis*—is subject to the laws of general evolution theory.

As we learn those laws from comparative studies of the histories of geogenesis, biogenesis, and noogenesis, we may develop the capability to guide our own sociogenesis, and to participate in the creation of our own future. This points to a new science of the future, a true social science, with mathematical models and observational laws, with understanding and wisdom, and with a basis in history and social philosophy. Many of its elements exist today: systems theory, complex dynamics, general evolution theory, the various social sciences. The integration of these elements into a new understanding and vision of sociogenesis awaits the computer revolution, chaos theory, and complexity theory, which are all necessary components of the evolution to come.

Holarchic Dynamical Models: Society and Mind

The relation between sociogenesis (cultural evolution, the evolution of cultural cognitive maps) and noogenesis (the history of consciousness) is particularly important for our future, and has been the special study of theoretical biologists like Conrad Waddington, Gregory Bateson, and Rupert Sheldrake.[12] In the introduction to his last book, in 1979, Bateson wrote:

> I want to tell you why I have been a biologist all my life, what it is that I have been trying to study. What thoughts can I share regarding the total biological world in which we live and have our being?
>
> What now must be said is difficult, appears to be quite *empty,* and is of very great and deep importance to you and to me. At this historic juncture, I believe it to be important to the survival of the whole biosphere, which you know is threatened.
>
> What is the pattern which connects all the living creatures? . . . The *pattern which connects is a metapattern.* It is a pattern of patterns. It is that metapattern which defines the vast generalization that, indeed, *it is patterns which connect.*[13]

"What now must be said is difficult, appears to be quite empty, and is of very great and deep importance to you and to me. At this historic juncture, I believe it to be important to the survival of the whole biosphere, which you know is threatened."

Erodynamics, or holarchic dynamics, is the mathematics of metapatterns, that is, patterns of patterns in space and in time, rhythms and undulations and symmetries. To some, this study of metapatterns is the new definition of mathematics itself.[14] Its applications to the physical, biological, social, psychological, and collective supraconscious realms were fundamental to the early coevolution of mathematics and culture. The social and metaphysical connections were gradually lost, however, after the Renaissance, and now, with the Chaos Revolution, they revive in a postmodern trinity, to span the Spirit bridge between Body and Soul.

OUR NEXT SOCIAL TRANSFORMATION

The definitive theorist of social transformation through utopian thought is Paul Tillich. He embeds the two aspects of utopology (see chapter 9 for a summary)—the positive-creative and the negative-destructive—into an essentially human activity that drives history through alternating cycles of falling from an ideal, then gaining new possibilities.[15]

The social and ecological crises of these times . . . have stimulated a great wish in the collective consciousness of human society, for a magical solution . . .

The social and ecological crises of these times, sometimes collectively called the *world problematique,* have stimulated a great wish in the collective consciousness of human society, for a magical solution, which we may call the *world mystique.* An early version of this wish was the *omega point* concept of Teilhard de Chardin.[16] After extensive analysis of the coupled evolutionary processes following the *alpha point* (creation) of our history, Teilhard proposed a divine resolution at the end of the upcoming crises, which he called the omega point.[17] This he saw as a catastrophic evolutionary event involving deep transformations of individuals and societies, a sort of phase transition of the noosphere, and the reunion of the noosphere with the denser spheres (geosphere and biosphere) into a conscious (and loving) hierarchy.[18] This reunited universe is Nature Reborn, Gaia herself (see figure 6.1).

More recent versions of this great Wish for Omega are the idea of a spontaneous transformation to the Aquarian Age[19] and the global Harmonic Convergence ritual observance of 1989.[20]

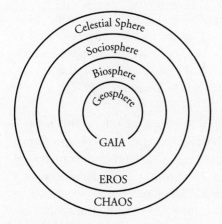

FIGURE 6.1

Chaos, Gaia, and Eros as the Three Concentric Spheres of Heaven, Earth, and Noosphere: Nature Reborn

Drawing by Diane Rigoli, © Ralph Abraham, 1994.

These contemporary expressions of the world mystique have been extensively criticized in the political press as a wish-fulfillment dream, potentially working against the urgent necessity of political action. This criticism begs the main question: *What action is possible and desirable in the present?* One popular answer to this pressing question is individual work, aimed at one's personal transformation. An outstanding summary of this view has been presented by Ralph Metzner.[21] If this individual approach to noogenesis is correct, we may be approaching the omega transition at a good pace, as there seems to be in process a tremendous groundswell in personal efforts toward individual transformation in many societies today.

INTERNATIONAL COOPERATION

A substantial increase in cooperation among peoples and societies is prerequisite to solution of world problems and the continued evolution of a planetary society. This is the view of Arthur Koestler, in his general theory of holarchic evolution, in which the balance of two main tendencies of holons (self-assertive and integrative, the two faces of Janus) is prerequisite for a stable evolution. If this holistic view is correct, individual work would be insufficient to achieve a healthy planetary society, even if all people were to work on themselves full-time! New strategies of holarchic cooperation and collective action would be necessary as well. The discovery of these new strategies is our eventual goal. Ruth Benedict's concept of social synergy is also relevant here, as a necessary condition for international stability.[22]

ERODYNAMICS

The integration of a planetary society needs many strategies. In the last chapter of this book, we will discuss just one among these, based on mathematical models and computer simulation. This is the current form of a strategy introduced by the ancient Greeks, and called by them *mechanikos* (mechanics). The hope for progress based on this strategy, and the creation of a universal theory of evolution according to mathematical principles, is an extrapolation of the wondrous success of mechanics in the physical and biological sciences. One explanation of this success is the philosophical theory of mathematical structuralism, which holds that natural evolution, in the phenomenal universe, is constrained by overlying mathematical structures.

Summary

There are many mathematical modeling strategies. This book is based upon just one of these, called *dynamical systems theory,* which has evolved extensively since Newton in the crucible of the physical sciences. One of its concepts, the *bifurcation* of a dynamical scheme, is fundamental to our strategy for modeling the critical moments in an evolutionary process. The application of these concepts to model a holarchic system requires the combination of separate dynamical schemes (*the model holons*) into a complex, hierarchical network (*the model holarchy*). These structures are the target of much research on the frontiers of dynamics today, which we call complex dynamical systems theory, or syn-

✹

onymously, *holarchic dynamics*. One outstanding problem we're faced with is to discover how the dynamical behavior of a holarchy is determined by its component holons, their interconnections, and (as yet unknown) holonomic rules. Another major problem is to discover what properties of a holarchy are not determined by its holons. We might call this domain the *canon of holarchic law,* or as José Argüelles says, *holonomy.*[23] We will return to these considerations in part 3.

Summary of Part 1

According to the dynamical scheme for viewing history presented in part 1, the history of our culture may be divided into three epochs, dominated by the dynamical metaphors of the static, periodic, and chaotic attractors of modern mathematics. This is close to the schemes of Giambattista Vico and William Irwin Thompson, and is compatible with further divisions into finer periods. Moreover, the bifurcations to an anticipated New Age, in our fantasy, coincide with a stepwise coevolution of our cultural cognitive map to new levels of dynamical complexity. Thus:

- The development of language empowered the emergence of static concepts (nouns), which materialized (during this interglacial) as domesticated plants and animals.
- The understanding of the starry sky empowered the emergence of periodic concepts, models of cyclical temporal processes, and materialized as the wheel.
- The understanding of mathematical models for the solar system empowered the emergence of chaotic concepts, models for chaotic temporal processes, which materialized as computer simulations of chaotic attractors.

Further, as I stated in the first conjecture from the introduction:

The meanderings of human history and prehistory during these past 25,000 years reveal a persistent pattern of cyclic recurrence in three phases, associated with the three root concepts of the Orphic trinity. This pattern is recognizable today in the context of the new mathematics of space-time patterns called chaos theory.

The meanderings of human history and prehistory during these past 25,000 years reveal a persistent pattern of cyclic recurrence in three phases, associated with the three root concepts of the Orphic trinity. This pattern is recognizable today in the context of the new mathematics of space-time patterns called chaos theory.

Mythogenesis is a space-time pattern of evolution in the cultural cognitive map, the noosphere. *Sociogenesis*—the evolution and transformation of social, religious, political, and technological structures—is a space-time pattern on the surface of the sociosphere. These two patterns coevolve in resonance.

The sense of our judgment is that, as a cultural transformation, the Chaos Revolution is comparable to the advent of the wheel. Like the wheel, the Garden, the Patriarchy, and all other major social transformations, the Chaos Revolution is emerging as a space-time pattern bringing chaotic order out of chaotic disorder. In the words of Gregory Bateson, this is *the pattern which connects.*

PART TWO

The Orphic Trinity in Myth

The theme that threads throughout this book is a perennial and overlooked mythic undercurrent in European civilization. Born before 25,000 B.C., in the goddess-worshiping partnership societies of the Paleolithic era, this tradition was overpowered and absorbed by the patriarchal dominator society after 4000 B.C., in Neolithic times. Because the emergence of this tradition into the historical record coincides with *Orphism,* the most important religion of ancient Greece, we shall refer to the entire cultural current as *the long line of Orphism,* or *the Orphic tradition.* Like a great river system, the Orphic tradition arose in a pure spring of partnership culture, flowed through time from the remote past with many branchings and combinations, became brackish with cultural debris, and was replenished occasionally by a succession of *Orphic revivals,* each followed inevitably by a backlash of repression.

An Orphic revival is characterized by a return of the partnership values of prehistory, a renewal of creativity in the arts, a striving for the rights of women and of animals, for the preservation of the environment, and for peace between nations and people. Fundamental to the conflict between the partnership way and the dominator paradigm is the *dichotomy of chaos and order.* The patriarchal religion worships order, striving always to defeat chaos, while the partnership way accepts both chaos and order, apparently without conflict.

In part 2 we'll look at the mythological context that frames recent upheavals in science, philosophy, and spirituality. The deepest roots of the now reemerging concepts of Chaos, Gaia, and Eros have been uncovered in evidence for a planetwide religion of the Mother Goddess that characterized the Late Paleolithic world of 25,000 years ago. This area of archaeological scholarship provides us with a basis for important shifts in our historical images.[1]

Riane Eisler, one of the contemporary chroniclers of early Neolithic cultural evolution (from roughly 10,000 B.C.), has introduced the terms *gylany* and *partnership society* to describe

---

An Orphic revival is characterized by a return of the partnership values of prehistory.

the more peaceful and egalitarian goddess-worshiping societies that she believes were predominant during the late Paleolithic and early Neolithic eras. She has also introduced the terms *androcracy* and *dominator society* to describe the more warlike and male-dominant god-worshiping form of society that began with patriarchal incursions about six thousand years ago, and still characterizes our current culture.[2] In her theory the partnership society survived for some time after the dominator phase began, dwindling in Europe to the single exemplary culture of Minoan Crete, at the dawn of written records.

As a viable society, the gylanic Minoans died out completely around 1400 B.C., taken over by the androcratic Mycenaeans. The religion, ritual, and mythology of Minoan Crete and its gylanic root culture were incorporated and preserved in the Mycenaean culture, and later in ancient Greece, in the form of Orphism. The long line of Orphism refers to this whole root system, including:

- the Paleolithic religion of the Mother Goddess since 25,000 B.C.

- the gylanic planetary culture of the early Neolithic after 10,000 B.C.
- its climax at Catal Huyuk, 6000 B.C.
- its partial erosion in Sumer, 4000 B.C.
- its defeat in Babylon, 2000 B.C.
- its postflorescence in Minoan Crete, 1500 B.C.
- its gender transformation in Mycenae, 1200 B.C.
- its reconstitution in the Orphic and mystery traditions in ancient Greece, around 600 B.C.
- their vestigial remains in European civilization up to the present time

As we will see, the early Orphic tradition in Crete was contemporaneous with parallel traditions in Mesopotamia, Ugarit, and Egypt from 3000 B.C. to about A.D. 400. These four traditions—Sumerian/Babylonian, Egyptian, Ugaritic, and Cretan—constitute the root system of European civilization. The trinity is characteristic of the Orphic tradition, since the origin of this tradition is in the goddess culture of TriVia. The rise of Christianity out of Judaism combined the three into one, but the long line of Orphism carries on, in the collective uncon-

scious, and in some of the trinities, sciences, and secret societies of our time.

The miracle of ancient Greece, which preserved some aspects of partnership culture—including Greek Orphism—underneath the veneer of a strong dominator overlay, is epitomized by the Academe of Plato and the Lykeion of Aristotle, both in Athens, and their successor university, the Alexandrian Museion. Despite the male dominance that was already a feature of these times, Hypatia was one of the most famous professors of Alexandria, along with Euclid and Eratosthenes. The fall of ancient Greece and the Orphic tradition, with the concomitant rise of Christianity, is symbolized by the murder of Hypatia by a Christian mob in A.D. 415.

ORPHIC REVIVALS

There have been several reformations within the Orphic tradition:

- Orpheus reformed Dionysism
- Pythagoras reformed Orphism
- Plotinus reformed Platonic Neopythagoreanism

Reformation is an archetypal form of social transformation, as is revival, which repeats an earlier reformation. Many important social transformations since the fall of ancient Greece have Orphic features. For example, the rise of early Christianity may be regarded as an Orphic revival because of its early themes of gnosis, the trinity, and love, which are clearly Orphic and Neoplatonic, as is the later theme of the Holy Mother. There are numerous parallels between the historical and mythical figures of Orpheus and Jesus. Both reformers, they led people toward an increased sensitivity and love for all life, including plants, animals, women, and men; and both were also saviors, identified with hope for the salvation of individuals, and of the world. The troubadour renaissance in the south of France in the eleventh century[3] and the Neoplatonic/Hermetic Renaissance in northern Italy in the fifteenth century have been described as *gylanic resurgence waves* by Eisler.[4] We will call them *Orphic revivals*. Each of these historical events incorporates:

- a movement toward partnership of the genders

- more freedom in sexual behavior
- a florescence of the arts
- a renewal of spirituality

The social upheaval in the United States and Europe in the 1960s also fits this pattern. From this most recent Orphic revival were born the three recent paradigm shifts within the sciences, described in part 3. These three are all derived from the mathematical theories of dynamical systems, chaos, and bifurcations. The cultural transformations of the 1960s affected the evolution of dynamical systems theory, and the lives of the mathematicians (such as myself) working in this field; chaos theory was the result.[5]

THE CONJECTURE

Three paradigm shifts in modern science, all occurring in the 1970s, carry the names of Chaos, Gaia, and Eros. At that time probably no one involved knew that these three names belonged to the three most important concepts of early Orphism, the Orphic trinity of Hesiod. The original significance of the Orphic trinity of Chaos, Gaia, and Eros is determined by Orphic mythology, to which we now turn, in search of the evidence for Conjecture 2 of our theory:

The three concepts, Chaos, Gaia, and Eros, have a continuous tradition from the Paleolithic past to the present. The trinity form from the Paleolithic Goddess religion survives even today.

Our vision of the long line of Orphism is based on the thesis of Mellaart, Gimbutas, and Eisler, of a major social bifurcation around 4000 B.C. from a partnership society to a dominator system. Orphism, the most important religion of ancient Greece, straddled the shift from a partnership society that worshiped the Divine Mother and her Divine Son or Lover to a male-centered, dominator society. Thus the long line of Orphism connects our utopian past and

---

The three concepts, Chaos, Gaia, and Eros, have a continuous tradition from the Paleolithic past to the present. The trinity form from the Paleolithic Goddess religion survives even today.

future, like Ariadne's thread, strung through the labyrinth of our troubled present.

The next six chapters are a tour of the Orphic tradition—from the Paleolithic goddess TriVia, through the religious rituals of Sumer, Babylonia, Canaan, Ugarit, Egypt, Crete, Mycenae, and Greece, up to early Christianity and its various trinities. We will note the transformation from the worship of the Great Goddess to the One God, from Chaos to Order, from matriliny to patriliny, from Gaia the sacred Earth to the destruction of Nature, and from the Eros of divine Love to the sick Eros of the family disease.

The first three chapters of this part tour the origins of the Orphic tradition in detail, paying particular attention to gender issues, and the shift from the Great Goddess to the One God. The second triad of chapters delves into the myriad meanings of the cosmic principles of the Orphic trinity, Chaos, Gaia, and Eros, tracing the changes of meaning as the three principles transit the shift from goddesses to gods.

THE ORPHIC TRADITION

The Goddess TriVia

CHAPTER 7

In 1968 I moved from Princeton University to the University of California at Santa Cruz, which was then the apex of the counterculture. The Sons of Eternity played to capacity crowds of crazed hippies at The Barn, in front of fluorescent murals by Uzek (Joe) Lysowski. The musicians lived in trees in the Santa Cruz mountains, and their instruments were welded steel sculptures made by Ron Boise. I lived in a twenty-four-room Victorian mansion at 724 California Street, where one of the musicians came to visit me. His name was Zoo.

Zoo: They say you're a mathematician.
Me: Yep.
Zoo: Well, can you tell me about one plus one?
Me: Do you mean two?
Zoo: No. I mean, like me and my partner.

Some years passed before I understood that numbers were emotionally real to Zoo, as they became real to me, too, and as they were to Pythagoras and the Pythagoreans from ancient times to the recent past. I now know that numbers, such as the Three of the trinity, are fundamental to our cultural evolution. I am grateful to Zoo for his instruction.

Prehistorical Chaos

The word *Chaos* first appears, along with Gaia and Eros, in Hesiod's *Theogony*, as the three cosmic principles from which all else derives. These three constitute what we call the *Orphic trinity*. To Hesiod, the word *chaos* meant a gap, or yawning chasm. The current meaning of the word *chaos*, as disorder, goes back

81

further than the actual word. Tracing it back through history, we arrive at the earliest written records, in Sumer and Egypt, where chaos appears in a context of goddesses and serpents. The chaos concept did not arise concomitantly with writing, and we must therefore seek its source in prehistory, where we cannot avoid speculation. This chapter is a speculation on the prehistory and early history of the Orphic trinity.

Social Bifurcations

Horseback riding seems to have originated around 4300 B.C.[1] This contributed to the rapid spread of the Indo-Europeans and the patriarchy. Around 4000 B.C., pottery wheels were developed in Mesopotamia (see chapter 13), and after the horse and the wheel came the cart. After the cart, came the city. The technical developments of the wheel and the cart led to the Urban Revolution in the Middle East, which comprises a major evolutionary event, a *social transformation*.

From the perspective of cultural history, such transformations are the most interesting phenomena in the evolution of human society. And these transformations are events that may be illuminated by the new mathematics, dynamical systems theory. The mathematical theory provides transformational models called *bifurcations*, which may help us to understand these social transformations. (This application was described in part 1.) The Urban Revolution is an example of a major social transformation, or bifurcation. Literacy is another.

One, Two, and Three Cultures

One possible evolutionary scenario for the early civilizations of the ancient Near East begins somewhere on the plain, where a group worshiped a certain goddess or god. Eventually, they built a temple, a scene that attracted or repelled other people. If attractive, a city formed, growing up as the materialization of an original mythic plan. Cities formed, evolved, matured, and died, resulting in the early civilizations of Anatolia, the Indus valley, Mesopotamia, Egypt, and Crete, cultures naturally selected to succeed, out of many possible mutations.[2]

Each protoculture developed its system of myths, worldviews, and social structures around a certain seed, or mental structure . . . a cognitive map. Mythology is the verbal residue of an antique cognitive map.

Each protoculture developed its system of myths, worldviews, and social structures around a certain seed, or mental structure. We call this a *cognitive map*. *Mythology* is the verbal residue of an antique cognitive map. One of the simplest attributes of such a mythology is the number of figures, root concepts, or gods in its pantheon. Thus there have been:

- *One* cultures (that is, cultures with a monotheistic religion, such as Judaism)

THE ORPHIC TRINITY IN MYTH

FIGURE 7.1
**Classical Greek TriVia:
Hecate Triformis**

From Creutzer (1825).

Stone Age

TRIVIAL PURSUITS

- *Two* cultures (with dualistic religion, such as Islam)
- *Three* cultures (such as the prehistoric culture of the goddess TriVia, or ancient Egypt)

Chuang Tzu says,

We have already become one, so how can I say anything? But I have just said that we are one, so how can I not be saying something? The one and what I said about it make two, and two and the original one make three. If we go on this way, then even the cleverest mathematician can't tell where we'll end, much less an ordinary man.[3]

Christianity began with a jump from One to Three. According to theologian Paul Tillich,

Trinitarian monotheism is not a matter of the number three. It is a qualitative and not a quantitative characterization of God. It is an attempt to speak of the living God, the God in whom the ultimate and the concrete are united. . . . The trinitarian problem is the problem of the unity between ultimacy and concreteness in the living God. Trinitarian monotheism is concrete monotheism, the affirmation of the living God. The trinitarian problem is a perennial feature of the history of religion.[4]

Archaeologically, Three cultures seem to be more numerous and long-lived than Ones, Twos, or Fours. Christian mythology and religion, derived from the One type structure of the Israelites, is fundamentally a Three type structure. This constitutes experiential evidence for some evolutionary advantage, or stability, of Three. The rest of this chapter gives a genealogy of our own trinity.

The late Paleolithic (25,000 B.C.–10,000 B.C.) and early Neolithic (10,000 B.C.–4000 B.C.) eras were characterized by an amazing uniformity of religion and culture. The approximate dates of these eras depend on location.[5] (See table 4.2.)

As revealed by recent feminist scholarship, a large part of the human population of the planet once shared a goddess religion.[6] Apparently, this religion was trinitarian, and early planetary society was a Three culture.[7] We will accept this as a working hypothesis.

The Stone Age trinity comprises three goddesses in one, called *TriVia* (the accent is on the second syllable), the triple-headed goddess (see figure 7.1). In Catal Huyuk, around 6000 B.C., the triple goddess appeared as the first holy trinity of Maiden, Mother, and Crone.[8]

This early trinity may be a combination of vegetable, sky, and chaos (dragon) goddesses in one figure. It may also be derived from the phases of the moon—waxing, full, and waning—interpreted in connection with the menstrual cycle.[9] The Latin name, TriVia, meaning *the crossing of three roads,* derives from the placement of goddess figures at crossroads (and perhaps from the outline of the crotch).[10] The Greek letter *upsilon,* our Y, was an important sign for the Pythagoreans, signifying the moral and immoral paths that might be chosen at maturity. The Pythagorean Y was a classic survival of the Paleolithic TriVia (three roads meeting).

Mesopotamian History

Written history begins in Sumer.[11] At this point, around 2500 B.C., the goddess TriVia becomes historical, more detailed, and more convincing. The Sumerians arrived from mountains to the northeast of Sumer (see map in figure 7.2) around 4000 B.C.

Their written records began around 2500 B.C. (see the chronology in table 7.1), recording a language unrelated to any one surviving today, which became extinct around 1600 B.C.[12] Their political dominance in the region passed to the Babylonians to the north, and then to the Assyrians. Both of these cultures spoke Akkadian, a Semitic language related to Minoan. Cities like Ur and Lagash, before 3000 B.C., were close to the seashore, which subsequently moved some 150 miles to the south. Sumerian died as a spoken language around 1600 B.C., but continued in use as a liturgical language until A.D. 100. Thanks to the library of the Assyrian King Assurbanipal in Nineveh, collected around 650 B.C., hundreds of cuneiform tablets have been recently translated and interpreted. All of this we shall call Mesopotamian history. It is the beginning of a continuous historical (that is, written) tradition, from Sumer, to Akkadia, to Canaan, Egypt, Crete, Mycenae, Greece, and to modern Europe.

SUMERIAN TRIADS

An early triad is the Sumerian An or Anu (heaven), Ki (earth), and Lil (air). An was created by Apsu, the underworld ocean, and Tiamat, the goddess of primeval chaos. Originally, An had a consort, Antu; but in the historical period Antu was replaced by Inanna (Akkadian Ishtar).[13] Another form of the trinity is An (heaven), Enlil (heaven and earth), and Nintu (also known as Aruru and Ninhursag, Enlil's sister, Mother Earth), who led the Sumerian pantheon, along with Enki (water, wisdom).[14] En-ki, meaning Lord of the Earth, evolved from En-kur, or Lord of the

Kur, the underworld. His earlier name reflects Enki's victory over the serpent, the monster of the underworld.

Throughout Sumerian history these four led the pantheon: An, Enlil, Ninhursag, and Enki. In earlier times the first three were the primary triad, and Enki was secondary. Later, around 2100 B.C., Enki was promoted above Ninhursag.[15] A second triad comprised Sin, the Moon god, Shamash, the Sun god, and Hadad, the storm god. (See table 7.3, later in this chapter, for a compilation of triads.)

THE SHIFT

In this period, apparently, the balance of power shifted from the goddess to the god, and from partnership to domination; priestesses were replaced by priests.[16] These changes coincided with a

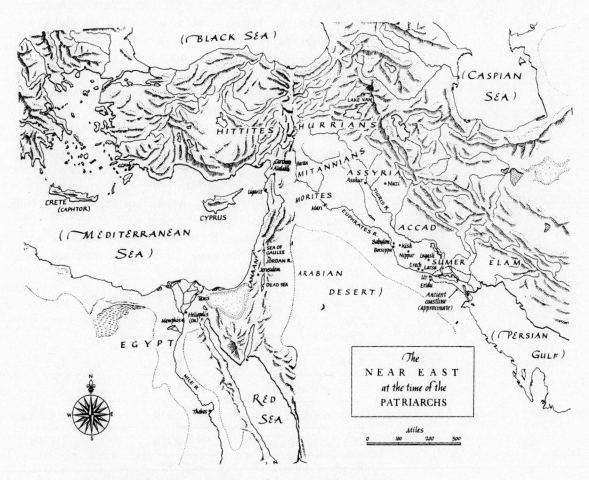

FIGURE 7.2 **Map of Babylonia at the Time of the Patriarchs, 2000 B.C.**
From Sarna (1966/1970).

change in climate, as we will see in chapter 18. At the same time, political power shifted from the priestly cast to the military commander and king.[17]

An old Babylonian theogony begins with the names of fifteen matched pairs of gods and goddesses, such as Enki and Ninki, Enmul and Ninmul, Enul and Ninul. According to Frank Cross, these divine pairs are characteristic of theogonies, in which creation is described using the language of sexual procreation. The trinity of ancient Babylonia arose by the syncretization of three separate gods: Anu (sky), Bel or Enlil (earth), and Ea (the deep, water) from the northern, central, and southern parts of Chaldea, respectively, around 2000 B.C.[18]

Ea is the Semitic name for the Sumerian Enki, acquired around 2500 B.C.. The center of his cult was at Eridu, and he was attended by the craftsman god, Mummu, his consort, Damkina, and his son, Marduk.[19] His domain was Apsu, the watery deep. Thus the Babylonian triad Anu/Enlil/Ea is derived from the Sumerian triad An/Enlil/Enki. Triads were characteristic of Babylonian religion from its earliest forms.[20]

Inanna rose from obscurity to become the main Sumerian goddess. Originally the familiar of the second trinity of Sumerian gods (Sin, Shumash, Hadad), she became the consort of Anu, and then the primary goddess in the Sumerian pantheon. Her Sumerian consort was Dumuzi (true son, the Shepherd.) In a legend important for the Orphic tradition, Inanna descends to the underworld to visit her sister, Erishkegal, is confined, then

TABLE 7.1
Chronology of Mesopotamian History

Period	From	To
Old Sumerian	2500 B.C.	2200 B.C.
Neo-Sumerian	2200 B.C.	1900 B.C.
Old Babylonian	1900 B.C.	1600 B.C.
Middle Babylonian	1600 B.C.	1300 B.C.
Late Babylonian	1300 B.C.	A.D. 100

THE ORPHIC TRINITY IN MYTH

released on condition of sending a substitute, for which she chose Dumuzi.

The origin of the Inanna cult has been placed at the Halafian site of Arpachiyah, around 5000 B.C., long before the beginning of the Sumerian civilization.[21] This suggests a diffusion from Catal Huyuk, around 6500 B.C., to Arpachiyah, Sumer, and the Indus.

ISHTAR

With the shift from Sumerian to Babylonian hegemony in the region, Inanna acquired the Semitic name Ishtar, while Anu remained Anu, Dumuzi became Tammuz, and Erishkegal became Allatu. This triad (Inanna/Ishtar, Dumuzi/Tammuz, Erishkegal/Allatu) recurs throughout our story.[22] In Babylonian mythology (and later in Canaan, and in the Old Testament) Tammuz is the vegetation god, dying each fall, to be reborn in the spring. This theme of eternal return, an early development in Babylonian religion, is basic to the later Babylonian New Year festival, described in detail in the next chapter.

The Babylonian center of the Ishtar cult was at Erech, where she was served by priests and priestesses, as the goddess of love and procreation.[23] Ishtar is important in the Gilgamesh and Flood stories of Babylonia, and is the model for the goddess Isis and her cult in Egypt.

MARDUK AND ASHUR

The Babylonian god Marduk eventually ascended to the head of the pantheon. Later, as Assyria displaced Babylonia in Akkadian regional dominance, the Assyrian god Ashur replaced the Babylonian Marduk as the chief god.

At about this time, the spoked wheel displaced the solid wheel on carts and chariots. The new chariots were faster and lighter, giving added advantage in war. This accelerated the advance of the dominator society in which this technological development occurred. Marduk was frequently depicted driving a war chariot, and the spoked wheel came to symbolize the dominance of Order over Chaos, and of men over women.

Egypt

The pantheon of Egypt included groupings of various number; for example, dyads (of two), triads (of three), ogdoads (of eight), and enneads (of nine). The eight primordial gods of Egypt, the Ogdoad of Hermopolis, consisted of four theogonic pairs: Nun and Nawnet, Huh and Hawhet, Kuk and Kawket, Amun and

Amawnet. Nun (the weary), Huh (endlessness), and Kuk (darkness) represent features of the chaos preceding creation.[24] There was a huge pantheon of gods, including several enneads. Although nine is three times three, Egyptologists agree that trinities (such as Tum, Ra, and Harmakhis, or Osiris, Isis, and Horus) made a late entry to Egyptian religion. They believe that the evolution of the Egyptian cultural map progressed from One, to Nine, then to Three.[25]

The Sun cult centered in Heliopolis (the city of On in the Bible), in Lower Egypt, had a basic trinity of Atum (the creator), Shu (the god of the air or void), and Tefnut (the goddess of moisture). From these arose six others to make an Ennead: Geb (the earth), Nut (the heavens), and their four children, Osiris and Seth (brother gods), Isis and Nephthys (sister goddesses).[26]

Memphis was the premier city of Middle Egypt, a religious and administrative center that flourished until Roman times. In the Memphis theology, the triad of Osiris, Isis, and Horus evolved from Three back to One (Horus or Osiris).[27]

THE MEMPHIS TRIAD

The triad of Isis, Osiris, and Horus is particularly important in the long line of the Orphic tradition. Osiris may have evolved from Ashur, the chief god of the Assyrians.[28] Death and reincarnation, the periodic flooding of the Nile, and the annual return of the seasons, were associated with Osiris, and were fundamental to the annual Mysteries of Osiris.[29] As we will see, Osiris became the early Greek Orpheus, while Isis became the goddess of late Greek antiquity in Alexandria, and thence Mary, the mother of Christianity.[30]

This triad, based on predynastic myths, was a model royal family: the goddess Isis, her husband (and brother) Osiris, the god of the dead, and their son, the falcon-sky god, Horus. Osiris was the firstborn of Nut and Geb, and he inherited the kingship of Egypt from his father. He taught agriculture to the Egyptians, and pacified the whole world with music. His brother Seth, jealous, set upon Osiris and killed him. Isis found the body in Phoenicia, grieved over it, temporarily resuscitated it with breath from her wings, embraced it, and conceived a son, Horus, destined to avenge his father. Meanwhile, Seth had taken over the throne of Egypt. Eventually, he found the body of Osiris, which he tore in fourteen pieces and scattered. Osiris then became king of the underworld. Thoth, the ibis, made peace between Horus and Seth, and Seth had to accept a divine position secondary to Osiris.[31] Horus gained the throne.

Crete

Crete was settled in the early Neolithic by people from Asia Minor. It was an Anatolian colony, speaking a language related to Dravidian.[32] The Neolithic goddess religion was introduced to Crete about 4000 B.C. from Anatolia. The early Halafian period in Mesopotamia dates from about 4000 B.C.[33] The excavations of 1933 at the Halafian site of Arpachiyah, near Nineveh, revealed goddess figurines, bull and double-axe symbols, and cave-like structures for the worship of the Mother goddess, very similar to those of Minoan Crete. Similarities with the Shaivite rites of the Indus have also been noted.[34]

The Minoan culture of Crete began around 3000 B.C.,[35] after the rise of Egyptian civilization nearby, and developed into a unique and spectacular culture. This, in turn, influenced the Mycenaean and early Greek cultures, and thus our own European civilization. While the patriarchal, dominator form of society began to overtake the earlier goddess religion in Sumer at the time of the discovery of the solid wheel (about 4000 B.C.), and buried it in Babylon after the advent of the spoked wheel (around 2000 B.C.), the matriarchal, partnership form, with its goddess religion, lingered on in Minoan Crete until about 1400 B.C.[36]

The Minoan religion featured a mature goddess, and a young god named Zan, later Zeus. This dyad configuration is similar to the pairs Inanna/Dumuzi of Sumer, Ishtar/Tammuz of Babylonia, and Shiva/Parvati of Shaivism in the Indus valley.[37] The later Cretan god, Zagreus or Dionysos (the son of Zeus) has been traced back to 6500 B.C. in the Zagros mountains of the Neolithic Near East.[38] The close comparison of many details of the Zagros and Cretan religions leaves no doubt as to the diffusion of the Dionysian/Orphic tradition from Anatolia to Greece.

THE GENDER TRANSFORMATION

The Minoan culture is a watershed in our history, important for our understanding of bifurcations in the evolution of our own cognitive maps. This is because of its unique longevity as a partnership society—the only one to survive into historical times—and because of the transformational process in which its triple goddess became, step-by-step, the triple god of our culture.

The religion of early Cretans from Anatolia (as well as that of the Dravidians of the Indus valley) was a cult of caves, trees, and pillars. The divine was manifest in bird forms, signifying epiphany, spiritual illumination. The primary Earth Mother goddess appeared frequently with her paramour, a young male.[39] This dyad, the Mother goddess and the Master of Animals, is derived from the widespread goddess culture of Stone Age Asia

Minor and Old Europe. In the second millennium B.C., Mycenaeans moved to Crete, and Mycenaean culture, although patriarchal, evolved along Cretan lines. Mycenaea dominated Crete after about 1400 B.C. (just as the Indo-European Vedic Aryans completed their conquest of the Indus), and Cretan culture migrated to Greece.[40] The cave cult continued, and the Mother goddess became Athene, Artemis, Demeter, and Aphrodite in Greek mythology; while the Master of Animals became the bull, Dionysos, Kouros, then Zeus. In time, the goddess declined, and was replaced by the bull.[41] Nevertheless, the Cretan goddesses survived in the Greek pantheon, as Hera, Athena, Artemis, Ariadne, and Helen.[42]

Although Cretan culture developed writing, its surviving literature is very limited. Our knowledge of Cretan lore has been excavated and interpreted by brilliant scholarship, from derived mythologies extensively represented in the classical literature of Greece and India. From this excavation there is evidence of a Cretan trinity. For example, in the sanctuary of Gournia in eastern Crete, around 1500 B.C., were found cult objects including a figure of the snake goddess Eileithyia at a low earthen table with three legs, surrounded by three tubular vessels.[43] Gertrude Levy has suggested that this goddess, her daughter, and younger son provided the model for the trinity of Eleusis, the Greek center of the Orphic mysteries.[44]

India

As we dig and discover more layers of data, sudden revisions of history and of our cognitive maps become more frequent. Some recent examples of these revisions are listed in table 7.2. Early among these is the discovery of Sanskrit literature by the West in 1785.[45]

The Vedic Aryans arrived in northern India from Asia Minor around 2000 B.C., some time after the patriarchal bifurcation.[46] Classical Sanskrit literature began with the writing of the Vedas, an already ancient oral tradition, about 1500 B.C. There are four Vedas: the Rig Veda, its derivative Sama Veda and Yajur Veda, and the later Atharva Veda. The next phase of the Vedic period produced the Brahmanas, the Aranyakas, and the Upanishads. The final (Vedanta) phase of the Vedic period produced the Sutras, completed by 200 B.C.

In the early Vedic period, Hindu mythology comprised a large pantheon of gods and goddesses. In the Rig Veda we find Indra (the sky, Zeus), Varuna (the Just), Virtra (the serpent), Krishna (the Absolute, the cowherd), Vayu (the wind), the

Maruts (terrible storms), Rudra (the howler, the militant, later Shiva), Usas (a goddess), Aditi (the goddess of the infinite), Saraswati (the goddess of learning), Vak (the goddess of speech), Aranyani (the goddess of the forest), Agni (fire), Brahma or Hiranyagarbha (the creator), and many others.

In the Atharva Veda there emerged a monotheistic tendency, and the gods were collected in three classes, of the earth, of the air, and of the sky. Skambha (also known as Prajapati, Purusa, and Brahman) emerges as the ultimate principle. Skambha has been identified with the axis of the celestial sphere.[47] Rudra (Shiva) became the lord of animals. In the Yajur Veda, Vishnu rose in importance, and in the Brahmanas, the trinity of Brahma, Vishnu, and Shiva emerged as fundamental principles.[48] In the Upanishads, after about 1000 B.C., these three became the Hindu trinity.

TABLE 7.2
Paleography and Archaeology

Date	Decoder	Language	Text
1785	Wilkins	Sanskrit	Negari
1800	Napolean	Egyptian	Pyramids
1822	Champollion	Egyptian	Hieroglyphs
1847	Layard	Assyrian	Nimrud
1850	Rawlinson	Babylonian	Cuneiform
1853	Rassam	Assyrian	Nineveh
1870	Schliemann	Greek	Troy
1872	Smith	Cypriot	Script
1890	Petrie	Egyptian	Giza
1900	Evans	Cretan	Minos
1950	Solecki	Persian	Shanidar
1952	Ventris	Mycenaean	Linear B
1952	Mellaart	Anatolian	Catal Huyuk
1966	Gordon	Minoan	Linear A

There is the One (Brahman), and it is Three (Brahma, Vishnu, and Shiva). The sacred syllable, AUM, represents the One, and also the Three, as "A" is Brahma the creator, "U" is Vishnu the preserver, and "M" is Shiva the destroyer. Altogether, AUM, or Brahman, signifies the hermeneutic circle, the creative cycle of evolution, the eternal pattern of growth and life.

Greece

In the evolution of consciousness from Minoan Crete to ancient Greece . . . the goddess submerged into the collective unconscious, while her statues underwent gender-change operations.

PYTHAGORAS

In sum, there is the One (Brahman), and it is Three (Brahma, Vishnu, and Shiva). The sacred syllable, AUM, represents the One, and also the Three, as "A" is Brahma the creator, "U" is Vishnu the preserver, and "M" is Shiva the destroyer. Altogether, AUM, or Brahman, signifies the hermeneutic circle, the creative cycle of evolution, the eternal pattern of growth and life. Here again we recognize a concordance with TriVia as Maid, Mother, and Crone. As Mary Daly says, "Since we are by now familiar with innumerable myths of the triple goddess, many of which originated in the Middle East, the thought that in a religion of reversals the triple goddess would be presented disguised as three wise kings is indeed a Nagging thought."[49]

There's a gap in our knowledge of the evolution of consciousness from Minoan Crete to ancient Greece, which may be the result of the intentional destruction of the records of the older culture by the leaders of the new one. The goddess submerged into the collective unconscious, while her statues underwent gender-change operations. It has been suggested by David Loye that this action, the revision of history, is an intrinsic part of a social bifurcation, or paradigm shift, scenario.[50] Eventually, mathematical theories (of dynamical systems, chaos, and bifurcations) may provide us with models for these universal processes of transformation.

In any case, the shift from Mycenaean to Greek culture occurred in the darkness of prehistory, and when the lights came on, we had the epics of Homer and Hesiod, dating from about 800 B.C., although scholars agree that these epics go back as oral traditions into the Mycenaean age, and were originally chanted in the Minoan language.[51] We may regard Hesiod, in whom we have the original appearance of the Orphic trinity—Chaos, Gaia, Eros—as a prehistorian, mapping the fundamental trinity of Cretan prehistory onto the cognitive map of the early Greeks. We should also note the concordance between the Hindu and Greek trinities; all are shown in table 7.3.[52]

Also, note the correspondence between Zagreus/Dumuzi/Zan/Osiris/Dionysos/Orpheus/Zeus/Shiva/Phanes/Eros.[53] The actual significance of Chaos, Gaia, and Eros, and the related correspondences, Orpheus/Buddha and Orpheus/Christ, will be discussed more fully in chapters 8 through 12.

The Pythagorean tradition is also fundamental to an understanding of the Greek phase of the long line of Orphism, which will be discussed in future chapters. Pythagoras, a reformer of Orphism, was said to have been initiated in the Idaean Cave on Crete, a sacred site of the cult of Zeus, derived from Catal Huyuk.[54] He was associated with the god Apollo and the goddess Demeter.[55]

GREEK MAIDEN TRINITIES

The early Greek goddesses frequently appeared in pairs of Maiden and Mother. The trinitarian form, which may have evolved from the twofold form, or may be a survival of the prehistoric goddess TriVia, is confined primarily to goddesses. Not every pair evolved into a trinity, but those that did developed further into a triple of maiden goddesses, not mothers. Hence the *maiden-trinity* formula of the Greek pantheon.[56] Many Greek goddesses, notably Demeter, had three aspects. *The triple muse theme* is also a survival of the prehistoric TriVia.[57] A few of the

TABLE 7.3
Traditional Triads

TRIVIAL	Crone	Mother	Maid
EGYPTIAN	Osiris	Isis	Horus
SUMERIAN	An	Nintu	Enlil
SUMERIAN	Inanna	Erishkegal	Dumuzi
BABYLONIAN	Anu	Ea	Enlil
BABYLONIAN	Apsu	Tiamat	Mummu
UGARITIC	El	Ashtoreth	Baal
CRETAN	Zeus	Semele	Dionysos
HINDU	Brahma	Vishnu	Shiva
EARLY GREEK	Chaos	Gaia	Eros
CLASSIC GREEK	Pluto	Demeter	Persephone
ALEXANDRIAN	Serapis	Isis	Anubis
PHILONIC	Yahweh	Sophia	Logos
NEOPLATONIC	One	Intellect	Soul
NEOPLATONIC	Soul	Body	Spirit
CHRISTIAN	Father	Son	Spirit

Greek gods, such as Dionysos, also had three aspects.[58] These may also be regarded as descendants of TriVia.[59]

THE DEMETER STORY

Demeter was the goddess of grain in classical Greece, and sister of Zeus and Hades. Her name (note the similarity to Tiamat) meant *Mother De*, the trinitarian Mother of the delta or triangle.[60] Her priestesses initiated young people in the arts of love. She was a main figure in the Orphic Mysteries at Eleusis, and the mother of Persephone. Hades, who ruled Tartarus, the underworld, fell in love with Persephone, and asked Zeus for permission to marry her. When Zeus did not consent, Hades abducted Persephone from Eleusis, and imprisoned her in Tartarus. Enraged, Demeter forbade the earth to produce food. Finally, a compromise was made in which Persephone would spend three months every year with Hades and the rest of the year at Eleusis. Kore, Persephone, and Hecate were maiden, nymph, and crone aspects of the same figure, goddess of the crossroads between this world and the underworld.[61]

Philo of Alexandria

Shortly after the death of Jesus, Philo the Jew (20 B.C.–A.D. 50) became the integrator of pagan and Jewish Gnosticism. His syncretism was fundamental to the development of early Christian philosophy, as well as for the Neoplatonic tradition. He revised the Platonic cosmography into a trinity:

- God
- his mate, Wisdom (Sophia)
- their child, the Logos, a kind of elastic medium connecting God to the intelligible world[62]

Neoplatonic

Six centuries after Plato, after Jesus and Philo, Greek philosophers in Alexandria renewed and simplified Plato's system into a philosophy called Neoplatonism. The main figures in this movement were Ammonius Saccas, his student Plotinus (204–262), and his student Porphyry (233–306). Other important persons of this school were Iamblichus, Hypatia, and Proclus. The teachings of Plotinus, collected in the *Enneads* by Porphyry, are organized around trinities. The highest trinity consists of the *One,* the *Intellectual Principle,* and the *All Soul.* God comprises these three in one.

Celtic

Triads of gods were important in Celtic religion, which spanned Europe in the centuries before Christ. The most important of the Celtic deities is the triple goddess Brigit. She was celebrated on

THE ORPHIC TRINITY IN MYTH

her day, Imbolc, the first of February, which survives in modern times as Candelmas, or the feast of Saint Brigid. Her three aspects ruled over the sky, earth, and underworld.[63]

Christian

The Israelite religion includes the One of the Sanskrit pantheon (monotheism), but not the Three. Perhaps the shift to Christianity, for which the Trinity of Father, Son, and Holy Spirit is a chief feature, may be interpreted as a forceful resurgence of the Three. The Christian trinity was derived from the Neoplatonic trinity by Justin Martyr in the second century.[64] The actual significance of the three principles is not well understood, however, and is still debated vigorously in theological texts.[65]

Without entering into this controversy at present (we will return to it in a later chapter), we simply propose the concordance shown in the last line of table 7.3. Here, the three aspects of the goddess TriVia (Crone, Mother, Maiden) are mapped to the Christian trinity (Father, Son, and Holy Spirit). Also, the Memphis trinity (Osiris, Isis, Horus) maps onto another Christian trinity, the model nuclear family of Father, Mother, and Son. This evolution took place in Alexandria, where by 340, two-thirds of the population had converted to Christianity.[66]

Christianity also took over the Neoplatonic triad (Soul, Body, and Spirit), but cast out the spirit (by a vote of the bishops) in the Council of Byzantium of 879. Perhaps this accounts for the confusion of soul and spirit that is so widespread today.[67]

Quaternity

We've discussed cultures that embody One, Two, and Three root concepts, arguing for the evolutionary advantage of the Three. Carl Jung, the pioneer psychoanalyst, discovered special meanings for the concept of Four in his therapeutic practice.[68] In dream and fantasy material, he found four to be an ordering principle in "a chaotic assortment of images." In his numerological scheme,

- one = unity
- two = duality, conflict
- three = union of opposites
- four = completeness

Jung viewed quaternities as psychic images of wholeness, with the climax of the therapeutic process represented as the center of a cross or square. He regarded the four as three plus one, the emergence of order from chaos . . .

Jung found triads rare and associated them with chaos. He viewed quaternities as psychic images of wholeness, with the climax of the therapeutic process represented as the center of a cross or square. He regarded the four as three plus one, the emergence of order from chaos, and associated this transformation with alchemy.[69] This alchemical arithmetic is illustrated in figure 7.3.

The addition of Inanna to the Sumerian triad of Anu/Enlil/Ea, as well as the position of Mary in the Christian trinity, may be related to this process of 4 = 3 + 1. The syncresis of a Three culture with a Four culture might result in a Twelve, as in the solar zodiac.

Summary

The distant past is nearly as ephemeral as the distant future, and I will not insist on a firm chronology for our prehistoric roots. Here I've proposed a possible path out of Paleolithic culture, with its earth-shaped triple goddess, through the gender transformations of goddesses to gods in Mesopotamia, to the mythic trinities of the present.[70] Here is an outline of the sequence proposed:

FIGURE 7.3

Jung's Quaternity: The Python as Three Plus One

From German alchemical work, ca. 1600. See Jung (1967).

- The triune goddess of the late Ice Age (25,000–10,000 B.C.) had various faces, such as Maid, Mother, and Crone; also seen as creative void, created form, and dissolution.
- As the ice receded and agriculture evolved (10,000–7500 B.C.), the goddess trinity took on vegetative and Earth Mother forms.
- In the early civilizations of Europe and Anatolia (7500–5000 B.C.) masculine forms (especially the bull) ascended.
- Around 4000 B.C., the patriarchal transformation gradually began.
- In early Sumer (2500–2000 B.C.), the goddess, the trinity, and partnership society gradually gave way to masculine forms, such as An/Ki/Lil and An/Enlil/Nintu.
- The Sumerian triads migrated to Babylonia, Ugarit, Canaan, Egypt, Crete, Mycenae, and Greece, along with their myths and rituals.
- Hesiod transmitted one of these triads into Greek literature; subsequent evolution brought the basic trinities into Alexandrian Christianity, and eventually to the modern world.

In the rest of this part, we seek to understand the trinity of Chaos, Gaia, Eros, as a basis for understanding our own culture and its transformations.[71]

New Year Festivals

CHAPTER 8

$$\ast 52 \cdot 01. \quad 1 = \hat{a} \{ (\exists x) . a = \iota' x \} \;\; \mathbf{Df}$$

FIGURE 8.1
The Definition of One
From Whitehead and Russell (1959).

The house I grew up in was close to the campus of the University of Vermont. Early in life I discovered the pleasures of cruising its library. At about age fifteen, I pulled Whitehead and Russell's *Principia Mathematica* from the shelf.[1] I was astonished and fascinated to see a book with a Latin title, written entirely in hieroglyphs! (See figure 8.1.)

I resolved to learn to read it, and about four years later, thanks to the innovative teaching of Professor Raymond Wilder at the University of Michigan, I did. It turned out to be a magical creation myth, in which the entire mathematical landscape emerges, by a process of "consideration," from nearly nothing.[2]

The Power of the Spade

The archaeologist's spade is responsible for more paradigm shifts than any other scientific instrument.

The archaeologist's spade is responsible for more paradigm shifts than any other scientific instrument. When Mariette uncovered the Serapeum at Saqqara, or Schliemann found Troy, or Evans excavated the Palace of Minos, or Rassam uncovered Nineveh, whole histories had to be rewritten. Popular culture was drastically affected as well. It's said that two publications were primarily responsible for destroying popular belief in the Bible: Darwin's *Origin of Species* in 1859, and Smith's *The Chaldean Account of the Flood* in 1873.[3] This chapter is devoted to one of Smith's discoveries. We will dig up the roots of the chaos concept (as the goddess Tiamat) in Mesopotamian antiquity, finding them already defeated and underground in the New Year festivals that have maintained and stabilized society for the past four thousand years.

Professor Simcha (Samuel Noah) Kramer died November 26, 1990, at age ninety-three. Through his sixty years of work excavating and translating Sumerian cuneiform tablets (1930–90), he was personally responsible for a major revision of history. He created the entire field of Sumerology, and wrote artfully for a lay audience about his fabulous discoveries in clay.[4] Besides deciphering Sumerian mythology and history, and establishing the priority of Sumer in many of our own traditions, he proposed a theory of the origin of the Sumerian gods in the Harappan civilization of the Indus River valley.[5] If true, his theory provides an important clue in the mystery of the social transformation from matriliny to patriliny, from the goddess to the god. Much of this chapter is based upon his work.

Mesopotamian History

FIGURE 8.2
View of Babylon from the New Town
After Ungar. See MacQueen (1964).

In Mesopotamia the dominance of Sumer was succeeded by Babylon, then Assyria and Persia. (These are shown on the map in figure 7.2.) Babylon, shown in figures 8.2 and 8.3, was a great city of stone, a wonder of the ancient world. Here were created, in advance of later Egyptian developments, some of the roots of modern mathematics and astronomy. Pictographic writing was developed around 3000 B.C., and evolved into cuneiform by 2700 B.C. The first great florescence of Babylonian culture occurred during the First Dynasty, from 1894 to 1595 B.C. By this time the dominator form of society, embodied in the Code of Hammurabi (published around 1780 B.C.), had already replaced the partnership society of Sumer.

Eventually, the Babylonians were conquered by the Assyrians and the capital moved north again, to Nineveh. Here, under Assurbanipal (ruled 669–629 B.C.), a vast library was collected, only to be destroyed around 600 B.C. by the Babylonians. Soon thereafter, the Persians took over, under Darius (ruled 521–485 B.C.). The recent excavation of the library has provided a wealth of historical information about the roots of our civilization in Sumerian culture and religion.[6]

Sumer

Many of our traditions can be traced back to Sumer, where written history began. We may only speculate on the prehistoric evolution of these themes. In the Sumerian literature that has survived in vast quantity are found root forms of the trinity, the origins of goddesses and gods, the partnership of the stars and Earth, the travels of the individual soul, and the struggle of

Many of our traditions can be traced back to Sumer, where written history began . . . the trinity, the origins of goddesses and gods, the partnership of the stars and Earth, the travels of the individual soul, and the struggle of Cosmos with Chaos.

Cosmos with Chaos. We know through the written record that the partnership form of society survived in early Sumer. We are particularly concerned here with three Sumerian legends:

- the sacred marriage
- the defeat of chaos
- the eternal descent and return

All of these were part of the annual New Year festival, involving a cast of Sumerian characters.

INANNA

Inanna is the Sumerian Venus, queen of heaven and goddess of love. Her older sister, Erishkegal, is the goddess of death and gloom, ruling the underworld. Inanna has a consort, Dumuzi, the shepherd-god. Inanna eventually becomes the Akkadian Ishtar, the Egyptian Isis, the Cretan Semele, the Greek Demeter. Dumuzi becomes the Akkadian Tammuz, the Greek Dionysos,

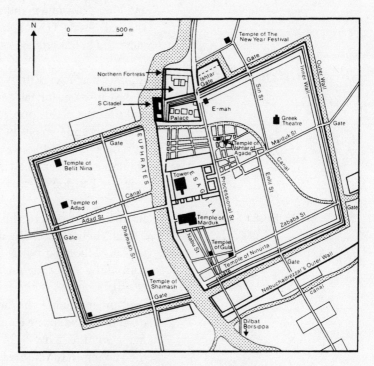

FIGURE 8.3 **Plan of the Inner City of Babylon in the Neo-Babylonian Period**

From Oates (1979, 1986). Courtesy of Thames and Hudson, London. Reprinted with permission.

Orpheus, Zeus, and so on. Erishkegal becomes the Akkadian Allatu.[7]

The sacred marriage, or *hieros gamos* tradition, was one of the central components of the New Year festival ritual and myth complex. The partnership of Inanna and Dumuzi was an early model for this sacred marriage, in which the king enjoys a marriage ceremony and nuptial bed with a priestess, the *hierogam*, playing the role of the goddess.[8] The fertile power and divine authority of the goddess was thus given to the mortal king.

Dating from around 3000 B.C. in Uruk, this alliance was renewed each year in the Sumerian New Year festival.[9] Originally in the spring, the marriage renewed the support of the goddess for the success of the agricultural season, after her return from wintering in the underworld. The sacred marriage survived throughout Neolithic times, and into historical mythology as the Babylonian Marduk and Ishtar,[10] the Cretan Zeus and Hera,[11] in the Greek mysteries at Eleusis,[12] and in the Psalms of the Old Testament. This mythical survival of the partnership of goddesses and kings, of women and men, is one of the few remains of the late Paleolithic Garden of Eden. Progressively, the god king increased in importance, while the goddess faded into servitude.

THE DEFEAT OF CHAOS

Another character, Kur, is a dragon, or underworld demon, one of the earliest historical identifications of chaos, the underworld, and thus the prehistoric goddess.[13] In another Sumerian myth, "The Feats and Exploits of Ninurta," a demon called Asag lives in Kur, the underworld, and is killed by Ninurta, the son of Enlil.[14] Ninurta is a Sumerian champion of order, who survived for millennia in Babylonian ritual.

THE ETERNAL DESCENT AND RETURN

Inanna descended to the underworld and returned, sending Dumuzi in her place. The descent is the mythic representation of the fall of the solar power at the end of the summer season. The path of the Sun along the ecliptic, where it descends below the celestial equator at the fall equinox, is the solar descent into the "underground," the land of the dead, the watery deep, and dragons. At the spring equinox, the Sun returns to the land of the living and the light.[15] The king is identified with Dumuzi, and the Sun may return if Erishkegal permits.

The Babylonian New Year festival, the Akitu (to which we will turn in a moment), combines these three Sumerian myths (sacred marriage, defeat of chaos, and eternal return) into one festival. More than a New Year festival, it was a celebration and performance of periodicity, devoted to the cycles of the soil, the year, and the annual victory of Order over Chaos.[16]

Digging Up the Past

In 1802 the British established a consulate in Baghdad. The first resident, Claudius Rich, surveyed archaeological sites and collected seven thousand pounds of antiquities. After his death in 1821, this hoard, including one thousand pounds of clay with cuneiform inscriptions, was sent to the British Museum.[17]

COLONEL RAWLINSON

Rich's contemporary, Henry Rawlinson (1810–95), was sent to India by his employer, the East India Company, where he learned Persian, Arabic, and Hindi. In 1835 he was sent to Iran as military adviser to a provincial governor at Kirmanshah (in Kurdistan, in the north of Iran), and on the way he heard about two cuneiform inscriptions on Mount Elvend, near Hamadan, which he copied and studied. He deduced that they concerned Darius and his son Xerxes. In Kirmanshah he heard about a huge inscription with reliefs on a mountain wall at Behiston, twenty-two miles to the east, shown in figure 8.4.

The inscriptions turned out to be trilingual, in Old Persian, Babylonian, and Elamite. In 1836 and 1837, at the risk of life and limb, Rawlinson scaled the Behiston cliff and copied the Old Persian inscriptions. He was able to decipher them, and sent the results to the Royal Asiatic Society in London in 1838. In 1847 he returned to the site to copy the Babylonian version. With the help of a wild Kurdish boy, climbing like a human fly, he obtained a paper squeeze of the inscription, opening up the whole field of Assyriology.[18] Rawlinson left his own name carved on the cliffs, and became known as the "Father of Cuneiform."

THE FIRST EXCAVATIONS

The first major excavation in northern Mesopotamia was carried out by French archaeologist Paul Emile Botta, in 1843. Botta dug out the capital of the Assyrian King Sargon II.[19]

Henry Austin Layard rode across the Ottoman Empire and Persia as a lark in 1839. He excavated what he thought was Nineveh in 1845, but it turned out to be Nimrud.[20]

Hormuzd Rassam, Layard's successor, saw French archaeologists approach a likely looking mound in 1853. Not to be outdone, he hurriedly dug into it at night, finding the library of Assurbanipal, the last great king of the Assyrian empire (669–633 B.C.), and destroying much of it in ignorance. Later, he learned how to bake the clay tablets to preserve them. This great cuneiform library contained the Gilgamesh Epic, a twelve-tablet masterpiece. More than 90,000 tablets and fragments were sent to the British Museum in London between 1872 and 1889.[21]

GEORGE SMITH

At the age of fourteen, George Smith (1840–76) was apprenticed to a firm to learn banknote engraving. He was fascinated by biblical archaeology, and spent his spare time at the British Museum, studying the exhibits of antiquities from Nineveh and Babylon.

FIGURE 8.4 **The Behiston Cliffs. Nagshe-I-Rustam, Tomb of Darius I, and Zoroastrian Fire, 486 B.C., Behiston, Iran.**
Photo: The Ancient Art and Architecture Collection. Reprinted with permission.

THE ORPHIC TRINITY IN MYTH

He became so familiar that the museum offered him a job as a repairer, in 1861. He looked through hundreds of fragments of tablets from the Nineveh library, seeking pieces from the same tablet that could then be joined, and in the process learned to read cuneiform. In 1872 he found a large fragment of the Gilgamesh Epic containing the Babylonian version of the Flood story. Tearing off his clothes, he ran naked around the museum shouting, "I am the first man to read that after more than two thousand years of oblivion!" The fragment turned out to be part of the eleventh tablet of the twelve-tablet epic. On December 3, 1872, he presented his discovery to the Society of Biblical Archaeology in London, demonstrating that the Flood story in Genesis was derived from earlier Babylonian literature.

The following month, the *London Daily Telegraph* offered Smith a grant to go to Nineveh to recover the remaining fragments of the Gilgamesh story. He went to Nineveh and actually found the missing fragment, returning to London in a matter of days! Returning to Nineveh the following year, 1874, under the auspices of the British Museum, and again in 1876, he died there of dysentery.[22]

"WHEN ABOVE"

We are interested in George Smith here not only for his discovery of the Gilgamesh Epic, nor for his decipherment of the Cypriotic script from Crete, but for yet another discovery.[23] Alexander Heidel's book, *The Babylonian Genesis,* opens with:

> Of all the Semitic inscriptions composed in cuneiform writing few have awakened as great a general interest as the epic known among the Babylonians and Assyrians as *Enuma Elish* ("When above"), which takes its name from the opening words of the poem. Aside from linguistic considerations, this widespread popularity of *Enuma Elish* is in part due to its great significance for the study of the theogonic and cosmogonic views of the Mesopotamians, and thus for a comparative study of ancient Near Eastern religion in general; but above all else it is due to the fact that *Enuma Elish* presents quite a number of analogies to the first two chapters of the Book of Genesis.[24]

This classic, discovered by Layard, Rassam, and Smith among the ruins of Assurbanipal's library at Nineveh between 1848 and 1876, consists of about one thousand lines, written on seven tablets (part of tablet V is still missing). This version was written in the First Babylonian Dynasty (1894–1595 B.C.), under

King Hammurabi (1792–1750 B.C.) (see figure 8.5), based upon an older Sumerian myth.[25]

George Smith revealed its meaning to the public in a letter to the editor of the *London Daily Telegraph* in 1875, and then in his second book, published posthumously.[26] The epic includes a creation story, on two tablets, which we will examine in detail in a later chapter. The creation story begins with the trinity of Apsu, Tiamat, and Mummu.

The Akitu Festival

In Babylon, from the time of Hammurabi, the New Year was celebrated by an eleven-day festival in honor of Marduk, the city god of Babylon, marking his annual battle with the forces of chaos. This period was an intercalary, in which the calendar waited for the sun to catch up. As no god was assigned to keep order during this time, it was associated with chaos, and the renewal of the year followed this brief period, requiring a new defeat of the dragon.[27] Enuma Elish was both recited and enacted during the festival.[28] According to E. O. James,

> The Annual Festival, or *Akitu*, in Babylon in the month of Nissan centered in the liberation of the captive god, Marduk, the reenactment of the creation Epic (the *Enuma Elish*), the humiliation and reinstatement of the king, and his ritual marriage with the goddess in his Tammuz capacity to renew the process of vegetation, to secure the fertility of the land and to determine the destinies at the beginning of the New Year.[29]

The similarity of these events to the Eleusinian mysteries will be described in the next chapter. The Akitu festival was originally a harvest celebration, from the third millennium B.C. down to Hellenistic times (300 B.C. or later).[30] After Hammurabi, it took place instead from the first to the eleventh of Nisan (March–April). Some scholars think that two festivals, the sacred marriage and the Akitu ritual, were combined to produce the New Year festival. The theme of combat between Order and Chaos, already established in the earlier Sumerian ritual, was enacted in the Akitu by a foot race between Ninurta and Zu, in which Zu is overtaken and slain.[31]

Akitu included a dramatic representation of the death and resurrection of Marduk. The myth begins with Marduk *dead in the mountain*.[32] Cylinder seals depict the slain god in the mountain, with a goddess kneeling nearby, as shown in figure 8.6.

This may have been a survival of the earlier Sumerian legend, in which Inanna/Ishtar mourns the sojourn of Dumuzi/

THE ORPHIC TRINITY IN MYTH

Tammuz in the underground. This older component of the ritual, Akitu, is not mentioned in the more recent myth, Enuma Elish.

E-SAGILA

The temple complex of E-sagila was the predominant feature of Babylon in the times of Hammurabi, around 1700 B.C. A sacred paved road approached it on the north side through a triumphal arch, the *Ishtar Gate*. The walled temple complex, situated a mile further on the east bank of the Euphrates, enclosed a vast sanctuary. Within was found the famous ziggurat (stepped pyramid), with its chapels for Marduk, and other gods and goddesses. Akitu referred to both the New Year festival and the temple of Marduk within the E-sagila walls. The confinement of the god/king was in a chamber, the *giguna,* under the ziggurat, while the sacred marriage was consummated on its top.[33]

THE PROGRAM

The first few days of the Akitu were devoted to ablutions and prayers. On the second day (the second of Nisan), the *urigallu* (chief priest) called upon the god to bless the city and face the temple of Marduk, the E-sagila. On the third day, craftsmen made images for use later, on the sixth day. Late in the evening of the fourth day, Enuma Elish was recited by the high priest, before the image of Marduk. The next day, the fifth of Nisan, a sheep was sacrificed, the king appeared for the first time, and was

FIGURE 8.6
Gods of Order. Cylinder seal of Marduk with Sahmash, Sun god (left), and agriculture god (right), third millennium B.C., Tell Mesopotamia

Photo: Art and Architecture Collection. Reprinted with permission.

humiliated by the priests of Marduk, the *urigallu* striking him in the face. In the evening, a white bull was sacrificed, signifying the victory of Marduk over his enemies (especially, the dragons of chaos). On the sixth day, the god Nabu arrived in his boat. Anu, Enlil, and other gods arrived as well.

Firm details of days seven through eleven have not been discovered, but we know the main events:

1. The sacred procession and parade down Babylon's Processional Way, through the Ishtar Gate, from Marduk's temple at E-sagila, to the Festival house outside the city, Bit Akitu, led by the king, holding hands with Marduk.
2. The enactment of the creation myth, Enuma Elish, with the king playing Marduk (more on this later).
3. The death and resurrection of Marduk, enacted by the king.
4. The fixing of the fates for the coming year, on the eighth and eleventh days.
5. The ritual marriage concluding the festival on the eleventh evening, publicly enacted by the king and a hierogam, a priestess of high rank, in the bridal chamber, the *giguna,* on a stage-tower atop the ziggurat.[34] A priestess of the goddess played the bride, and sacred prostitution may have originated in this ritual.[35]

These five elements were common to annual festivals of renewal throughout the cultural region.[36]

Egypt

In Egypt there were similar New Year festivals, involving the annual Great Procession of Osiris, and the erection of the Djed Pillar. The Osiris mysteries at Denderah and Medinet Habu occupied three weeks in the month of Khiak, culminating at the winter solstice. The mysteries celebrated the passion, death, and resurrection of Osiris. The Djed column lying on the ground expressed his death, and its erection by the king in person symbolized the resurrection.[37] This public spectacle gave rise to the sacred role of obelisks in Egyptian culture.

Cult Patterns

Neighboring cultures had similar New Year festivals. Besides the Osiris festival in Egypt, the Dionysos celebration in Crete and the Sukkot (Tabernacles) ritual in Canaan (and still celebrated by Jewish people today) are the main examples.[38] The comparative study of these rituals reveals a common pattern, characteristic of patriarchal societies. We will return to this repeatedly in this part of the book.[39] Table 8.1 presents a comparative tableau.

THE ORPHIC TRINITY IN MYTH

TABLE 8.1
New Year Festivals

PLACE	FESTIVAL	SEASON
Babylon	Akitu	Spring
Egypt	Osiris	Winter
Canaan	Sukkot	Fall
Crete	Dionysos	Summer
Greece	Eleusis	Fall
India	Diwali	Fall

Summary

The New Year festivals of the ancient Near East combined prehistoric prototypes into a major ritual event that kept cultural evolution on the track of law and order, and maintained the bond between society and nature.

The New Year festivals of the ancient Near East combined prehistoric prototypes into a major ritual event that kept cultural evolution on the track of law and order, and maintained the bond between society and nature.[40] Three myths predominated: the sacred marriage, the eternal return, and the defeat of chaos. The fixing of the fates and the sacred procession also relate to order, and to the calendar. In particular, the creation myth of Enuma Elish evolved from Sumerian precedents. Its role in the annual Akitu (New Year) festival, and renewal of the victory of Order over Chaos, dominate history from Babylon to the present. Thanks to the recent translation of Sumerian literature, we now have the outlines of a complete evolutionary trajectory, from the prehistoric goddess tradition in Anatolia, to Harappa and the Indus cultures, to Sumer, and to us. In the next chapter, we will examine this theme of Order and Chaos more closely. We will see this trajectory carried forward through Egypt and Crete to ancient Greece, connecting seamlessly with the Orphic religion in the long line of Orphism.

The Long Line of Orphism

In 1983 I was invited to a dynamical systems theory conference on Crete. For a week in September, we were ensconced in a lovely resort hotel on the Aegean coast. One day had been set aside for sightseeing. On Sunday, September 4, I found myself on a bus headed for Mount Ida with a group of mathematicians. Our destination was the site of the Idaean Cave.[1] Later I learned that the cult of Idaean Zeus was centered on this cave, and that Pythagoras, Plato, Magellan, and many other famous figures of history had made pilgrimages to it.

Upon arrival, we walked from the bus to the cave entrance, the path going steeply down to a small balcony, below which the cave descended to a muddy pit from which archaeologists were digging up votive offerings left by pilgrims over three thousand years ago. As we stood in a circle around the archaeologist in charge, who was explaining all this, my mind wandered. I saw the shadow of a tree near the entrance, projected on the wall of the cave above us, as the sun prepared to set. I felt sure that Plato's allegory in the *Republic* was inspired by his visit to this cave. At that moment my attention was called back to the present, as I heard the archaeologist describe Plato's visit. Carried away by my thoughts, I left the group and ascended to the entrance, going outside to be alone. In standing meditation, I received a vision, in which the role of caves in the evolution of con-

In standing meditation, I received a vision, in which the role of caves in the evolution of consciousness, from the Paleolithic to the present, unrolled like a movie.

sciousness, from the Paleolithic to the present, unrolled like a movie.

The Orphic Path

Orphism was the most important religion of ancient Greece. What we encompass by *the long line of Orphism,* or equivalently, *the Orphic tradition,* is an amazing evolutionary sequence of myths, rituals, and paradigms. This path spans, in one continuous sweep, the late Paleolithic to the present: from late-Paleolithic TriVia, through the Agricultural Revolution of the early Neolithic, to the great partnership civilizations of Anatolia, to the discovery of the wheel and the associated Urban Revolution in the middle Neolithic, to the first great cultures of Sumer, Babylon, Egypt, India, Canaan, Crete, Mycenae, and Greece.

Of course, the tradition did not encounter the name Orphism until it broke the surface of history in ancient Greece, and perhaps we should call it the goddess tradition, but that suggests a much larger compass. Greek Orphism is a key point on this long line, the midpoint of the transformation from the Great Goddess to the One God. It sweeps on from Greece and Rome to Alexandria, Byzantium, Baghdad, Cordoba, Florence, to us, and beyond. In spite of being the subject of an enormous scholarly literature spanning two thousand years, the long line of Orphism is little recognized today. Its rediscovery is a perennial occurrence, basic to the evolutionary dynamics of consciousness. What follows is a brief outline of the chief features of the line, including pointers to the literature.[2]

The Root

The goddess religion of the late Paleolithic (best known for its cave art in Europe) and that of the early Neolithic (recently unearthed in Asia Minor) may be taken, for our present purposes, as the source of this evolutionary sequence. Diffusion led to a stable equilibrium of this culture over a wide range, covering most of the inhabited world. The parallels between the religion in the Zagros mountains of northern Mesopotamia in the seventh millennium B.C., that of Catal Huyuk in the fifth millennium B.C., the Cretan cult of Dionysos in the second millennium B.C., and Greek Orphism in the first millennium B.C., are very striking.[3]

Patriarchal culture apparently arrived in waves from the northern steppes of Asia, after 4000 B.C., along with horses and the solid-wheeled chariot.[4] This initiated a long conflict, culminating in the replacement of the goddesses by gods. The first phase of this gender transformation was complete by 2000 B.C., in Babylon, along with the arrival of the spoked wheel and improved war chariots. Meanwhile, various aspects of the earlier form survived as underground cults. Thus our story is a continuous undercurrent in the religious history of Europe and Asia.

Bifurcations

In the mathematics of dynamical systems created by Newton and Poincaré to model the solar system and the rhythms of the sky, one of the most important concepts is that of *bifurcation*. The word suggests a fork in the road, but dynamical theory knows three different types of bifurcation.

1. A *subtle bifurcation* refers to a gradual change in the type of dynamics of a system, such as a change from the rest state to one of very subtle vibration.
2. An *explosive bifurcation* refers to an unsubtle change in which the range of a state of dynamical equilibrium suddenly increases. An example is the sudden increase in the noise made by an engine, when something has broken.
3. A *catastrophic bifurcation,* or *catastrophe,* refers to the disappearance of an equilibrium state, followed by a rapid fall to a new equilibrium. A canonical example is the toggle switch.

We imagine, in the future of the social sciences, a time when models for social processes exist, and the dynamical theory of bifurcations may help us to understand social transformations and paradigm shifts, like early Christianity or the Renaissance.

THE GODDESS/GOD BIFURCATION

After 4000 B.C. the diffusion of Neolithic Orphism from its Anatolian homeland to the west was driven underground by the Kurgan waves, and their patriarchal aftermath. In far corners of civilization, the Orphic culture survived longer. For example, in the British Isles, it was not replaced until the arrival of the Druids in the second millennium B.C.[5] The Sumerian goddess Belili was transformed into the Babylonian god Bel.

Meanwhile, Orphism diffused eastward over a longer stretch, finding fertile ground among the Dravidians of the Indus valley.[6] There it evolved into Shaivism, Jainism, then Sankhya, Yoga, Advaita, Tantrism, and Buddhism.[7] After the arrival of the

Vedic Aryans in the second millennium B.C., the Indian branch of the Orphic path also became overrun by the patriarchal tendency, while retaining other overt characteristics of Orphism, including the transmigration of the soul, the cycle of births, karma theory, Tantrism, love for all life, and vegetarianism.

The Aryan domination of Dravidian India culminated around 1400 B.C., just as the Minoan culture on Crete was finally suppressed. While the partnership society and its Orphic ideas were repressed in the Mediterranean into secret societies, mystery schools, and the unconscious, they survived more overtly in the East. When the spoked chariot wheels ground to a halt in the foothills of the Himalayas, and their baggage of patriarchy and writing settled down, the lines were drawn for history as we know it today.

DIONYSOS/SHIVA

In India, the earlier form of Orphism survived as Shaivism.[8] In Minoan Crete, Zeus displaced the goddess.[9] Knossos, the earliest known settlement on Crete, was founded around 6000 B.C. by colonists from Anatolia, along with the Dionysian religion, including the Mother goddess and her sacred animals.[10] Crete is covered with places sacred to Zeus, such as the Idaean cave. Zagreus, the son of Zeus and Semele (Persephone), was devoured by the Titans, but was reborn as Dionysos.[11] Semele, another name of the primeval goddess, means *earth* in Phrygian.

In the migration from Crete to Mycenae, Dionysos rose in importance. While previously thought to have originated as a Thracian god, the discovery and translation of Linear B tablets from Pylos established his Minoan origin.[12] The Dionysian cult in Thrace included the immortality of the soul, in common with the contemporary Egyptian and Indian beliefs.[13] Other cult features included ecstasy and orgiastic rites. From Thrace, the cult of Dionysos made its way into Greece by way of Asia Minor, around the time of Hesiod's *Theogony,* 700 B.C.[14]

The similarities between the Shaivite cult in India, the Dionysian in Crete, and the priestly cult in Egypt are particularly interesting. Trade routes from Mesopotamia extended westward to Asia Minor, Crete, and Egypt, and eastward to the Indus; the development of writing followed these routes, from Sumer to the Indus, while the myths of the Harappan culture came the other way. The origin of similar cults in the Paleolithic goddess religion, and its culmination in Neolithic Anatolia around 7000 B.C., is obscured by the gender changes resulting from the patriarchal bifurcation, beginning around 4000 B.C. In summary, we are proposing, like Daniélou, a common Neolithic origin to Chalcolithic Orphism and Shaivism.[15]

Orpheus

Orpheus was a reformer of the Dionysian religion, restoring some of its basic principles, rejecting others. Later, the Buddha performed a similar function in India. Orpheus was a vegetarian, particularly objecting to *omophagia,* the Dionysian rite of the animal sacrifice. In fact, for the Orphics, omophagia was the original sin.[16]

In Greek legend Orpheus was an Argonaut, who lived around 1200 B.C., long before Homer and Hesiod. Some believe that Orpheus was a Cretan from a much earlier period.[17] Some scholars doubt that he ever existed as an actual person. According to Garth Fowden:

> The ambiguity of a figure who hovered between the divine and human worlds will have struck many as an advantage and attraction. Late paganism cultivated with enthusiasm such figures as Heracles, Dionysos, Asclepius, and Orpheus. Hermes was one more of these intermediaries, who were much in demand in a world increasingly fascinated by the transcendental quality of the Divine.[18]

Another characteristic of Orpheus, also derived from Mesopotamian roots, was his mastery of music, and its sacred and medical powers.[19] Physician, bard, and spiritual leader, he epitomized the functions of a shaman in primitive societies.[20]

THE GREEK LEGENDS OF ORPHEUS

To the Greeks and Romans of the fifth century B.C., Orpheus was a Thracian of the Golden Age preceding Homer. He was the son of a Muse, Kalliope, and the Thracian river god, Oiagros. Although not a warrior, he earned a place among the Argonauts because of his skill with the lyre, which was needed to survive the Sirens. In the later Roman version of the myth, he descended to the underground in search of the shade of his wife, Euridice, who was killed by a snake. This resembles the myth of Dionysos, who similarly rescued Semele. Orpheus was said to be the creator of homosexuality, for which he was killed by the promiscuous Maenads.[21] About this aspect of the Orpheus legend, Proclus (the fifth-century Neoplatonic philosopher) wrote: "Orpheus, as the founder of the Dionysiac mysteries, is said in the myths to have suffered the same fate as the god himself; and the tearing in pieces is one of the Dionysiac rites."[22]

Pythagoras/Buddha

Pythagoras was another initiate of Cretan rites (perhaps in the Idaean cave). Proclus (410–485 A.D.), Neoplatonist of Alexandria, says that Pythagoras was an initiate of the Orphic mysteries. Pythagoras, Mahavira (the last prophet of the Jains), and Gautama Buddha were contemporaries.[23] In his *Life of Pythagoras,* Porphyry wrote:

> What he said to his disciples, no man can tell for certain, for they preserved an exceptional silence. However, the following facts in particular became universally known: first, that he held the soul to be immortal, next that it migrates into other kinds of animals, further that events repeat themselves in a cyclical process and nothing is new in an absolute sense, and finally that one must regard all living things as kindred. These are the beliefs that Pythagoras is said to have been the first to introduce into Greece.[24]

Further, Pythagoras is regarded as one of the founders of Greek mathematics.

The Roots of Orphism

Herodotus, Greek historian of the fifth century B.C., described the Orphic practices (his is our most ancient surviving testimony of them) as Egyptian and Pythagorean.[25] Diodorus Siculus, in 50 B.C., proposed a theory of mythic diffusion, giving as an example the transformation of the Egyptian Osiris into the Greek Orpheus. Further, he wrote:

> The initiatory ceremony of the Athenians at Eleusis, which is, I suppose, the most magnificent of all, and that in Samothrace, and that in Thrace among the Kikones (the country of Orpheus the initiator), all these, they say, are divulged in the form of mysteries, but at Knossos in Crete it is the custom, and has been since ancient times, to let all partake openly of these rites.[26]

In 1903 Jane Ellen Harrison (1850–1928), a turn-of-the-century professor of classical archaeology at Cambridge University specializing in Greek art and religion, "hazarded the conjecture that Orpheus came from Crete bringing with him, perhaps ultimately from Egypt, a religion of spiritual asceticism, which yet included the ecstasy of the religion of Dionysos."[27]

Certainly the mythic episode of the dismemberment of the Greek Orpheus by the Maenads (Dionysian priestesses, or women, of Thrace) is similar to that of Osiris by his brother, Seth/Typhon.[28] Later on, in 1932, S. H. Hooke wrote, "There is a clear thread leading back through the Dionysiac rites of dismemberment to the Osirian mysteries and the ritual of the deification of the king."[29]

Thus a thread leads back from Orpheus to Dionysos, to Osiris, and to the Akitu festival, in which Marduk is imprisoned in the mountain. In Greek legend Orpheus founded the Dionysiac initiation mysteries along with the secret Orphic sects, which worshiped Dionysos. The mystery rites of Eleusis derived from these, and Orphism has been more famous and controversial than any other phenomenon of Greek religion. Unlike its predecessors, it has an extensive literature, and was the first Greek religion to have sacred books. Because of this relative certainty, we've extended the name *Orphic tradition* over the entire path, from the Cro-Magnon to the present (see table 9.1).

The Orphic Sects

Both Orphics and Pythagoreans were vegetarians, and ascetics, as Plato related.[30] The ancient themes of the death and rebirth of the Lover (Dumuzi, Tammuz, Osiris, Dionysos, Zeus, Orpheus), of the Earth goddess (Inanna, Ishtar, Isis, Semele, Demeter, Euridice), and the transmigration of the soul were fundamental, and were symbolized in the rites. These themes are among the oldest of the Ancient Near East, and probably derive from early Neolithic Anatolia.[31]

For true Orphics, each life was a preparation for the next. They had to participate in an animal sacrifice once (symbolizing the fate of Zagreus) and thereafter abstain from eating flesh or eggs, be chaste, and wear only linen clothes.[32] Orpheus transformed the Dionysian religion of Crete, with its rites of music, dance, intoxicants, sexual license, and the rending of animals, replacing licentiousness with asceticism.[33]

The Rhapsodic Theogony

The Orphic Bible, a canon of sacred writings associated with Orphism, was traditionally ascribed to Orpheus himself. Among the most important of these writings is the so-called Rhapsodic Theogony, an amalgam of twenty-four fragments.[34] In 1968 Frank Cross, the biblical archaeologist, introduced a useful distinction between two types of creation myth.

> One type is the *theogony*, the birth and succession of the gods, especially the old gods. Only at the end of the theogony proper do we reach the active or young deities, the great gods of the cult. The second type is the *cosmogony*, characterized by a conflict

THE ORPHIC TRINITY IN MYTH

TABLE 9.1
The Long Line of Orphism

1.	15,000 B.C.	Old Europe: *Goddess*
2.	7000 B.C.	Catal Huyuk: *Bull*
3a.	4000 B.C.	Sumer: *Innana, Dumuzi*
3b.	4000 B.C.	India: *Shakti, Shiva*
4a.	2000 B.C.	Babylon: *Marduk, Tiamat*
4b.	2000 B.C.	Canaan: *Tammuz, Ishtar*
4c.	2000 B.C.	Egypt: *Osiris, Isis*
4d.	2000 B.C.	Crete: *Dionysos, Demeter*
5.	1000 B.C.	Greece: *Orpheus, Physis*
6.	1 B.C.	Rome: *Bacchus, Natura*
7.	A.D. 1400	Florence: *Orpheus, Euridice*

The numbers in the left column refer to the map of figure 9.1.

between the old and the young gods out of which order, especially kingship, is established in the cosmos.[35]

The Rhapsodic fragments comprise a theogony in this sense. (In writings of this sort, the word *god* is used for both gods and goddesses.) From the feminist perspective, Cosmos means not just order, but patriarchal order; the acceptance of patriarchy, the transfer of power from the goddess to the god. Thus cosmogony is interpreted as the creation of patriarchal order.

The central doctrine of the Orphic theogony of the Rhapsodies is that "Everything comes to be out of One and is resolved into One." It has been compressed as follows.

> In the beginning was water and slime; and out of the water and slime was born Kronos (Time), brooding over the universe, a serpent with the head of a bull and a lion at the side and the face of a god between. "Of this Kronos, the ageless one . . . was born Aither the bright shining air and a great yawning gulf" and in the "divine Aither great Kronos fashioned a silvery egg." The egg splits open, and from it hatches Phanes, the first creator deity who is also called Erikepaios, Eros (Love), Dionysos, Zeus, or Protogonos (firstborn). Phanes is the shining one, the revealer; he has "four eyes looking this way and that . . . golden wings moving this way and that . . . and he utters the voice of a bull and of a glaring lion." He is "the key of the mind" who "cherishes in his heart swift and sightless Love." He is bisexual, beyond difference, a "very whole animal." As "female and father" he brings forth Night; darkness and light unite to produce Heaven and Earth (Uranos and Ge). At this point the normal "Hesiodic" mythology takes over . . .[36]

Note that the gender transformation of the goddess (snake) into a god (bull) is well advanced here. There are many versions of the Orphic cosmogony in later Orphic literature. But according to Nilsson, one of the most respected scholars of Greek mythology, writing in 1935,

> The Orphic poems were dependent on earlier epic poetry. It may perhaps be said that they used and reworked it according to their purposes, as later Orphic poets are known to do. This is corroborated by the fact that no other poem is so frequently quoted in the Orphic fragments as precisely the Theogony of Hesiod.[37]

The appearance of Kronos (Time) in the primary role is significant, as he was identified with the Sumerian Enki by the

Babylonian priest Berossus, in the third century B.C. This is further evidence for the continuity of the Orphic tradition from earliest Sumerian history up to early Christian times. The dating of the Rhapsodic Theogony is still uncertain, but we may assume here the opinion of Guthrie in 1952, that the Orphic religion took shape in the sixth century B.C., from a medley of Cretan and Thracian traditions, and that Phanes, Eros, Dionysos, and Zeus are one. We will take Hesiod's version as the original Orphic theogony. Thus three writings play special roles in the story of this chapter: a theogony (Hesiod), a cosmogony (Enuma Elish), and a creation myth (Genesis).[38]

Orphism and India

The sacred texts of Jainism and Buddhism are roughly contemporary with the Orphic Bible. It's possible, as Daniélou suggests, that the Orphic path came to India from Anatolia in the early Neolithic, developed as early Shaivism among the Dravidians, diffused to Sumer, Egypt, and Crete as Dionysism before the arrival of the Vedic Aryans in India around 1400 B.C., and then moved on to Greece as Orphism.[39] In any case, our prehistoric Orphism is identical to Daniélou's prehistoric Shaivism, both of which will be described in more detail in the next chapter.

The Mysteries

Orphism in Greece, although originally an underground cult, evolved into a cultural institution, much like the Masonic Lodge of our own times. Called the *mysteries,* there were various versions established at different temples. The most famous and influential were the *Eleusinian mysteries,* said to derive originally from the Egyptian rites of Osiris and Isis, before the cult of Orpheus.[40] After a millennium or so, the arrival of Orphism transformed the mysteries, adding the Sumerian tradition of the Sacred Marriage, and the Sacred Birth (rites of union with the divine, which became central to the Eleusinian mysteries), as well as the doctrine of the eternal return: the immortality and reincarnation of the soul.[41]

DEMETER

Recall from chapter 7 that Demeter was the Greek goddess of grain. When her daughter, Persephone, was abducted by Hades, the ruler of the underworld, Demeter rushed to the rescue. In Homer's *Hymn to Demeter,* the goddess interrupts her search at the home of the King of Eleusis, stopping there in disguise, taking a job as nursemaid to the king's infant son. When discovered,

THE ORPHIC TRINITY IN MYTH

she withholds the sprouting of the grain until Persephone is returned, at least for part of the year.[42]

THE ORPHIC MYSTERIES OF ELEUSIS

Demeter marks the transition of the Eleusinian mysteries from their ancient form to the rites of Orphism. The prehistoric goddess was replaced by Demeter, her husband by Zagreus/ Dionysos/Bacchus, their son by Iacchos, and their daughter by Kore/Persephone. In the most important festival of the mysteries, Kore and Iacchos were married.[43] These rites were so secret that to reveal them carried the death penalty, but there are many oblique references to them in ancient Greek literature. Some of these references were collected, translated, and woven into a commentary by Thomas Taylor (1758–1835), the English Platonist who influenced Blake and the Transcendentalists.[44]

Celebrated every fifth year for eight days beginning on the fifteenth of September, the Eleusinian rites included the initiation, or lesser mysteries (training in the meaning of the rites, fasting, purification, washing in holy water), sacrifices, processions, games, singing, and dancing. The myths of Demeter, Persephone, and their consort Dionysos (the Orphic trinity in Greek dress) were recited. Finally, the initiation in the *telesterion*, the mystic temple, included sacred orgies and an epiphany. This divine illumination has been described by Gordon Wasson and others as a group psychedelic experience.[45] These rites were celebrated at Eleusis regularly for over two thousand years, until the fourth century A.D. Note the similarity of the Eleusinian mysteries with the Akitu festival of Babylon, the Egyptian mysteries of Osiris and Isis, and the Cretan rites of Dionysos described in the preceding chapter.[46]

Natura

The goddess TriVia survived in ancient Greece as Physis, celebrated in the Orphic hymns, and in Rome as Natura. Ovid began his cosmogony with a description of chaos, in which cold battles with hot, wet with dry, soft with hard, heavy with light. Natura, a powerful goddess and cosmic power, ended the strife. She is transcendental, tremendously vital, all-wise, firstborn, immortal, creative, and she has power over individual souls.[47]

Bacchus

In Roman times Dionysos was renamed Bacchus; his followers, Bacchantes; and the rites, Bacchanalia. The mysteries and rites of Dionysos/Bacchus continued in various forms into the Christian era, were revived in the Middle Ages and the Renaissance, and again in our own time by hippies in the 1960s.[48]

Orpheus/Christ

In competing theories, Christianity is seen as developing from either Judaism or Orphism. Recalling Philo the Jew of Alexandria, a contemporary of Jesus, we may simply assume a synthesis of traditions. In any case, a number of parallels have been noted between the myths of Orpheus and Christ.[49] Both were anglers, fishers of the soul. Both were shepherds, saviors of souls. Both fed people with bread and fish. There are numerous Orphic images in the literature of the early Christians, including the image of Orpheus with his lyre among the animals.

Two Roots

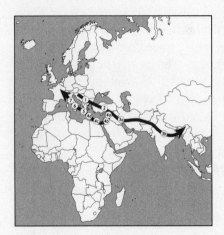

FIGURE 9.1
The Two Streams
Drawing by Diane Rigoli, © Ralph H. Abraham.

A river of Orphic diffusion is apparent; running from Old Europe and Asia Minor to Sumer and Babylonia, to the Holy Land, to Egypt and Crete, to Mycenae, to Greece, and to us. Another current goes from Asia Minor to India, and through all of Asia. Note that the route from Babylon to Ugarit to Crete to Mycenae to Athens is practically a straight line. So is the route from Babylon to the Indus and to the Lumbini Grove of Gautama's birth. Two streams merge in this river: the Great Mother stream from Neolithic Anatolia, and the patriarchal stream of the Divine King and Son of god (perhaps from the proto-Indo-Europeans) (see figure 9.1).

In the European mind, these two streams become, respectively, the underworld, or collective unconscious, and the mundane world, or consensual reality. The mysteries of Isis in ancient Rome and Alexandria shaped the veneration of the Virgin Mary in early Christian circles.[50] In the East the two currents became different cults of organized religion, such as the Mahayana and Hinayana traditions of Buddhism. Meanwhile, Jainism and Shaivism joined, creating Mahayana Tantrism, and this variety of Orphism was protected in Tibet and elsewhere in Asia, reaching us intact in modern times.

Salomon Reinach

The story related in these first three chapters of part 2 is rarely told, but not new. At the turn of this century, Salomon Reinach, the distinguished French historian of religion, published his book *Orpheus, a History of Religions*. This text of five hundred pages or so traces the history of Christianity from Babylonia and Egypt to the modern day. The book was phenomenally popular, and went through thirty-eight editions in French, as well as many in English and other languages. In the preface, he answers

THE ORPHIC TRINITY IN MYTH

the question, why does the name Orpheus appear on the title page?

> Because he was not merely "the first singer," though the Greeks knew of poems by him which they held to be much earlier than those of Homer. Orpheus was also, to the ancients, the theologian *par excellence,* founder of those mysteries which ensured the salvation of mankind, and no less essential to it as the interpreter of the gods. Horace designates him thus: *Sacer interpresque deorum.* He it was who revealed first to the Thracians and afterward to the other Greeks the necessary knowledge of things divine.[51]

Summary

In this chapter we've reconstructed an evolutionary sequence, from the widespread goddess religion of the late Paleolithic up to the Middle Ages, under the name the Long Line of Orphism. The main steps of this sequence are:

- the Magdalenian religion of the Lascaux cave
- the goddess religion of Old Europe
- the cult of Zagreus of the Zagros mountain villages
- the Dionysian religion of Catal Huyuk
- the Shaivite cult of the Indus valley
- the Dionysian religion of Minoan Crete
- the New Year festivals along the Mesopotamian line: Sumer, Babylonia, Ugarit, Egypt
- ancient Greek Orphism
- the Bacchanalia of the Roman Empire

Subsequently, we will extend this to:

- the Isis mysteries of late antiquity at Alexandria and Rome
- early Christianity, and the cult of Mary
- the Gothic revival of the goddess
- the Florentine Renaissance
- the Elizabethan Renaissance
- the Theosophic Renaissance

Classical Orphism, the most important religion of ancient Greece, is the midpoint of this long line, and of the transformation of the goddess into the god. Among the recognizable features of this tradition are vitalism, animism, reincarnation, the soul, vegetarianism, mystical illumination, sexual and ecstatic rites, asceticism, and feminism.[52]

The Eleusinian mysteries are particularly important, in the context of our current revolutions of Chaos, Gaia, and Eros, as a model partnership of Chaos and Order. The derivatives of

Among the fruits of the Orphic tree in our own culture are the Chaos Revolution, the Gaia Hypothesis, and the erodynamic movement in the sciences, as well as the growth of Green Buddhism in Europe and North America.

Orphism include Neopythagoreanism, Neoplatonism, Buddhism, the troubadours, the Renaissance, and the fabulous social transformations of the present century. A bolus of Orphic energy was apparently released during the 1960s, which is bringing forth from the European unconscious a massive revival of Orphic features. Among the fruits of the Orphic tree in our own culture are the Chaos Revolution, the Gaia Hypothesis, and the Erodynamic movement in the sciences, as well as the growth of Green Buddhism in Europe and North America. Our future may depend vitally on the nourishment and recovery of this lost pagan heritage, because our passion for order and control is throttling the life out of Nature. Not all the goddesses and gods of pagan antiquity need be revived, but we are especially in need of Chaos, Gaia, and Eros—the Soul, Body, and Spirit.

THE ORPHIC TRINITY

Creation Myths

In spring 1979 I made eight pounds of tofu every Sunday morning, to last through the week. It was a family affair. On one of these mornings, my mother called from her home in Florida.

Mom: Hi! What's doing?
Me: John and Marianne and I are making tofu.
Mom: *Tohu wabohu!* That's chaos in the Torah.

Two years later, on Monday, the sixth of July, 1981, I was visiting Otto Rössler, the chaos pioneer whose father was a theologian, at his home in Tübingen, and he confirmed to me, "*Tohu wabohu* in Genesis means chaos."

At this point I resolved to look into the matter. Cursory examination of various versions of the Bible led nowhere, however. Another two years passed. In 1983 I was invited to the Cosmos Conference of the Institute of Ecotechnics, in Provence. There, on the eighteenth of November, I met physicist David Finkelstein, a storehouse of rabbinical knowledge. I asked him about *Tohu wabohu*. He said, "*Wa*, in Akkadian, means 'and.' *Tohu wabohu* means '*Tohu* and *Bohu*,' the Babylonian gods." Now, at last, I had a clue. There must be two Babylonian gods of chaos! My career as a chaos historian was thereby launched.

Chaos Revolution

One by one, scientific disciplines are falling into the chaotic attraction of a new paradigm. The recent history of this wave began a century ago, with the mathematical discoveries of Henri

Poincaré. In response to a prize offered by King Oscar II of Sweden for a mathematical proof that the solar system was stable and orderly, Poincaré showed that the classical methods of Newton were inadequate to prove this, and went on to invent totally new methods for the geometric analysis of the problem. His work cast doubt on the orderliness of the solar system, but won the prize anyway. Later, in 1899, using his new geometric methods, he observed chaotic behavior in the solar system model. (More of this story is told in part 3.)

In spite of the existence of a mathematical model for chaos (that is, very unruly dynamical behavior) in Poincaré's model solar system, few people knew of it until the advent of the computer revolution. Then came an explosion of new understanding, in the computer graphics of Ueda and Lorenz in the 1960s.[1] In the 1970s the mathematical waves of chaos theory crashed on the beaches of the sciences. First struck, in 1971, was fluid dynamics, an event occasioned by the proposal of Ruelle and Takens to model turbulence in fluids with a chaotic attractor.[2] Then, in 1975, population dynamics was given a chaotic mathematical model.[3] Rapidly, the other physical and biological sciences followed suit. Recently, the earth sciences, social sciences, and even psychoanalysis, have fallen into the new paradigm of chaos.[4] Some of the major upheavals now in progress include the Chaos Revolution in planetary astronomy, the Gaia Hypothesis in earth physiology, and Erodynamics in the social sciences.

In this chapter we will continue to dig up the roots of this paradigm shift. In our archaeological search, we find a rich layer of material in the ancient creation myths of our culture. This layer in the world of ideas is known to specialists as *cosmogony,* as described in the preceding chapter. In historical cosmogony we find the remains of a vital struggle between Chaos and Order. In the New Year festivals of Sumer, Babylon, and Canaan, the god must annually reconquer the dragons of chaos, resetting the planets on their orderly (periodic) ways. This struggle between Order and Chaos is still going on in the various branches of science, where papers on chaos are being rejected for publication, and the best young experts remain unemployed. The mythic struggle between Chaos and Order is the emotional motor driving (and resisting) the Scientific Revolution now in progress. In later chapters we will see how Newton and Poincaré joined the fray. Both foreshadowed the Chaos Revolution, and both were cautious enough to keep their chaotic ideas to themselves.

The mythic struggle between Chaos and Order is the emotional motor driving (and resisting) the Scientific Revolution now in progress.

THE ORPHIC TRINITY IN MYTH

Cosmogonies

Cosmos means order or arrangement, and *cosmogony* means a theory of the origin of order in the physical (or social) universe (the root *gony* signifies birth)—a creation myth.[5] Most cultures seem to have a developed cosmogony, and this is seen as an indicator of cultural sophistication by anthropologists.[6]

Our own cosmogony (including the version prevalent among astrophysicists, in which the universe was created from nothing in a Big Bang about 15 billion years ago) may be understood as an outgrowth of the ancient Babylonian precedent.[7] In these early myths, *chaos* plays a special role. Although "chaos" today means "disorder" to most people, in the older myths there are important variant meanings.[8] In its first occurrence, in Hesiod's *Theogony*, Chaos meant the gap between heaven and earth. The biosphere, the atmosphere, the sociosphere, and the noosphere all occupy this gap. We live in Hesiod's Chaos.

Creation Myths

Apparently, humans must have a cosmogony—every tribe or town creates one, sooner or later.

Apparently, humans must have a cosmogony—every tribe or town creates one, sooner or later. Usually, it's the first indication that a society has risen above the primitive level.[9] In any case, this comes fairly late in the game of creation; for we must have language and a considerable degree of sophistication to make a cosmogony. *Cosmogonification* is an important step in creation itself, a kind of cultural self-reference.

Much is known of prehistorical cosmogonies from various cultures,[10] but here we will be satisfied with the written (historical) record, beginning in Mesopotamia, within a milieu of patriarchal dominance, while the mythology of the displaced goddess culture is still in a process of transformation.[11] Some outstanding features of the widespread goddess culture of the early Neolithic are peace, partnership of women and men, and love of the earth. It has been suggested that the partnership of Chaos and Order existed before patriarchal domination was established around 4000 B.C.[12]

Sumer

Sumer, like all other cultures, had cosmogonical myths, but in its written records only fragments survive. Thus our first historical cosmogony is incomplete. The main components we find are the triad of An (heaven) and Ki (earth, a dome on a flat disk), enclosing Lil (air). This universe, Anki, was created out of the primeval sea. Then came Enlil, Enki, Ninhursag, Inanna, and Dumuzi, as described in chapter 7. In another early Sumerian myth, Enlil's son Ninurta defeats the dragons of chaos, including Usumgal, or

Basmu, the equivalent of Tiamat, and the bird-god, Zu.[13] An early historical cosmogony known from a Sumerian cuneiform text, circa 2000 B.C., refers to Nammu, the Sumerian goddess who gives birth to heaven and earth, by an ideogram signifying *sea*.[14] A concordance of cosmogonical principles is given in table 10.1.

Babylonia

One of the earliest surviving written cosmogonies documents the goddess worship of the Semitic people of Mesopotamia. Of Ishtar, worshiped since 5000 B.C., it is said (in the rendering of Merlin Stone),

> Queen of Heaven, Goddess of the Universe, the One who walked in terrible chaos and brought life by the law of love and out of chaos brought us harmony and from chaos She has led us by the hand . . .[15]

Another early historical cosmogony, from Eridu, a Babylonian seaside town (see figure 7.2), is known from a bilingual (Sumerian and Babylonian) cuneiform tablet dating from before 700 B.C. and discovered in 1882 by Hormuzd Rassam (see figure 10.1).[16]

TABLE 10.1
Cosmogonical Principles

Sumer	Babylon	Hebrew	Greek	English	Meaning
—	Apsu	Tehom	Oceanus	Deep	father, ocean
Nammu	Tiamat	Tohu	Chaos	Void	mother, sea serpent
Enki	Ea, Mummu	—	—	Flood	mist
Enlil	Marduk	Yahweh	Zeus	God	order, cosmos
Ki	—	—	Gaia	Earth	matter
Inanna	—	—	Eros	Desire	spirit
An	Anu	—	Ouranos	Sky	heaven
—	—	—	Tartarus	Underworld	—

THE ORPHIC TRINITY IN MYTH

Enuma Elish

The cast of characters include Apsu, the Deep, the waters of chaos before the Creation, the watery home of Ea, the culture-god; Tiamat (Hebrew Tehom), the watery chaos, enemy of the gods of light and law, pictured as a dragon (see figure 10.2); and Mummu, represented by cloud banks or mist.[17] Recall that the dragon was a common symbol for the goddess in ancient times. Apsu and Tiamat are the male and female aspects of the watery deep, harking back to the Sumerian Nammu.[18]

This partnership derived from the syncresis of the earlier Tiamat, from Nippur, and Apsu, from Eridu.[19] Apsu is a Sumerian loan word in Akkadian, and is an old synonym for the Sumerian Enki, lord of the earth, also the Akkadian Ea.[20] Some have ascribed to Tiamat a celestial origin: the Milky Way.[21] The Old Testament Lilith, Adam's first wife, may be a Hebrew version of Tiamat.[22] The origin of the Akkadian Mummu is uncertain, but it probably derived from the Sumerian *mud-mud,* or creator.[23]

The creation story begins:

No holy house, no house of the gods
in an holy place had as yet been built,
No reed had grown, no tree planted,
No bricks been made, no brick-mold formed.
No house been built, no city founded,
No city built, no man made to stand upright;
The deep was uncreated, Eridu unbuilt,
The seat of its holy house, the house of the gods, unerected:
All the earth was sea,
While within the sea was a current . . .[24]

A later story (ca. 1800 B.C.[25]) is the better known Enuma Elish, also known as the Epic of Creation. This is the cosmogony discovered by George Smith, as described in chapter 8, which was recited twice during the Akitu festival. By this time Babylon had become the culture capital of Mesopotamia, and Bel-Merodach (better known as Marduk, the city god of Babylon) had replaced Ea (the culture-god of Eridu) as God (figure 10.3).[26] Bel was a masculine form of Belili, the Sumerian mother goddess,[27] epitomizing the gender changes many goddesses underwent during the cultural transformation from a partnership to a patriarchal society.

FIGURE 10.2
Babylonian Image of Tiamat, from the Ishtar Gate, Babylon, 605–564 B.C.

Photo: Erich Lessing/Art Resource, New York.
Reprinted with permission.

FIGURE 10.3
Babylonian Drawing of Marduk

From Heidel (1942).

Enuma Elish is an epic hymn in honor of Marduk and his overthrow of Tiamat and the powers of chaos. In the translation of Archibald Henry Sayce (1845–1933), Professor of Assyriology at Oxford University at the turn of this century, the Epic begins thus:

> When above unnamed was the heaven,
> And earth below by a name was uncalled,
> Apsu in the beginning being their begetter,
> And the flood of Tiamat the mother of them all,
> Their waters were embosomed together (in one place),
> But no reed had been harvested,
> no marsh-plant seen;
> At that time the gods had not appeared,
> any one of them.
> By no name were they called, no destiny was fixed.
> Then were the gods created in the midst of heaven, . . .[28]

In another translation by Professor Sayce, based on a commentary by the philosopher Damascius,

> When above unnamed was the heaven,
> the earth below by a name was uncalled,
> the primeval deep was their begetter,
> the chaos of Tiamat was the mother of them all.[29]

At this point, Professor Sayce comments, "The word I have rendered 'chaos' is *mummu*. Damascius explains it as 'the world of thought' or 'ideas.'"

Here is a more recent translation, for comparison, by Mrs. H. A. Groenewegen Frankfort:

> When a sky above had not been mentioned
> And the name of firm ground below has not been thought of;
> When only primeval Apsu, their begetter,
> and Mummu and Tiamat—she who gave birth to them all—
> Were mingling their waters in one;
> When no bog had formed and no island could be found;
> When no god whosoever had appeared,
> Had been named by name, had been determined as to lot,
> Then were gods formed within them (Apsu, Mummu, and
> Tiamat).[30]

This basic trinity of chaos gave life to the pantheon: Apsu represents sweet water, Tiamat the sea, and Mummu, clouds and mist. The creation scenario unrolls on six tablets. Here is the rest of the epic in outline form.[31]

THE ORPHIC TRINITY IN MYTH

TABLET I.   The primeval gods are created:
- Lakhmu and Lakhamu, half-bestial man and consort
- Ansar and Kisar, the upper and lower firmament, or heaven and earth
- Anu, Bel, and Ea, a triad symbolizing sky, earth, and water.

The younger gods of light and order (Ansar and Kisar, Anu and Ea) rebel against the primeval water gods (Apsu, Mummu, and Tiamat).[32] The older gods decide to destroy the rebels. On hearing this, Ea kills Apsu and locks up Mummu. Tiamat, the dragon of chaos, creates ten monsters to subdue the rebels

TABLET II.   Tiamat prepares for battle, Ea attacks but is defeated, Anu fails as well. Marduk offers to fight Tiamat in exchange for a promotion to chief god.

TABLET III.   All the younger gods (the Igigi and the Anunnaki) assemble; they accept Marduk's offer.

TABLET IV.   Marduk is empowered with new weapons, and engages Tiamat in battle. Then the forces of darkness and chaos are overthrown by Marduk.

> The lord rested beholding the cadaver,
> As he divided the monster,
> devising cunning things.
> He split her into two parts,
> like an oyster.
> Half of her he set up
> and made the heavens as a covering.

He fixes the abode of the three gods of the trinity: Anu, Enlil, and Ea (earth, air, and light).[33]

TABLET V.   The regulation of the solar system, zodiac, and calendar.

TABLET VI.   The making of man. Marduk creates Babylon, its temple, E-sagila, and the Akitu festival.[34]

In still another Babylonian cosmogony, from Nippur in the north, Tiamat, the dragon of the subterranean waters of chaos, is the source of creation.

The cosmogony of Enuma Elish was later summarized by Damascius, one of the last Neoplatonic philosophers (born about

A.D. 480) and a contemporary of Justinian I (483–565, Roman emperor, 527–565) thus:

> The Babylonians, like the rest of the barbarians, pass over in silence the one principle of the universe and constitute two, Tiamat and Apsu, making Apsu the husband of Tiamat, and denominating her the "mother of the gods." And from these proceeds an only-begotten son Mummu, which, I conceive, is no other than the intelligible world proceeding from the two principles.

Mummu (the flood) represents chaos, and is identified with Tiamat and Apsu in the cuneiform text. By the time of Damascius, apparently, a bifurcation (that is, one splits into two) has occurred, and Mummu has become the child of Tiamat and Apsu.[35] This suggests a concordance of the Babylonian trinity (Apsu, Tiamat, Mummu) with the three hypostases of Neoplatonism (see table 7.3).[36]

Egypt

Egyptian mythology also has creation myths. On the walls of the pyramid of Pepi I is inscribed:

> Pepi . . . was born of his father Tum. At that time the heaven was not, the earth was not, men did not exist, the gods were not born, there was no death.[37]

This is very close to the opening lines of Enuma Elish. Most interesting for us, however, is the creation myth of the god Re, from Heliopolis. In this story the primeval hill, the *ben-ben*, arose from the primordial waters of chaos, the Nun. The creator, Atum, appeared on the *ben-ben,* and made Shu, the god of air or the void, and Tefnut, the goddess of moisture, and thus a divine trinity was created. (Again, see table 7.3.) From these came Geb, the earth (male), and Nut, the heavens (female). Then Shu created the gods Osiris and Seth, and the goddesses Isis and Nephthys, to form the ennead of Heliopolis.[38] Later, the Sun god, Re, climbed the *ben-ben,* subdued the powers of Chaos, instituted Ma-a-t (the world order, Cosmos, harmony), and became king of the universe.[39] From this myth is derived the tradition of burial in pyramids.[40]

Ugarit

Canaan, between Egypt and Babylon, was inhabited (like Babylon) by Semites. Its literature, on the Ras Shamra tablets dating from 1400 B.C., was discovered in 1928, on the site of its capital city, Ugarit.[41] In its cosmogony, El is the father of the

THE ORPHIC TRINITY IN MYTH

gods, his wife, Ashtoreth, is the mother of the gods, their son, Baal, is the god of fertility (see table 7.3). His brother Yam-Nahar is the god of seas and rivers, while Asherah is the Lady of the Sea.

One of the main themes of the Ugaritic mythology concerns a family feud involving all of these characters. Yam-Nahar is favored by El, and Baal is in revolt against his father. Asherah covets the throne of Baal for her son, Ashtar. Eventually, Baal defeats Yam-Nahar. In another myth, Baal slays the seven-headed dragon, Lotan (the Hebrew Leviathan). This defeat of the forces of disorder and chaos appears to derive from the Marduk and Tiamat lore of Babylonia. In turn, the Baal legends were taken over by the Hebrews when they settled in Canaan.[42] The dark side of the patrilineal paradigm, and its correlates, the nuclear family and male dominance, are clearly presented in these myths of family violence and mayhem.

Crete

In Cretan mythology there is a cosmogony in which Gaia brings forth Earth and Eros from Chaos.[43] As described in chapter 3, the Orphic tradition in Greece derives from Crete.

Greece

The older Greek literature includes Homer (*Iliad, Odyssey*) and Hesiod (*Theogony, Works and Days*). In Homer, there is a cosmogony in which Night is the supreme principle, and Oceanus and Tethys are the father and mother of the gods, including Zeus, who is modeled on the Sumerian Marduk. It's not certain which of these two traditions (Homer or Hesiod) is older.[44]

Hesiod

In Hesiod's *Theogony* is another cosmogony (verses 116–36, among the oldest), in which Chaos (feminine) is supreme. Here are verses 116–22, in the faithful translation of Athanassakis:

> Chaos was born first and after her came Gaia
> the broad-breasted, the firm seat of all
> the immortals who hold the peaks of snowy Olympos,
> and the misty Tartaros in the depths of broad-pathed earth
> and Eros, the fairest of the deathless gods;
> he unstrings the limbs and subdues both mind
> and sensible thought in the breasts of all gods and all men.[45]

Then came Erebos and Night, Aether and Day, Ouranos and the other gods. Here is the first known occurrence of the actual word Chaos,[46] as far as we know. It's most probable meaning is *gap;*[47] that is, the gap between sky and earth;[48] or the gloomy cavern between Earth and Tartaros;[49] or *gaping void.*[50] Chaos did not acquire its current meaning, *any condition or place of total disorder or confusion,*[51] until the Stoics (300 B.C.) at least.[52] In order to prevent the confusion of Hesiod's Chaos with disorder, it's sometimes translated as Void rather than Chaos.[53] Note that Void suggests Tiamat, even without the attribute of disorder, as Marduk split her in two to make heaven and earth.

In Hesiod, Gaia means Earth, or more broadly, the physical universe; and Eros is Desire, the immanent creative energy, the soul of all the divine unions of the creation story.[54] More abstractly, we may think of Gaia and Eros as Matter and Spirit.[55] For Hesiod, there are three primal cosmic forces: Chaos, Gaia, and Eros. From Chaos issues Darkness and Light, Night and Day. From Gaia comes Mountains, Sea, and Sky. From these are born all the other deities, in four generations (Eros has no issue).

The Orphics

In the Rhapsodic Theogony of the Orphic canon, as described in the preceding chapter, the first principles are Earth, Night, and Heaven. A later Orphic theogony (probably sixth century B.C.) begins with Kronos (time), from which Aether and Chaos emerge.[56] Kronos was the Orphic name for the serpent, and to Pythagoras the serpent was the psyche of the universe.[57]

Philo

The concept of the Logos evolved through many versions in Ancient Greece. A late phase, en route to the Christian Logos, is that of Philo of Alexandria, already discussed in chapter 1. To Philo, the Logos, besides belonging to the divine trinity (see table 7.3), contains the totality of all archetypical ideas (like the intelligible sphere of Plato, and later, of Neoplatonists like Damascius). Thus the Logos may be identified with Tiamat.[58]

Hebrew

Finally, we may consider the Hebrew cosmogony from the Old Testament. Genesis 1 is said to date from the early post-exilic period, before 800 B.C., but is based on older myths, derived from Babylonia.[59] In the English of the Dartmouth Bible, it begins:[60]

1. In the beginning God created the heaven and the earth.
2. And the earth was without form, and void;
   and darkness was upon the face of the deep.
   And the Spirit of God moved upon the face of the waters.

THE ORPHIC TRINITY IN MYTH

Here we may recognize Babylonian influence:

1. *God created the heaven and the earth:* Marduk rearranged Tiamat's oyster shell.
2. *without form, and void* (Hebrew *Tohu wabohu*): the watery chaos aspect of Apsu and Tiamat[61] and *the waters* (Hebrew *Tehom,* which is philologically related to Tiamat[62]): Mummu, the flood, offspring of Apsu and Tiamat. A tentative concordance is shown in table 10.1.

TOHU WABOHU

The phrase *Tohu wabohu,* from the Genesis creation story, remains a mystery. Werner Wolff, who made a new translation of the first two chapters of Genesis in 1951, rendered the first two verses,

1. From the foundation Elohim hewed out the two heavens and the earth.
2. And the earth was confusion and emptiness and darkness was over the abyss and the Tempest-Elohim was brooding upon the waters.[63]

Here, *tohu* is translated as a state of volcanic confusion associated with Tiamat, and *bohu* is a state of emptiness of life. According to C. Westerman, *tohu* means *desert, wasteland, nothingness.* According to J. Ebach, *Tohu wabohu* means *Tohu and Bohu,* but *Bohu* has no independent meaning. Later he suggested the association of *Bohu* with *Baau,* the Phoenician goddess of night.[64] R. Kilian suggests an Egyptian origin, where *Tohu wabohu* means *a trackless, water wasteland,* and may be identified with Heh, the Egyptian god of chaos, from Hermopolis. Görg favors the identification of *Tohu* with Heh, and *Bohu* with Niau, another Egyptian god of chaos. He also suggests an Egyptian translation for Baau: *the night sky, which must be split open to allow the light to come through.* This recalls Tiamat in Enuma Elish.[65] *Tohu wabohu* is translated *chaos and emptiness* by Graves,[66] and as *empty and void* by Niditch.[67] Apparently, David Finkelstein was correct when he said *Tohu wabohu* may be Apsu and Tiamat—chaos.

Israel

Returning now to the theme of cult patterns in the New Year festivals of Babylon, Egypt, Canaan, and Crete, described above in chapter 8, we note once more that these festivals contain common elements. According to the Old Testament scholar A. R.

Johnson writing in 1933, as summarized in Voegelin, the phases of the Israelite Feast of Tabernacles (Sukkot) are:

1. Yahweh, the leader of the Forces of Light, triumphs over the Forces of Darkness as represented by the Chaos of waters or primeval monsters;
2. Yahweh's enthronement as King over the Floods and Ruler in the Assembly of the Gods;
3. Yahweh's mysterious works in Creation.[68]

Similarly, Mowinkel has written about the Hebrew New Year,

One of the chief ideas was the enthronement of Yahweh as king of the world, the symbolic representation of His victory over His enemies, both the forces of chaos and the historical enemies of Israel. The result of this victory was the renewal of creation, election, and the covenant, ideas and rites from the old fertility festivals which lay behind the historical festival.[69]

Further, the Sukkot festival included the Joy of the House of Water Drawing, the most elaborate yearly ritual performed in the Second Temple of Jerusalem. This mysterious festivity occupied the whole night, for each of the seven nights of the festival. It included beating the alter with willow branches, a torch dance, the water-drawing and libation, and the *lightheadedness,* which led to the building of special galleries for the women. All these elements have been correlated with features of Enuma Elish.[70]

The Judeo-Christian tradition took over many elements of earlier cultures, including the annual festivals that featured Sacred Marriage, a Great Procession, the defeat of chaos, and the eternal cycle of death and rebirth.

India

Indra's slaying of the serpent Vritra is the chief myth of the Vedic Aryans and is closely related to the Babylonian myth of Tiamat and Marduk.[71] In the myth of "the incomparable mighty churn" and the Sea of Milk, from the Sanskrit classic *Mahabharata,* Vishnu sits atop the axis of the universe, representing Cosmic Order, and seen as a "mighty churn." This is turned by the conflict of Krishna (a Deva) and Kansa (an Asura), engaged in a tug-of-war with a rope resembling a dragon, hence the goddess Chaos, or Tiamat. This myth may be derived from the Egyptian legend of Osiris, Seth, and Horus[72] (see figure 10.4).

The connections between Hindu myths and the long line of the Orphic tradition from Sumer to Alexandria are strong. The books of Alain Daniélou excavate and clarify these connections.[73] This strong concordance is understandable, as the Vedic Aryans were Indo-Europeans, and it's a short route from Mesopotamia to the Indus River valley.

China

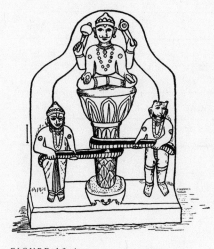

FIGURE 10.4
The Mighty Churn

From Smithsonian Trust Press, 1894. See Santillana and von Deschend (1969).

The connections between Chinese myths and the Orphic tradition are also strong, and are delineated by N. J. Girardot.[74] This is more distant than the Shiva/Orpheus connection, but here nevertheless. The two basic texts for this story on the chaos theme in Taoism are Lao Tzu (the *Tao Te Ching*) and Chuang Tzu, from the times of Pythagoras and Plato, respectively.

In chapter 25 of the *Tao Te Ching,* we find,

> There was something chaotic yet complete, Which existed before the creation of heaven and earth. Without sound and formless, It stands alone and does not change. It pervades all and is free from danger; It can be regarded then as the mother of the world. I do not know its name but will call it Tao.[75]

This suggests a correspondence of Tao and Chaos, or *Tohu wabohu.* In Chuang Tzu, at the end of chapter 7, is the story of the Emperor Hun-tun of the Center.

> The Emperor of the South was called Shu. The Emperor of the North was called Hu. And the Emperor of the Center was called Hun-tun. Shu and Hu at times mutually came together and met in Hun-tun's territory. Hun-tun treated them very generously. Shu and Hu, then, discussed how they could reciprocate Hun-tun's virtue saying: "Men all have seven openings in order to see, hear, eat, and breathe. He alone doesn't have any. Let's try boring him some." Each day they bored one hole, and on the seventh day Hun-tun died.[76]

Hun-tun is ordinarily translated as chaos. The extensive myths around this character include creation from a cosmic egg, and other Orphic elements.

Summary

The creation of the universe, in our tradition, means the subjugation of Chaos by Cosmos. Ours is a universe of law and order.

The creation of the universe, in our tradition, means the subjugation of Chaos by Cosmos. Ours is a universe of law and order.[77] This tradition dates from Eridu, as early as 2000 B.C., at least. We will take a closer look at this aspect of dominance in the next chapter. Note that throughout, creation means creation in form, order from chaos, cosmogony, not creation from nothing. The creation of the universe of matter and energy from absolutely nothing is not the kind of creation our cosmogonies try to explain. Some of the more important traditions in the collage of ideas presented in this chapter are summarized in table 10.2.

TABLE 10.2
Mythic Themes

Theme	Egypt	Sumer	Babylon	Greek	China
Disorder	Nun/Heh	Kur/Zu	Tiamat	Chaos	Hun-tun
Order	Re	Enki	Marduk	Apollo	North
Marriage	Osiris/Isis	Inanna/Dumuzi	Ishtar/Tammuz	Demeter	Tao
Underworld	Osiris	Erishkegal	Allatu	Pluto	South
Cycle	Osiris	Dumuzi	Tammuz	Orpheus	

THE ORPHIC TRINITY IN MYTH

Chaos and Cosmos

CHAPTER 11

In fall 1940, after my fourth birthday, came my first day at school. Preschool, actually. Along with the rules and schedules came my first experience of cosmos, at the expense of the chaos that had prevailed at home during my long days of solitude and freedom. Here also, with Tommy Knight's snowball attacks, came my first experience of the dominator paradigm. Little did I suspect the tight partnership of these two evils: violence and the defeat of chaos.

The Defeat

The Babylonian cosmogony of Enuma Elish (read twice during the New Year festival) begins with the chaos trinity of Apsu, Mummu, and Tiamat, from which are born all the gods. Ea (Enki) kills Apsu, and locks up Mummu. Later, Marduk, the son of Ea, kills Tiamat. In these violent steps, Cosmos is established over Chaos by force.[1] Tiamat is variously interpreted to represent the Great Mother goddess, Chaos, the Milky Way, the Red Sea, the flooding of the Tigris and Euphrates rivers, the Void, and the slipping of the celestial pole from its fixed position in the sky. Marduk represents Order, the Creator King, the fixed position of the celestial pole, and associated constellations of the vernal equinox.[2] The New Year festivals were meant to restore Cosmos, cosmic order, the revolutions of the stars and seasons, and to defeat Chaos in all its forms.[3] The defeat of Chaos is part of the social transformation that elevated the gods over the goddess.[4]

The defeat of Chaos is part of the social transformation that elevated the gods over the goddess.

The Serpent

An important element in Enuma Elish is the cosmic battle with a snake god, common throughout the Near East.[5] In the Babylonian myths, the serpent is identified with the disorderly currents in the ocean, which connect with the current meaning of the word *chaos* as disorder (see figure 11.1).

137

When *chaos* emerged as a word around 800 B.C., in Hesiod's *Theogony,* it meant the gap between the sky and earth. Void was implied, rather than formlessness. But within a few centuries, it acquired our modern meaning, disorder, which is the significance of Tiamat.[6] Further, it seems likely that Tiamat developed in Sumer from earlier mythical serpents, representing disorder and creativity in the goddess religion of the early Neolithic.[7] One of the principal images in Cretan religion is the snake goddess, Eileithyia.[8] Thus Hesiod's concept of Chaos merged with an earlier tradition, to form our modern concept of chaos.

Genesis

When Genesis 1:1–2 was written, Chaos and Tiamat reappeared as *Tohu wabohu* and *Tehom.*[9] Beyond the obvious similarities, there are also important differences between Enuma Elish and Genesis.[10] Chief among these is the omission in Genesis of the cosmic battle as a major theme, which is common to most of the Near Eastern precedents, in which Order subdues Chaos after a titanic struggle. Monotheism may be the basis for this transcendence of conflict in creation. Nevertheless, Yahweh always defeats the forces of evil, and remnants of the pagan combat theme do survive in Genesis, where "they practically always appear as a literary device expressing the evil deeds and punish-

FIGURE 11.1
Battle of Cosmos and Chaos

From Heidel (1942).

THE ORPHIC TRINITY IN MYTH

ment of the human wicked in terms of the mythical conflict of God with the rebellious forces of primeval chaos."[11]

Here *primeval chaos and evil are identified,* a bad omen for the essential chaos of life, which is necessary for evolution and is the source of all creativity.

Duality

Joseph Campbell has identified the Cosmos/Chaos battle theme as the origin of the mythical concepts of heaven and hell.[12] The dialectic of good and evil is an aspect of Two, a number beset by conflict (see the discussion in chapter 1 about the concepts of One cultures, Two cultures, and so on).[13] In the monist approach of the number One, Apsu and Tiamat, sky and underworld, male and female, Order and Chaos, heaven and hell, good and evil: all are merged in One. As Heraclitus says,

> Listening not to me but to the Logos,
> it is wise to acknowledge that all things are one.[14]

The Two tendency predominates in the Bible, where we read:

> And there was war in heaven: Michael and his angels fought against the dragon; and the dragon fought and his angels, And prevailed not; neither was their place found any more in heaven. And the great dragon was cast out, that old serpent, called the Devil, and Satan, which deceiveth the whole world: he was cast out into the earth, and his angels were cast out with him.[15]

Shortly after, we have

> And he laid hold on the dragon, the old serpent, which is the Devil and Satan, and bound him up for a thousand years and cast him into the abyss, and shut it, and sealed it over him, that he should deceive the nations no more, until a thousand years should be finished: after this he must be loosed for a little time.[16]

Further, it's nearly certain that the biblical theme of Yahweh and the dragon derived from a Canaanite version of the Marduk-Tiamat myth,[17] in which Baal, the king of gods, defeats Leviathan (or Lotan), the primordial dragon of chaos.[18]

Greek

The early Greek cosmogonies of Hesiod and Orpheus, reviewed previously, show Chaos in her rightful place of honor and partnership. Later in the Greek miracle, however, she was demoted. For example, in Plato, we have

TIMAEUS: Let us therefore state the reason why the framer of this universe of change framed it at all. He was good, and what is good has no particle of envy in it; being therefore without envy he wished all things to be as like himself as possible. This is as valid a principle for the origin of the world of change as we shall discover from the wisdom of men, and we should accept it. God therefore, wishing that all things should be good, and so far as possible nothing be imperfect, and finding the visible universe in a state not of rest but of inharmonious and disorderly motion, reduced it to order from disorder, as he judged that order was in every way better.[19]

Anaxagoras preceded Plato in this view of creation.[20] It's difficult to disagree with Anaxagoras and Plato, but we must always question authority! And so we ask: *Is order really better in every way?*

One meaning of the Chaos Revolution is that it is not really better, and that the restoration of chaos to full partnership with order is desirable. (This idea is explored in more detail in part 3.) This renewed partnership is part of the Orphic revival, recovering the balanced view of Nature that was lost in the patriarchal takeover.

Christianity

Christianity derived from Hebrew monotheism. In the early evolution of Christianity, One became Three, a very stable paradigm. In the further evolution of the church, Three became Two (by casting out Spirit from the trinity of Body, Soul, and Spirit), and again One (by rejecting the Soul as well), which is unstable. Perhaps as a result of this instability, the history of Christianity is full of saints—some local, others universal, added to the Christian pantheon as attempts to regain the stability of the trinity.

Among the local saints of the English Christians are Saint Michael and Saint George, renowned for their skill in subduing dragons. These traditions are typical examples of the Marduk/ Tiamat paradigm, which seem to be ubiquitous in all places and historical times. In the Gnostic tradition of early Christianity, biblical values were reversed: the serpent being Eve's teacher, the wisest of all animals.[21] This inclusion of Babylonian tradition may be one reason behind the phenomenal success of early Christianity, in the field of Judaism and late paganism. The Hebrews had demoted chaos at an early stage, but the Kabbalists revived it in the sixteenth century.[22]

THE ORPHIC TRINITY IN MYTH

Scientism

Our challenge now is to restore goodness to chaos and disorder to a degree, and to reestablish the partnership of Cosmos and Chaos, so necessary to nature, to health, and to creation.

In our current patriarchal paradigm, Order is to Chaos as good is to evil, and this has been the status quo for the past four to six millennia. But in the new paradigm of the Chaos Revolution, chaos is the favorite state of Nature, where it is truly good.[23] In the Chaos Revolution of the sciences, we are now learning that chaos is essential to the survival of life. For example, the healthy heartbeat is more chaotic than the diseased heartbeat, and the normal brain is more chaotic than the dysfunctional brain, according to the new measures of chaos theory.[24] In these contexts, health and stability depend upon a moderate degree of chaos.

This truth has been banished to the collective unconscious for all these centuries. From the shadows of the unconscious, it pushes forth into our consciousness and literature in poetry and song, romance and struggle. It erects heretical monuments in the history of our art, architecture, music, science, and philosophy. The myth of evil chaos threatens our future, inclining us always and everywhere to try to impose on Nature an unhealthy, orderly state. The excessive order of our agricultural techniques, for example, contributes to global environmental problems. Our challenge now is to restore goodness to chaos and disorder to a degree, and to reestablish the partnership of Cosmos and Chaos, so necessary to nature, to health, and to creation. This requires a major modification to our mythological foundations, unchanged these past millennia, and this is *no mean feat.* In a sense, we must replace Tiamat on her rightful throne, in mythology and in daily life.

Review of Orphic Revivals

In *The Chalice and the Blade,* Riane Eisler proposes an anthropological theory in which there are two basic forms of social organization: the partnership, or *gylanic,* and dominator, or *androcratic*, forms. The partnership form gave way around 4000 B.C. to the dominator form.[25] This cultural transformation (or bifurcation, as it is called in mathematical theory) took several centuries, and coincides approximately with the discovery of the wheel (thus with the beginning of the Periodic Era now coming to a close, as explained in part 1). According to her theory, the peaceful partnership society of the Garden of Eden disappeared altogether by about 1500 B.C., but lives on in our collective unconscious as a memory. This racial memory wells up from time to time of itself, in waves of what Eisler calls *gylanic resurgence.* We also refer to these as *Orphic revivals,* and sometimes as

Chaos revivals. The rise of early Christianity, and the eleventh-century renaissance of the troubadours in the south of France, are examples of these gylanic resurgence waves. As Eisler says, in the language of the mathematical theory of dynamical systems,

> Moreover, these historical dynamics can be seen from a larger evolutionary perspective. As we saw in preceding chapters, the original cultural direction of our species during the formative years for human civilization was toward what we may call an early partnership, or protogylanic, model of society. Our cultural evolution was initially shaped by this model, and reached its early peak in the highly creative culture of Crete. Then came a period of increasing disequilibrium or chaos. Through wave after wave of invasions and through the step-by-step replicative force of sword and pen, androcracy first acted as a "chaotic" attractor and later became the well-seated "static" or "point" attractor for most of Western civilization. But all through recorded history, and particularly during periods of social instability, the gylanic model has continued to act as a much weaker but persistent "periodic" attractor. Like a plant that refuses to be killed no matter how often it is crushed or cut back, as the history we will now reexamine shows, gylany has again and again sought to reestablish its place in the sun.[26]

We now seek

- to regain the Garden of Eden
- to replace dominance with partnership, in a context of psychological and mythological factors deep within the collective unconscious system of global human society
- to create a sustainable future[27]

New Year Festivals

Returning again to the theme of cult patterns in the New Year festivals of Sumer, Babylon, Egypt, Canaan, and Crete, recall that these festivals contain, among their common elements, a reenactment of the defeat of Chaos by the god of Order. We've tried to reemphasize these common elements. According to Voegelin:

> These festivals, however, were not New Year celebrations in the modern sense, but were loaded with the representation of periodicity on the three levels of a renewal of the fertility of the soil, of the renewal of the sun period on which the fertility depended, and of the aeonic victory of order over chaos of which the solar revolution itself was the symbol. In all three respects the New Year festival was the expression of a new beginning, of a righting of all wrongs, of a cosmic redemption from chaotic evils.[28]

In these powerful festivals, continued in some form for the past four or five thousand years, the abhorrence of chaos has been drilled into our cultural map. The virtue and primacy of periodicity, in exact cyclic repetition on all these levels, has been maintained in myth and ritual since the discovery of the wheel. This is the reason for our view that the Chaos Revolution overturning the sciences today ranks in importance with the coming of the wheel, the principal cultural bifurcation of six thousand years ago.

The Underworld

The mythic theme of the underworld is fundamental to the long line of Orphism. The basic belief in a life of the soul after bodily death is accompanied by an abode, or spiritual world, through which we journey after death. At some point in the evolution of mind, a bifurcation occurred, into the collective conscious and the collective unconscious.

A persistent feature of this bicameral world of the soul is the eternal cycle of descent and return. In Sumer, Inanna goes down to witness the funeral of the husband of her sister, Erishkegal.[29] She returns, but sends her consort Dumuzi back in her place, and he is then subject to the eternal cycle. The partner of Hades, Persephone, is trapped in an annual eternal cycle of six months on earth, six in the underworld. In the Roman version of Virgil, written in 45 B.C., Orpheus goes down to regain his lost lover, Euridice.[30] (For more discussion of this myth, see chapter 13.)

In the context of our theory of the defeat of Chaos by Cosmos, it's possible that the formation of an inaccessible part of our unconscious system, the deep unconscious, is a consequence of the suppression of chaos.[31] In modern European history, the legend of Orpheus is all that remains of Orphism. The long line of Orphism arrives here as a favorite theme of opera, operetta, musical comedy, and film. Eros, love, the unconscious, chaos, creativity in music and the arts; all become one at the end of time.

Summary

The conflict of Chaos and Order has been described as the most basic opposition of human evolution, the fundamental duality of existence.[32] With Chaos and Cosmos, we have a conflict situation similar to, and related to, the gender-based cultural bifurcation described by Riane Eisler. During the millennia since the beginning of monotheism and the association of chaos and evil in our mythological and religious foundations, there have been revolutionaries of chaos, tossed up into history by chaotic revivals. Orpheus (1200 B.C.), Pythagoras (600 B.C.), Buddha (500 B.C.), Heraclitus (500 B.C.), Christ (A.D. 37), and Hypatia (415) are the best-known Orphic reformers and Chaos revolutionaries of ancient times. More recently, Marsilio Ficino (1450), John Dee (1575), Giordano Bruno (1600), William Whiston (1710), Immanuel Velikovsky (1950), and Wilhelm Reich (1957) stand out. All suffered some kind of calamity, including crucifixion, burning at the stake, dismemberment, or simply societal persecution.

Science, one of the primary watchdogs of the domination of society by law and order, is now in a major upheaval. Its main strategy has been to suppress any experience contrary to its dogma, somewhat like organized religion in the medieval period. Now science is rediscovering Chaos, Gaia, and Eros, and we see this as a major paradigm shift.[33] Chaos is inescapable in the rhythm of the planets, the climate, the metapatterns of history; Gaia is emerging in the earth sciences as the name of a new holistic view of the interconnection between climate and life; Eros is associated with new mathematical theories for the social sciences. This shift, a new Orphic revival, is the primary subject of this book. Perhaps, with conscious attention, we may direct this movement into a reenchantment of the world,[34] in which Chaos and Cosmos enter into partnership, and we regain the Garden of Eden with our creativity intact: Tiamat rejoined!

Gaia and Eros

CHAPTER 12

My father rejected organized religion. He had his own belief system, centered on an abstract principle of love and life. And now, in midlife, I find I was raised an Orphic.

Cosmic Principles

In Enuma Elish, there are four fundamental powers:

1. The power in the sky: authority
2. The power in the storm: force
3. The power in the earth: fertility
4. The power in the water: creativity[1]

All are derived from chaos. In the preceding chapters of this part, we've established the Orphic trinity of Hesiod as a triad of cosmic principles: Chaos, Gaia, and Eros. We've described some of the meanings of the Chaos principle, and now we turn to the meanings of Gaia and Eros. The popular implications of these words today, the Mother Earth goddess and the Child God of Love, insufficiently convey their original significance. Rather, they should be understood as basic elements of a protoscientific model, or cognitive map, of nature. The richer meanings of early Orphism were basic to the worldview of the ancient Greeks. In the words of Martin Nilsson, the late professor and rector of the University of Lund in Sweden and one of our greatest scholars of Greek folk religion, writing in 1925,

The popular implications of the words Gaia and Eros today, the Mother Earth goddess and the Child God of Love, insufficiently convey their original significance.

> Chaos, Erebos, Nyx, and other names in Hesiod stand for nothing but cosmic principles, although the words are spelt with an initial capital like personal names. . . . The fundamental distinction between matter and force is already dimly perceived by Hesiod, when he gives to Eros, Love, the driving force of generation, a place as one of the cosmic powers. Thus the aetiological tale in its highest form gives rise to the beginnings of science. The first

elements of a scientific explanation of the universe were among other peoples just as inseparably united with the mythical as Ouranos with Gaia in the myth of Hesiod.[2]

Aetiology, now usually spelled etiology, is the science of the origins or causes of things. Thus *aetiological tale,* in Nilsson, means creation myth, or theogony/cosmogony.

Hesiod's Gaia

Recall from chapter 10 that according to Hesiod, around 800 B.C.:

> Chaos was born first and after her came Gaia
> the broad-breasted, the firm seat of all
> the immortals . . . (v. 116–18)

Apparently, Gaia included the earth, yet was not the same as the earth. We may regard her as a more abstract geometric model for the abode of divinities; a divine space, larger than the physical universe of matter and energy. Gaia is derived from Semele, the Cretan Earth or Mother goddess, in turn derived from Cybele, the Great goddess of Asia Minor, around 4000 B.C.[3] For Hesiod, Gaia appears to be abstracted to a higher level of the hierarchy, as the divine space in which gods (including Mother goddesses) live, work, and play.

> the immortals who hold the peaks of snowy Olympos,
> and the misty Tartaros in the depths of broad-pathed earth
> and Eros . . . (v. 118–20)

Hesiod's Eros

Tartaros, also belonging to the first wave of creation, is more of a place than a divine principle.

> and Eros, the fairest of the deathless gods;
> he unstrings the limbs and subdues both mind
> and sensible thought in the breasts of all the gods and all men.
>   (v. 120–22)

Here, we must remember the divine plasticity characteristic of Orphism, in which gods and meanings are interchanged at will, and one god's name represents a collage of concepts belonging to different levels of the hierarchy. For example, Zagreus/Dionysos is originally the son of Zeus, but eventually becomes fused, as described in chapter 9. Just as Gaia is at once goddess and goddess abode, so Eros is at once immortal god, and spirit of all gods. The word *eros,* in ancient Greek, denotes "want," "lack," "yearning," "desire for that which is missing," or "demanding

THE ORPHIC TRINITY IN MYTH

love."[4] According to Athanassakis, the translator of Hesiod quoted above, the position of Eros in trinity with Chaos and Gaia implies a very fundamental role as demiurgic catalyst in the creation of the world.[5] In the interpretation of theologian Paul Tillich, Eros is "the unreflective striving for what is noble." We may regard Eros as the connection between Chaos and Gaia, as in the Neoplatonic trinity, in which Spirit (or Logos) connects Soul and Body (see table 7.3).

OURANOS

Chaos gave birth to Erebos and Night, from whom sprang Ether and Day. Then:

> Gaia now first gave birth to starry Ouranos,
> her match in size, to encompass all of her,
> and be the firm seat of all the blessed gods.
> (v. 125–27)

Gaia creates mountains, woodlands, and the sea, then she mates with Ouranos, producing a long list of gods and goddesses. All hate Ouranos, and eventually they attack and mutilate him in a story reminiscent of the Osiris and Orpheus legends. Ouranos is apparently on the same level of the hierarchy as Gaia; as her equal, he is also an abode for the gods. Together, they are housekeepers for the immortals, meta-earth and meta-sky, the universe of matter, energy, and space. Distinctions may be made between *Gaia* (earth) and *chthon* (ground), between *Ouranos* (Heaven) and *aither* (sky). Here we have a more-than-divine Two, but Gaia preceded Ouranos.

Gaia and Eros after Hesiod

The Orphic tradition, consolidated around 600 B.C., as described earlier in this part, provides no evolution of the Hesiodic principle of Chaos, and little of Gaia. The idea of Chaos as a cosmic principle devolved after the advent of Christianity, and vanished altogether in the eighteenth century.[6] Gaia obtained a role as the earliest of the Delphic oracles, before Poseidon, Dionysos, or Apollo.[7] The oracle voice was heard to issue from a cleft in the rock at *Delphys,* which means vagina, the entrance to Gaia, the womb of the earth.[8] In the cult of Zeus, Gaia was the mother of Zeus, and took him with her into the cave of Aigaion to nurse. Certain caves on Crete were pilgrimage sites for the devotees of Zeus (including Plato, as described above) throughout the history of ancient Greece.[9] The image of Gaia, Earth Mother goddess, although preserved in Mary, the mother of Jesus, was lost as a cosmic power early in the Christian era.[10]

The Eros principle has had an extensive development, continuing to this day. One reason for this is the role of love (*agape*) in Christianity. Another, related, is the enormous revival of Eros in the Renaissance.[11] The last chapter of Jane Ellen Harrison's *Prolegomena* provides an extensive history, in thirty-eight pages, of one thousand years of this development in ancient Greece. Semele and Dionysos/Zeus, the mother and son dyad of Minoan Crete, developed into Gaia and Eros in the Orphic religion. In this tradition Eros was the primary principle, and was also known as Phanes, and as Erikapaios. According to Hermann Gunkel, an early commentator on the connection between the Babylonian and biblical creation myths, the Greek concept of Eros corresponds to the divine principle *ruah elohim* in Genesis, and to the Phoenician concept *pneuma*.[12] The role of Phanes and the cosmic egg in the creation myth of the Orphic canon, the Rhapsodic Theogony, has been described in a preceding chapter. She/he is the model of the universe, and the source of all.[13]

Mysteries

The Eleusinian mysteries near Athens were originally a fall harvest festival that evolved from prehistoric rites. The mysteries of the sanctuary of the Great Mother at Phlya in Attica were even older than these. These mysteries incorporated the basic Cretan rites after 600 B.C., evolving into the Orphic mysteries.[14] The roles of Gaia and Eros in the Orphic mysteries of Phlya are those of the Earth goddess and the cosmic spirit. Gaia is at once mother and maid; Eros is the spirit of life and love. At Eleusis, Demeter, the grain goddess, and Dionysos/Zeus predominate.

Eventually, the Eleusinian mysteries overshadowed those of Phlya. Gaia was replaced by Demeter and Aphrodite, goddess of love, while Eros became the god of love. Later, the Pythagoreans revived the mother and matriarchism, while the Orphic hymns revived the earlier, more general Eros, under the names Phanes, Metis, and Erikapaios. Phanes is the name of Hesiod's Eros in the Rhapsodic Theogony, meaning divine light, as in *epiphany*. Metis means counsel, and Erikapaios denotes lifegiver. In sum, Dionysos/Bacchus and Phanes/Eros (they are two sides of the same cosmic power, rather than anthropomorphic gods) became the chief Orphic gods, while Gaia lost place as the men took over, the same as Tiamat in Babylon. The wings of Phanes/Eros suggest his Cretan origin. In Harrison's words, written in 1903,

> The gods whose worship Orpheus taught were two, Bacchus and
> Eros; in actual religion chiefly Bacchus, in mystical dogma Eros,
> and in ancient Greek religion these are the only real gods. . . . The

religion of Orpheus *is* religious in the sense that it is the worship of the real mysteries of life, of potencies rather than personal gods; it is the worship of life itself in its supreme mysteries of ecstasy and love. . . . To resume: the last word in ancient Greek religion was said by the Orphics, and the beautiful figure of Orpheus is strangely modern.[15]

The Orphic doctrines of Phanes and Kronos influenced other mystery religions, such as the Mithraic mysteries of Rome.[16] We may summarize the classical Eros as:

- the first of all gods
- son of Aphrodite
- god of athletic youth, mystery
- the cosmic power of love and procreation
- symbol of the Higher Self in its aspect of Love
- drawing things toward unity
- bringing order and harmony from chaos
- the creative action of the universe[17]

The Fall of Eros

To Carl Jung, Eros symbolized the psychic energy of relating, joining, and mediating.[18] More recently, Rollo May has described a devolution of the Eros concept in three stages:

- the healthy Eros of the Hesiodic *Theogony;* a cosmic principle of creativity, which persisted through the classical age
- the middle Eros of later antiquity, of Plato and Aristotle
- the sickly child Eros, or Cupid, of the Romans and the Middle Ages.[19]

The middle Eros was revived in the Renaissance, when the Neoplatonic doctrines of Marsilio Ficino and the Florentine Academy developed around the central concept of Eros.[20] The Florentines invoked the authority of Orpheus in this love-centered pantheon, and gave Eros a Christian interpretation.[21]

Trinity Again

In the Florentine Renaissance, Eros was identified with the Christian notion of the God of Love, and the Orphic Trinity was interpreted in the context of Christianity.[22] We may now regain the Orphic trinity in our own form, closer to the Neoplatonic. Chaos is the source of all form and creativity, the mother of invention, the soul. Gaia is the base of it all, the body, the world of energy and matter, the physical universe and the divine cosmos. Eros/Spirit is the connecting medium between Chaos/Soul and Gaia/Body, as shown in figure 12.1.

The subjugation of Chaos by Cosmos disempowers the trinity, which survives only in the collective unconscious. For this reason, creativity (an aspect of Chaos) proceeds from the unconscious, and romantic love is one of the few remaining avenues to Chaos, the mother of all. The recovery of Chaos from the unconscious, and the full partnership of Chaos and Cosmos, must be a primary goal in our revision of ritual and myth for a viable future.

The recovery of Chaos from the unconscious, and the full partnership of Chaos and Cosmos, must be a primary goal in our revision of ritual and myth for a viable future.

Summary

Hesiod's Gaia was divine geometry; his Eros, divine inspiration. These basic concepts of Gaia and Eros later degenerated from abstract cosmic principles to anthropomorphic gods, but were revived by the later Orphics. Meanwhile, Chaos degenerated into evil, the tricky snake, the dragon to be slayed by the forces of good. The Roman Orpheus tried unsuccessfully to rescue her from this inferior position, and we're still trying to work out this problem as sacred artists in our own struggle for a new myth. We're coming to realize that a healthy Eros requires Chaos and Gaia.

Summary of Part Two

From the fabric of creation myths and histories of the world, we've pulled out one strand for consideration, *the long line of Orphism*. From the Paleolithic goddess to the present, most of the Orphic tradition is shrouded in the mists of prehistory. The historic part of this line is only four thousand years long, from Sumer and Egypt to us. We've suggested that trinities have special value for cultural evolution, and connect the Orphic trinity (Chaos, Gaia, Eros) of Hesiod to TriVia, the triple-headed goddess of the early Neolithic.

The Orphic trinity may be mapped onto the cycle of birth, death, and regeneration. We've traced the traditional conflict between Cosmos and Chaos, and its annual reinforcement in New Year festivals throughout the cradle of (patriarchal) civilization, as background for the occasional Orphic revivals in our history. We've associated the suppression of Chaos by Cosmos and the defeat of disorder by order with the birth of the collective unconscious, the patriarchal takeover, the discovery of the wheel, the death of the spirit, and the killing of the dragon. Ever since this transformation, the suppressed system of chaos, creativity, and partnership perennially seeks to reemerge into the collective conscious, and into the mainstream of world culture. These resurgence waves—early Christianity, the troubadours, the Renaissance, the hippies—we call Orphic revivals. The recent

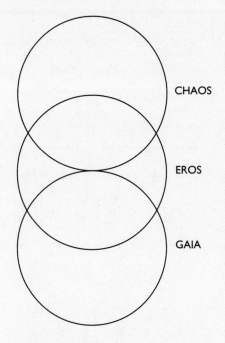

CHAOS

EROS

GAIA

FIGURE 12.1
The Three Spheres Arrayed Vertically

Drawing by Diane Rigoli, © Ralph H. Abraham.

resurrection of Chaos, Gaia, and Eros on the frontiers of mathematics and the sciences is such an Orphic revival, a step on the way to a new partnership of Father Sky and Mother Earth, Cosmos and Chaos, mental and emotional, stability and change, yang and yin. The world spirit, connecting world body to world soul, is reasserting itself. In this collage of observations we've glimpsed the progressive evolution of abstract cosmogonical themes from deepest spiritual feeling into ritual, mythic, and artistic traditions.

This concludes our case for the second conjecture from the Introduction:

The three concepts of the Orphic Trinity—Chaos, Gaia, and Eros—belong to a continuous tradition flowing from the Paleolithic past to the present. Occasionally, one or more of them has been suppressed, only to surface again. The meanings of these three abstract concepts (and the names, images, genders, and other aspects of their cultural representations) have undergone gradual (and occasionally sudden) changes over the past 25,000 thousand years.

The loss of Chaos and Gaia to the collective unconscious has left us with a weakened Eros. Numerous Orphic revivals have tried to restore the Orphic trinity without avail. And now we must try once again.

PART THREE

The Orphic Trinity in the Sciences

In part 1 we surveyed the history of history, tracing a dynamical scheme that maps the evolution of our culture according to three epochs, governed by the mathematical concepts of static, periodic, and chaotic attractors. We briefly surveyed the ongoing process of mythogenesis as it has affected our self-image as a culture, and the stories we tell about ourselves and our history. We explained why the Chaos Revolution underway today is one of the main bifurcations of our cultural evolution, comparable with the Periodic Revolution.

In part 2 we looked more closely at the process of mythogenesis and its effect on cultural forms. We described the Mesolithic Static Revolution, around 10,000 B.C., in which the chaos of the late Paleolithic partnership society gave way to the sedentary society of the farm. We described the Neolithic Periodic Revolution, the social transformation around 4000 B.C. that brought us the order of the heavens, the calendar, the zodiacal signs, the alphabet, the concept of history, horseback riding, the wheels of pot-

tery, carts and chariots, the urban revolution, and patriarchy. We described the arrival, with the wheel, of the ubiquitous New Year festival, with its ritual enthronement and divine marriage, accompanied by the ritual enactment of the creation myth, in which the God of Order triumphs over the Goddess of Chaos. This triumph apparently required annual renewal, as, in the celestially inspired solar religion, the Sun returns from the underworld each year at the spring equinox. Many features of the Paleolithic goddess religion, and its early Neolithic overlay of patriarchal values, entered Greek culture, and thus the European tradition, in the context of Orphism.

In part 3 we present examples of the Chaos Revolution in the sciences—physical, biological, and social—relating them to the Orphic trinity. In the first example, the physical science context of the heavens, we will see how Order has come to dominate Chaos in our model of the solar system, and how this is now giving way to a new form of creative partnership. As Order (Cosmos)

Order has come to dominate Chaos in our model of the solar system,
and this is now giving way to a new form of creative partnership.

denotes the cyclical regularity of the seasons, and of day and night, in the traditional paradigm of the wheel, Chaos refers to the possibility that spring will not arrive on time, or that the sun may not rise in the morning. In the new paradigm, as in early Orphism, chaos denotes the small irregularities associated with, and necessary for, romance and creativity.

In a second example, the biogeological context of the history of Earth's climate, we describe how cyclic models have given way to chaotic models for the occurrence of interglacial warm spells (called Gaian fevers by James Lovelock).

In a third example, in the context of the social sciences, we tell of the arrival of a new wave of mathematically based theories, emerging out of chaos theory.

In three apparently independent evolutionary transformations within the sciences, all occurring within the past two decades, all three cosmic principles of the Orphic trinity have surfaced again. In our three stories, spanning the past three centuries, we see Chaos emerging in the physical sciences, Gaia reappearing in biological science, and Eros entering the social sciences. The Orphic trinity returns!

THE CONJECTURE

All of this is evidence for the third conjecture:

The Chaos Revolution currently underway in the sciences, along with the related paradigm shifts associated with the names Gaia and Eros, signals one of these major phase shifts of history.

Taken together with the first conjecture, asserting the division of the past 25,000 years into three major epochs by the arrival of agriculture and the discovery of the wheel, this third conjecture implies that the Periodic Epoch has come to an end, ushering in another Chaotic Epoch.

In the first three chapters of this part, reviewing the discovery of the wheel, the mythogenesis of Orpheus, and the dogma of the Celestial Wheel, we will set the stage for the resurgence of Chaos in the halls of Science. In the final three chapters, we consider, one by one, the three revolutions associated with the principles of Chaos, Gaia, and Eros, and conclude our case: that the Orphic revival has arrived at the current frontiers of the physical, biological, and social sciences.

COSMOS, COMETS, *UND SO WEITER*

The Wheel

CHAPTER 13

My father was a merchant in Burlington, Vermont. He usually dressed meticulously in a three-piece suit, with a watch-chain across the vest. One day, when I was about eight years old, he showed me how to find North with his pocket watch, employing the hour hand and the Sun. The watch was particularly beautiful, his initials were engraved on the back: H.W. A. When he died in 1974, I inherited the watch.

It is the only such memento I have, and I still use it as my daily timepiece, keeping it in the upper-left pocket of my vest. In fact, this watch is the main reason I wear a vest. When I lecture on dynamical systems theory, I use Dad's watch as a pendulum to demonstrate Galileo's discovery of the isochronous property of the pendulum: the frequency of the oscillation is relatively independent of the width of the swing. This discovery was crucial to Galileo's invention of the pendulum clock, which revolutionized European society in the seventeenth century. And when I hold the chain in my hand, swinging the watch gently, I think of the pendulum inside the watch, the pendulum inside the pendulum, and I am reminded of my Dad and me.

Three Bifurcations

The Static Revolution (the advent of agriculture), the Periodic Revolution (the discovery of the material wheel), and the Chaos Revolution are the principal bifurcations in history, according to the scheme of dynamical epochs described in part 1. In fact, the developments of the wheel and of writing (and thus also of history) are parallel and concomitant. The wheel, the calendar, the clock, and writing, and a lot of other things, date from this particular cultural bifurcation of 4000 B.C. Table 13.1 presents the chronology of this bifurcation.

We can outline the bifurcation of the wheel in three phases: *before, during,* and *after* the event. The overall time frame of our outline is from the Pleistocene Age, beginning 2 million years ago, to the present, as shown in table 13.2.[1] (See also table 4.3.) The species involved, thus, are *Homo erectus, Neanderthal,* and *Homo sapiens.* The wheel, that is, the actual bifurcation, spans the interval between 4000 B.C. and 3000 B.C.

Through these three phases, we will pay attention to three parallel developments: the wheel (including the calendar and the clock), writing (pictographs and phonetic symbols), and social structure (partnership and dominator models). We view this sequence of developments within the *top-down paradigm.* That is, we see the emergence of the mathematical concept of cycle leading gradually to the material wheel. There is archaeological evidence for this primacy of mathematics and imagination in the history of consciousness, as proposed by Sir Flinders Petrie. A chronology of the sequence is shown in table 13.1.

Prehistory: Before the Bifurcation

The emergence of consciousness took place by starlight.

The emergence of consciousness took place by starlight. Prior to the domestication of fire, before 300,000 B.C., people probably spent a lot of time observing the night sky. Cognitive maps of countless tribes have been projected upon the celestial sphere, and the dynamics of the stars and the planets animate the myths of all times and places. In the north temperate zone, the most obvious features of the celestial dynamic are the circles of the polar constellations and the Milky Way. These were the hands of the first clock. An understanding of the annual variation of the polar constellations in the early evening was the first calendar.

HOMO ERECTUS

Homo erectus emerged in the middle of the Pleistocene Age, a million years ago, and eventually colonized most of Europe and Asia. Surely this required celestial navigation, and an idea of their methods survives today among many seafaring peoples.[2] Terra Amata is a site discovered in 1959 during the construction of a new building in Nice. Hurriedly excavated by a large group of students,

TABLE 13.1
Chronology of the Wheel

300,000 B.C.	seasonal migrations, fire
100,000 B.C.	speech
25,000 B.C.	lunar cycle, petroglyphs
18,000 B.C.	zodiac
8000 B.C.	sundial (gnomon)
6500 B.C.	Catal Huyuk, wheeled cross
4700 B.C.	Egyptian calendar
4500 B.C.	horseback riding
4000 B.C.	sky myths, cuneiform
3500 B.C.	pottery and cart wheels
3000 B.C.	Stonehenge, hieroglyphs
2000 B.C.	Egyptian temple alignments
2000 B.C.	precession of the equinoxes
2000 B.C.	the alphabet
2000 B.C.	spoked wheels
1850 B.C.	Tiamat and Marduk
600 B.C.	Ezekiel saw the wheel
400 B.C.	Greek epicycles
350 B.C.	the primitive sphere

remains were found of a seasonal lodge dating from 300,000 B.C. This is about the time of the emergence of *Homo sapiens*. These people returned to the same base annually, apparently on a round of seasonal migration determined by the polar constellations. They used fire and sophisticated stone tools. The lodge was a dome-shaped longhouse, with distinct areas for the fires and for tool industries. The domed roof and indoor fireplace suggest the possibility of a ritual in which the movements of the constellations was enacted—an early planetarium or armillary sphere.[3]

NEANDERTHAL

In an early example of the influence of climate change on human affairs, the Neanderthal people appeared in Europe during the early Paleolithic interglacial of 80,000 to 100,000 years ago. The Shanidar cave in northern Iraq provides a nearly continuous record of habitation from that time until the present.[4] Here was discovered the earliest evidence of belief in an afterlife. The cave was inhabited seasonally, indicating an understanding of the polar celestial calendar. As at Terra Amata, the domed ceiling of the cave, and the fireplace within, may have been used for rituals in which stellar myths were enacted. The gnomon, used as a sun-dial from very early times, also gives an indication of the season, in the annual variation of the length of the shadow at noon.

CRO-MAGNON

By 30,000 B.C. the Cro-Magnon people had colonized the entire globe, a tremendous accomplishment requiring sailing technology and celestial navigation.

It seems likely that the mythology of the polar constellations provided models for the earliest arts of Paleolithic peoples. The *Cro-Magnon* people arrived in Europe around 40,000 B.C. Like *Homo erectus* before them, they diffused widely. By 30,000 B.C. they had colonized the entire globe, a tremendous accomplishment requiring sailing technology and celestial navigation.

Their cave paintings of the middle and late Paleolithic at Lascaux, Altamira, and other caves in France and Spain suggest an understanding of cyclic order in the heavenly sphere. Here are found human and animal figures, geometrically organized in tableaux that may be cognitive maps, mythic groupings, or even sky maps.[5] This would be a logical evolution from the hypothetical fire-and-dome rituals of Terra Amata and Shanidar. At Lascaux there is actual evidence of rituals danced in the cave. These people developed a system of mathematics adequate to determine the cycle of phases of the moon, engraving a primitive graph of this cycle in a bone, around 25,000 B.C., according to the analysis of Alexander Marshack.[6] The bone is shown in figure 13.1.

THE ZODIAC

Later, the zodiacal constellations of the celestial equator, through which the Sun moves on its annual cycle around the celestial sphere, replaced the polar constellations as the calendar of the ancients. This required a further development of mathematical skill. Many people even today are ignorant of the complicated space-time pattern of the Sun and the zodiac. This is the step in the evolution of archaeoastronomy that led directly to the wheel. The zodiac may be visualized as a thick, solid wheel, revolving

TABLE 13.2
Two Million Years of Cultural Evolution

Age		Approximate Dates (B.C.E.)	Northwestern Continental Europe	West Central Europe	Egypt and the Near East	Human Types
NEOLITHIC		50	Iron Age Introduced	Historic Times Begin		Persisting Varieties of *Homo Sapiens*
		500		Iron Age Introduced		
		1000	Bronze Age Introduced		Iron Age Begins	
		1500	Traces of Copper	Bronze Age Introduced		
		2000	Late Neolithic	Copper Age Introduced	Bronze Age Begins	
		2500			Alloys in use	
		3000	Middle Neolithic	Late Neolithic	History Begins Writing Invented	
		3500			Amratian Industry	
		4000	Early Neolithic: Shell Mounds	Middle Neolithic Industries	Iron Use Begins	
		4500			Agriculture and Domestication of Animals	
		5000				
MESO-LITHIC		5500	Norse Petroglyphs	Early Neolithic Industries	Use of Copper Begins	
		6000	Maglemose Industry			
		6500				
Upper/Late	PALEOLITHIC	8500		Late Magdalenian	Probably beginning of a Neolithic culture in Nile valley floor silts	Předmost Cro-Magnon
				Early Magdalenian		
				Late Aurignacian		
Middle		15,5000		Early Aurignacian		Grimaldi Cro-Magnon
		18,5000				Emergence of Cro-Magnon
		35,000		Mousterian Culture		
Lower/Early		75,000				Emergence of Neanderthal
		100,000				
		600,000				Emergence of *Homo Erectus*
		1,000,000				
		2,000,000	*Start of Pleistocene*			

FIGURE 13.1

The Blanchard Bone. Engraved and shaped bone plaque from the rock shelter site of Blanchard (Dordogne), Aurignacian, ca. 28,000 B.C.

Photo: Alexander Marshack. Courtesy of Alexander Marshack. Reprinted with permission.

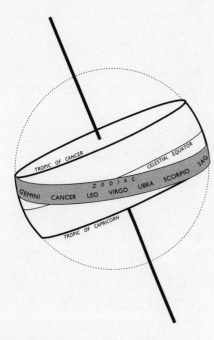

FIGURE 13.2

Hamlet's Mill. An early model of the solar system

Drawing by Diane Rigoli, © Ralph H. Abraham.

TERRESTRIAL CYCLES

SKY AND EARTH

on a spindle that's attached to the celestial sphere at its poles. On the outer surface of the solid wheel is painted a snake, representing the annual path of the Sun, which winds north in summer, south in winter, as shown in figure 13.2.

This wandering accounts for the annual change in the length of daytime.[7] In fact, it is very difficult to understand the dynamics of the Sun's motion without making such a model. The efforts of early astronomers to model this dynamical system may have led to a toy wheel, which later was enlarged and put to practical use.[8] This may be seen as the origin of dynamics, the branch of mathematics dealing with space-time patterns, as well as a crucial step in the discovery of the wheel.

The so-called Venus figurines, found all over the world and dating from the late Paleolithic, are symbols of the Earth goddess. Figure 13.3 shows one of these figurines, exhibiting a rhombic geometry common to them all.[9]

It's reasonable to assume that our Cro-Magnon ancestors may have known that Earth was round, and that these figurines were globes—intentional models of Earth. Perhaps some of them were incised with maps of continents, islands, and so on.[10] The rhombus figure discovered by Leroi-Gourhan also suggests that some of these figurines were suspended in a frame, within which they might turn freely.

These rotating globes may also have been used as models of the celestial sphere. The similarity of the models needed to understand the dynamics of these two spheres, the celestial and the terrestrial, is the basis for the dictum, *As above, so below;* and for the

THE ORPHIC TRINITY IN THE SCIENCES

The possibility of an advanced mathematics of great antiquity cannot be ruled out. This archaeomathematics would have been the basis of calendrics, timekeeping, navigation, and other sacred and secular applications, then as now.

idea of the partnership of Father Sky and Mother Earth, the ideal partnership model for the nuclear family; and for the two halves of humanity.[11] In any case, the possibility of an advanced mathematics of great antiquity cannot be ruled out. This archaeomathematics would have been the basis of calendrics, timekeeping, navigation, and other sacred and secular applications, then as now.

SEASONAL MIGRATIONS

The terrestrial cycle of the seasons determined annual population migrations, certain locations being occupied for long periods of time, determined by the slower variation of the climate and its ice ages. Eventually, regular routes were established, and homes (either constructions like Terra Amata or caves such as Shanidar and Lascaux) were reused at fixed times. At some of these sites, temples or Megalithic monuments were established for rituals, perhaps in worship of sky gods and Earth goddesses. The larger caves of the Cro-Magnon seem better adapted to worship than to habitation. At Glastonbury, in Neolithic England, the annual migration route was marked with zodiacal signs, indicating the dates of habitation of each of the sites, now called the Hides of Glastonbury.[12]

AGRICULTURE

Seasonal migrations were enabled by global climate warming, and by celestial calendrics and navigation, thus from an evolving theory of dynamics that became mathematics and astronomy. From the seasonal migrations evolved agriculture, around 9000 B.C. This great bifurcation did not occur as an instantaneous transformation. Rather, a seed was planted somewhere, then roots of a new technology grew outward in a gradual diffusion. There may have been several nuclei, and a complex space-time pattern of transformation.[13] As shown in table 13.2, for example, the early Neolithic progressed from Egypt, as early as 15,500 B.C., to western Europe around 6500 B.C., to northern Europe around 5000 B.C., and the wheel, as an artistic symbol, went along with it.[14] In the slowly developing new pattern of agriculture, people became attached to the land in settlements along old migration routes. The former space-time pattern survived within the new, as temples and rituals maintained the old sacred tempo. We still have seasonal gatherings, pilgrimages to ancient sacred sites, and repetitions of rituals, whose meanings are long forgotten.[15]

3500 B.C.–2000 B.C.: During the Bifurcation

We will describe three parallel developments in this period: writing, patriarchy, and the physical wheel.

WRITING

Writing began around 3000 B.C., with the cuneiform of Sumer, and then spread to Egypt. Egyptian hieroglyphs were the first to

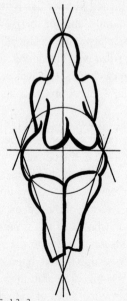

PATRIARCHY

TOY WHEELS

be deciphered, beginning with the work in 1636 of Jesuit mathematician Athanasius Kircher (1601–80).[16] Cuneiform was deciphered by Georg Grotefend (1775–1853) in 1802. Earlier, we told some of the story of Henry Rawlinson, who translated the cuneiform inscriptions of the Behiston cliffs in 1836. These systems are phonetic, but not truly alphabets.[17] Where did they come from? The cave signs and Old European alphabets may be compared suggestively. Previously, we suggested that the symbols appearing along with cave paintings might be astrological signs, and in the case of Native American petroglyphs, this has been firmly established.[18]

The origin of the first phonetic alphabet is still debated, but a consensus is emerging for the northwestern Semites around 1500 B.C. A strong case for the common origin, in the lunar zodiac, of two hundred phonetic alphabets has been made by Hugh Moran and David Kelley.[19] The lunar zodiac is older than the solar zodiac. Based on the polar constellations, it records the progress of the Moon through its twenty-eight-day cycle, with one constellation corresponding to each day of the lunar cycle. The theory of Moran and Kelley derives the alphabet from the symbols for these twenty-eight constellations.

According to the gylanic theory of James Mellaart, Marija Gimbutas, and Riane Eisler, the partnership society of the early Neolithic was the peaceful reign of the goddess, ended by the incursions of a warlike dominator society into Old Europe and Anatolia in the Copper Age. The Kurgans, who worshiped a warrior god and may have been Indo-European, were among these invaders, as were the Homeric Acheans and the Philistines. They arrived in three successive waves, overrunning the agricultural settlements of Old Europe and Anatolia. The dates of the three waves are 4300 B.C., 3400 B.C., and 3000 B.C.[20]

As described above, the top-down paradigm suggests the conjecture that toy wheels (perhaps models of the spinning earth) may have preceded full-size wheels, as an intermediate stage in the materialization of a mathematical idea. Suggestive toy carts have been found in Mayan ruins, and some remarkable disks, usually described as tops, have been found in Egyptian tombs.[21] A socket in the back receives a small stick, with which the disk may be rotated by the fingers. An excellent arrangement to model the solar zodiac, this could easily evolve into a top, a toy wheel, or a pottery wheel.

POTTERY WHEELS

The pottery wheel is a relatively new development in the long history of pottery. The earliest known pottery wheel, found at the Iranian site of Sialk, has been dated around 4000 B.C.[22] The pottery wheel was known in Sumer around 3500 B.C., a surviving portion of an actual potter's wheel having been found at the site of Ur, from 3250 B.C. As shards of wheel-made vases can be dated accurately, a snapshot can be made of the diffusion of the pottery wheel radiating outward from Sialk, reaching Egypt in 2750 B.C., Crete in 2000 B.C., and Scotland in A.D. 400.[23]

CART WHEELS

Transportation was revolutionized by the wheel soon after the transformation of the pottery industry. Two solid wheels (tripartite disks) were added to the sledge around 3500 B.C. in Sumer. First used for moving foodstuffs from the fields to the settlements, these farm carts enabled the Urban Revolution, in which larger towns sprang up quickly. By 3000 B.C. the war chariot was in action in Sumer, and the oldest wheeled vehicles actually surviving are hearses, buried in the royal tombs of Mesopotamia around 2500 B.C. Like the pottery wheel, the cart wheel and chariot wheel diffused slowly to Europe and Asia, reaching Crete by 2000 B.C., Egypt by 1600 B.C., and Britain by about 500 B.C.

SPOKED WHEELS

Spoked wheels appeared around 2000 B.C. in Mesopotamia, reaching Egypt by 1600 B.C., Crete and Mycenae by 1500 B.C., and China by 1300 B.C. These were more costly, and much better, than solid wheels, especially for war chariots.

WATER WHEELS

Wheels to harness water power to turn a millstone appeared around 100 B.C. in the Mesopotamian hills.[24]

History:
After the Bifurcation

After wheels, writing, and patriarchy were established, the evolution of the mathematical concept of the cycle continued at an increased pace. Here is a brief summary of some related developments, up to Roman times.

OBSERVATORIES

In this age of jet transport, it is hard to understand the slow pace of cultural diffusion in the early historical period. The wheel took three thousand years to get to Britain. Yet the cycle concept, from astronomy, is already found there by around 2500 B.C. This is the date of the earliest known *henge,* or Megalithic stone circle. About one hundred of these have been found in Britain, built over a period of fifteen hundred years.[25]

The discovery that these Megalithic monuments were astronomical observatories was first made by the astronomer Samuel Langley, in 1889.[26] Previously, a professor in Germany had discovered the astronomical orientations of ancient Egyptian temples, and Norman Lockyer went to Egypt in 1890 to begin his studies.[27] He discovered solar temples with astronomical alignments dating from 5000 B.C., and reported fully on his discoveries in his book, *The Dawn of Astronomy,* in 1893. Here he also commented on the astronomical source of Egyptian mythology, and related the myth of Horus to the circumpolar constellations (Horus being the rising Sun, which destroys the circumpolar stars). He further noted that much of Egyptian astronomy was motivated by the New Year festival, and predicting the arrival of the flood of the Nile, which was apparently complicated by the fact that their year had only 360 days.

CALENDARS

After the cycle concept had materialized, better models of the heavenly motions were possible. The understanding of celestial events such as the heliacal rising of Venus and the setting of Sirius improved. Thus calendars became more accurate. The adjustment of the Egyptian calendar in 747 B.C., from 360 to 365 days, was an early improvement.[28] Calendric revision is still underway, and the Mayan calendar is generally agreed to be the most accurate so far devised.

CLOCKS

Before the wheel, clocks existed, but were not very accurate. The gnomon, the sundial, and the water clock were already in use in Egypt and Mesopotamia. After the wheel, improved models of the solar system were built, allowing more accurate calendric timekeeping. Eventually, these were coupled to clocks, providing animated simulacra of the heavens in the form of planetaria, armillary (primitive) spheres, alarm clocks, and so on.[29] A sophisticated device for astronomical computations was in existence by 50 B.C.[30]

It was not until around A.D. 1600 that accurate clocks were developed. We can see that Greek models for heavenly mechanics gave rise to science as we know it today.

COGNITIVE MAPS

After five or six millennia, the wheel is so ubiquitous as to be almost invisible. In the mythology and religious images discussed earlier, we've seen it as a primary sacred symbol. To Plato, the circle represented divine perfection. Later scientists added epicycles, that is, circles upon circles, to explain all forms in terms of divine circles. The medicine wheel and other circular metaphors abound in sacred literature of the past millennia. Especially, we should note that Marduk rode a spoke-wheeled chariot to his attack upon Tiamat, around 2000 B.C. Ezekiel saw spoked wheels in his visions a little later, and Parmenides took his chariot ride to the Sun.

Summary

In this chapter we've outlined the Periodic Revolution for two purposes. First, the three dynamical epochs of history (the Static, the Periodic, and the Chaotic Epochs) are punctuated by the three bifurcations (the Periodic Revolution ends the Static Epoch and begins the Periodic Epoch, for example). Thus the Chaos Revolution is clarified by an outline of the parallel Periodic Revolution (the wheel), which preceded it by six thousand years. Second, the development of modern science has unrolled, until now, in the milieu of the Periodic Epoch. Thus the meaning of order has been specialized within the sciences into the special case of Periodic Order. This rigid paradigm is the backdrop for the Chaos Revolution in the sciences, to which we now turn.

Orpheus Revisited

Terence McKenna, Rupert Sheldrake, and I have shared great times talking into the night, blending our thoughts in synergy. Terence lives near me in California. Rupert lives in London and usually visits California in the fall, when we have our annual Trialogues. In fall 1988 we devised an experiment in exporting our experience to a public venue, a workshop at the Esalen Institute. In September of 1989, a thrilling interaction took place, entwining the themes of chaos, creativity, and the imagination.[1]

After the workshop we visited with Nancy Kaye Lunney, the Esalen program director. Nancy knows thousands of show tunes and has an uncanny ability to get people to sing them as she plays accompaniment on her piano. While Rupert was busy with his son Merlin, Terence and I had a transcendental experience singing "Irish Eyes," significantly strengthening our bond. Impressed by Nancy's skill in catalyzing this experience, I proposed to her that we do a workshop together on "The 3 Ms: Math, Music, and Myth." The original idea for the workshop was to seek hit songs that present, perhaps in disguise, the themes of Orphism, or the myth of Orpheus. She introduced me to her friend David Shire, a musical theater composer and fan of dynamical systems theory, and the workshop began to take form.

The workshop took place in July of 1990, and I learned a lot, including the information presented in this chapter.

A myth is an attractor in the world of ideas.

During this workshop David said to me, "A myth is an attractor in the world of ideas," which radically changed my approach to dynamics and history.

The Fable

The Long Line of Orphism extends from our Paleolithic past into the foreseeable future. Its characteristic features are encoded into the Roman fable of Orpheus and Euridice, one of the oldest still-living legends of the European tradition, somewhat like the Ramayana of India. From the point of view of the partnership/dominator theory of prehistory, we may interpret this fable as a vestige of the lost partnership of the past. Orpheus is the prototypical feminist male hero, seeking to restore the equality and partnership of the genders. Orphism survives in the modern day, and from the time of Christ onward, almost exclusively in this myth. This chapter is devoted to our heritage of the long line of Orphism, in the form of the Orpheus myth, and the mythogenesis of this theme from earliest Sumer (Inanna, Erishkegal, and Dumuzi) to the present.

THE BIFURCATION

From the perspective of general evolution theory, or mythogenesis, an entire myth complex constitutes an evolutionary sequence. The gods and goddesses all have interactions with each other extending over time. They get into fights, they don't speak to each other for a long time, there are horrible murders, rapes, and family feuds. We see, in the whole history of the mythological complex from Paleolithic times to the present, a gradual shift from the goddess to the god, from the partnership society—described so well in Riane Eisler's popular book, *The Chalice and the Blade*—to the patriarchy of 3500 B.C., which continues to the present. This shift is also manifest in the mythogenesis of Orpheus and Euridice.

THE SUMERIAN PROTOTYPE

As described in part 2, our earliest historical version of the myth of descent and return is the story of Inanna/Ishtar, Dumuzi/Tammuz, and Erishkegal/Allatu. Inanna (the replacement for the original Sumerian Mother goddess) visits the underground, is detained there by her older sister, Erishkegal, and is released on condition she send back a substitute. She sends Dumuzi, her young consort. In the mythogenesis of this tale, the Sumerian Dumuzi becomes Assyrian Tammuz, Egyptian Osiris, Cretan Dionysos, and Greek Orpheus.

If we look up Euridice in Graves, we find her name means *wide justice*. She is associated with serpents; she holds serpents in her hands, like the goddesses of Ras Shamra and Crete. And Orpheus is known in modern mythography to be a principal figure in the mythology of Minoan Crete, the last stronghold of the goddess religion and partnership culture of the Paleolithic past, enjoying peace and a successful economy, and living in harmony with its environment. In early Greek myth, Orpheus was the poet/musician who could move trees and animals with his art. He was one of the Argonauts, the unique nonwarrior, who fended off the Sirens with his music and founded the mysteries of Dionysos.[2] While both Orpheus and Euridice existed in the Greek pantheon, however, their relationship did not.

Greek myths were popular in Rome, and around 42 B.C. Virgil joined the Orpheus and Euridice legends into a single romantic fable.[3] In this version the father of Orpheus is Apollo, one of the leaders of the patriarchal takeover. When he was only seven months old, he got out his bow and arrows and slew Python, the serpent of the goddess and oracle of Delphi. Eventually, Apollo displaced the goddess at Delphi. Virgil's story is the first of the Orpheus legends in which Euridice appears. In it we have their courtship and marriage, her death, the daring rescue attempt by Orpheus, and so on.

The whole story is long, but Orpheus and Euridice are only mentioned in a portion of about seventy-five lines. The rest of the fable is about Aristeus, the older brother of Orpheus. He is the heir to the tradition of Apollo, devoted to the overthrow of the goddess. Like many Greek and Roman gods, he is a rapist, devoted to male dominance. He rapes Euridice, and in trying to escape, she steps on the snake (an aspect of the suppressed goddess tradition) and is called back to her own place: the underground (symbolizing the unconscious, and the diminished status of women in Greek and Roman society).

Orpheus and Euridice represent the two genders, and their loving relationship represents the partnership of the genders. We see that the three fundamental principles of Orphic religion—Chaos, Gaia, and Eros—are none other than Orpheus, Euridice, and their partnership. (Alternatively, as suggested below, the roles are given to Euridice, Demeter, and Orpheus.) Thus the fundamental principles of Orphism are encoded in history as our

The Roman fable of Orpheus deifies the feminist male hero, and calls forth the suppressed androgyne within us all.

heritage of Greek Orphism, itself a midstation on the path from a partnership to a dominator society. The Roman fable of Orpheus deifies the feminist male hero, and calls forth the suppressed androgyne within us all.

The Theories

In the Greek myth we witness the violent end of Orpheus at the hands of the Maenads, priestesses of Dionysos. Dionysism, and its degenerate practice of animal sacrifice, was the target of Orpheus' reformation. The Maenads tore him into pieces, which floated down various rivers. They not only eliminated Orpheus, but their own husbands. This is among the oldest aspects of the Orpheus legend. There are different theories as to what this means. Plato refers to the violent end of Orpheus in the Myth of Er, at the end of the *Republic*.

VIRGIL'S THEORY

Virgil disposes of this question with a single line: *the Thracian women are resentful.* Guthrie believed that Orphism was misogynistic.[4]

OVID'S THEORY

The next version of the legend is by Ovid, who was born about the same time that Virgil published his version. Virgil's one-liner is replaced by a different theory in Ovid, which occupies 650 lines—fully eight times the length of Virgil's entire poem![5] In Ovid's version, a love song in praise of boys and pederasty, there is an interesting kind of misogyny, in which the women are portrayed as being jealous and resentful. They are being ignored because men have found a way of doing without them. From the perspective of our partnership interpretation of the myth, the Maenads are women who support the dominator society, and act to preserve it by attacking partnership reformers, male or female.

PARTNERSHIP THEORY

According to the partnership/dominator theory, the myth may be interpreted as follows. After the partnership of Orpheus and Euridice (the prehistoric partnership of the genders) was terminated by his older brother, Aristeus (the patriarchal takeover), Euridice (womankind) was reclaimed by the serpent (Euridice's mother, the goddess) and retired to the underworld (of domination). Orpheus (the feminist male hero) tries to restore her to full partnership, but Hades tricks him and pulls Euridice back (the dominator backlash, which inevitably follows a partnership revival). The murder of Orpheus by the Maenads (women supporting the dominator system) points to the role of patriarchal women in defeating feminist men. To relate the Roman myth to the Orphic trinity, we may propose this concordance:

- Euridice/Chaos (slain by Aristeus/Marduk/Order, and captured by the underworld, like Tiamat)
- Demeter/Gaia (the Mother goddess)
- Orpheus/Eros (who goes back and forth, and is torn apart like Osiris/Dionysos)

The Long Line Again

The long line of Orphism began in the Paleolithic past with the goddess, partnership, and so on. Classical Greece is a midstation on this long line, a turning point in the transformation from gender partnership to male dominance. The Roman Orpheus fable of Virgil and Ovid is a representation of this transformation, in a simple myth for ordinary people, presented as Orphism submerged and the Roman empire, with its atheistic approach, took over. The essence of the story was packaged for posterity, and for us, by these possibly unconscious servants of the muses, Virgil and Ovid. The continuing popularity of this fable is due to our nostalgia and unconscious memory of the Golden Age of Partnership, the Garden of Eden, and our longing to recover from the Fall into the dominator paradigm. The rapid growth of Christianity in the Roman Empire may also derive from the identification of Christ, the *shepherd of being,* with the beloved Orpheus image.

THE CHRISTIAN SUPPRESSION

In Alexandria, different groups lived side by side: the native Egyptian community, the Neoplatonic Greeks, Jews, early Christians, and so on. Into this melting pot went pagan elements, and out came Christianity. Elements of Orphism were injected into the early church, and Orphism disappeared as Christianity exploded.

The Christian suppression of Orphism was a key factor in the development of European culture. Traditional features of pagan society—the detailed metaphysics of the celestial spheres of the Pythagorean and Neoplatonic traditions, the presence of Soul in all things, the sacred nature of the biosphere—which may be essential to an enduring society, were discarded. Besides the general intolerance of the church for all things pagan (and

Orphism is pagan), the trinitarian aspect of Orphism was most unacceptable to the early fathers. The trinity at the heart of the long line of Orphism in early Paleolithic times stabilized the early history of human consciousness. The Paleolithic TriVia—the triple-headed goddess, the trinity of three female principles—transmigrated to the divine triads of Sumer, Babylon, Egypt, Crete, Mycenae, Greece, Rome, and Christianity.[6] Gradually, their genders changed, and male gods got older and more aggressive. In Babylonia Order defeated Chaos when Marduk killed Tiamat. This gender transformation culminated in Judaism with the cult of Yahweh, and in Christianity with the suppression of Orphism and replacement of the Orphic trinity by the Christian trinity.

THE MIDDLE AGES

The medieval evolution of the myth made Orpheus into a Christ figure, troubadour, courtly lover, and singer of love songs.[7] This development accompanied the troubadour period in the south of France, a noted Orphic and gylanic resurgence.[8]

THE RENAISSANCE

A miraculous transformation began with the revival of classical paganism—the entire pagan myth complex, in rebellion from Christianity—around 1430 in Florence, with the financial support of Cosimo de Medici, who commissioned the collection of classical texts, and their translation into Latin by Marsilio Ficino. The classic myths were portrayed in all the arts: in paintings, music, and poetry. The mythogenesis of the Orpheus legend resumed. Merely to read the poem, to see the play, or to hear the music invoked anew these principles of the Orphic trinity: Chaos, Order, and the artistic bridge for going back and forth between the conscious and the unconscious, the overground and the underground, exemplified by the power of Orpheus' lute.

OPERA

Within this revival of pagan art, ritual, and myth, opera was born in intentional imitation of Greek tragedy. The beginning of opera is synonymous with Orpheus. The earliest recorded opera, written by Peri in 1600, is the story of Orpheus and Euridice. The second opera, by Caccini in 1602, is the story of Orpheus and Euridice. The third opera, by Monteverde in 1607, is the story of Orpheus and Euridice. There are at least twenty-six operas in the 1600s about Orpheus, and twenty-nine in the 1700s, including classics by Telemann, Gluck, Handel, and Haydn. And not only operas, but also operettas, beginning in 1858 with *Orpheus in the*

Underworld, by Offenbach (later accepted into the operatic oeuvre). Similarly, with musical theater and film, Orpheus is a traditional theme to this day. The Orphic mythogenesis goes on, incorporating pagan elements not allowed in church.

GOETHE'S NATURA

Ovid's cosmogony begins with Chaos, and progresses through a conflict between the goddess Natura (Physis of the Orphic hymns) and another god. Natura is cosmic power, the original Mother of All. She was a fundamental religious theme in the late pagan world, her power over human souls persisting throughout the Middle Ages (especially in the Gothic period.) An anonymous hymn to Natura, appearing in 1782, was attributed to Goethe. In 1828, after rereading it, he wrote: "Although I cannot remember composing these observations, they are quite in accord with the conceptions to which my mind then soared."[9]

Another Partnership Theory

The secret of the success of this theme has to do, ultimately, with our nostalgia for the Garden of Eden, the partnership society, a world of peace and plenty, and living in harmony with the environment. Our longing to reattain this world, which now exists only in the unconscious, is a collective memory not really accessible, in spite of the fact that we have poetic representations of it throughout history from Sumer until the present. Partnership is the theme, and Orpheus and Euridice the representation. Even Plato criticized this story, saying that if Orpheus were a true hero, he would have killed himself just to follow his lover to the underworld, rather than coming back without her.[10] As a partnership person, Orpheus was very unhappy without Euridice. Society seemed unworthy. In the end he goes up to heaven, saved by his divine parents, achieving immortality. The myth may be interpreted in terms of Eisler's partnership and dominator dichotomy of social structures. Alternatively, it may be seen as an expression of the utopian dialectic of Tillich's political theory; as foolish fantasy seen from hell/earth, or as ideal life in the kingdom of the gods.

A Modern Orphic Trinity

Recalling the Nietzschian dialectic of Apollo and Dionysos, Karl Kerenyi proposed in 1950 to interpose Orpheus as a unifying element. This concords with the concept of Eros unifying the binary of Chaos and Gaia in the ancient Orphic trinity, as shown in figure 12.1.[11]

THE ORPHIC TRINITY IN THE SCIENCES

Our Future

We can change the myth, and history may follow.

The Orphic mythogenesis continues. Prehistoric society had myth as oral history in place of written history. Greek society can be understood at least as well by its myths as by its history. We too, have oral history and myth, as well as written history.

The myth complex of a society is its cultural cognitive map, its collective self-representation, its view of itself. The evolution of myth is the evolution of the self-representation, or self-image, of society, which guides our behavior today, and tomorrow. If we reflect on our myth—seeing it as it is, grokking it, giving impetus to its evolution—we can participate consciously in the creation of our future. In the late Renaissance, for example, Monteverde and his librettist sat down and said, in so many words, *We don't want the Maenads, because that part of the story is misogynist. We don't want Aristeus, either; he is a racist and male supremacist, let's get rid of him.*

In the reinterpretation of a fable in each new time and presentation, different choices may be made. This might be our greatest leverage in the creation of the future. In mythogenesis, we can apply our creative hand, our will, our understanding. We can change the myth, and history may follow.

Summary

Every historical period has had big problems, but now they are bigger. The mere numerical strength of our species overpowers the planet. Our society is on a death track. We know we need a turn to the left or right, but do not know which way to turn. It could be that our self-consciousness on the mythic level—traditionally represented by the artist—is all that is needed to find the right turn, and to have a future. This is the optimism of the mythogenetic point of view.

Film is a great art, combining music, libretto, animation, coordinated speech, music, and visual music. Here we have the greatest power of illusion. Jean Cocteau made the first film on the Orpheus legend, *The Testament of Orpheus,* in 1939. In a preface called *The Film-maker as Hypnotist,* he wrote,

> I have often thought that it would be not only economical but admirable if a fakir were to hypnotize an entire auditorium. He could make his audience see a marvelous show, and moreover could order them not to forget it on waking. This, in a way, is the role of the screen—to practice a kind of hypnotism on the public and enable a large number of people to dream the same dream together.[12]

Applicable equally to the television medium today, Cocteau envisioned a sacred art of intentional intervention in creating the future, as in the Akitu festival in Babylon, with Greek tragedy in ancient Greek times, with Roman theater, and with opera in the Renaissance. We sense an opportunity to create a truly glorious future, adding to the sacred arts and rituals of the church a new wealth of secular art, like opera.[13]

Celestial Order

CHAPTER 15

FIGURE 15.1
Poor Will Whiston

Portrait by an unknown artist. Photo: Hulton Deutsch
Collection Limited. Reprinted with permission.

In mathematics one learns to focus on a single problem. After discovering dynamical systems theory in 1960, I worked singlemindedly on mathematical problems for several years without looking up. While this is a great way to progress in mathematics, it is no way to prepare for dealing with the politics of everyday life.

When I moved from Princeton University to the University of California, Santa Cruz, in the fall of 1968, the campus was embroiled in the political struggle for human rights. I got involved, and within a month or so of my arrival, the administration began persecuting me for organizing lectures without permission. The support of students and colleagues in Santa Cruz and around the world saved my career, after a two-year struggle.

This experience gave me a keen appreciation for the story of Poor Will Whiston, the seventeenth-century apostle of chaos (see figure 15.1).

Whiston's offense had to do, officially, with religion: He overtly agitated for an Arian-Trinitarian interpretation of the Bible in a time of Athanasian-Unitarian orthodoxy. Secondarily, he was guilty of believing in a scientific creation myth, involving chaos and the creative role of comets in forming the solar system.

Und So Weiter

Und so weiter (abbreviated USW) is German for *et cetera*. By the *USW Problem*, Husserl meant the question of the stability of the world of appearances. This is closely related to the *immer wieder principle* (sometimes translated as the *again-and-again principle*); as in, *I can do it again and again.* An important special case is the question, *Will the Sun rise tomorrow?* This matters to people on a very deep level, and it's very comforting to have a dogma that states categorically that the Sun will certainly rise.[1]

The question, Will the Sun rise tomorrow? matters to people on a very deep level, and it's very comforting to have a dogma that states categorically that the Sun will certainly rise.

This dogma is built into modern science, as it is in most religions. Under the name *the dogma of stability,* it has hounded celestial mechanics from Sir Isaac Newton to Immanuel Velikovsky, as we shall soon see.[2] A postmodern version of the USW question is our anxiety over the human damage to the environment. Publicists of this problem continue to be received like earlier heretics of planetary stability: Bruno, Whiston, and Velikovsky. See table 15.1.

Cusanus, 1440

We begin our story in 1440, when Nicholas Cusanus anticipated the theories of Copernicus. A follower of Alexandrian Neoplatonism (Hypatia) and John Scotus Erigena, he said Earth is spherical, but not really a sphere; the orbits are circular, but not perfect circles; and so on. As a channel for ancient science and philosophy, he was an important influence on Copernicus, who revived the ancient heliocentric model of the solar system. In this model the sacred and perfect order of the circle, as the path of the planets around Earth, was diminished. The paths of the planets around the Sun were obviously not perfect circles.

TABLE 15.1
Cometophiles 1400–2000

Dateline	1400	1500	1600	1700	1800	1900	2000
Cusanus (Italy)	▬▬						
Bruno (Italy)		▬▬					
Burnet (England)			▬▬▬				
Newton (England)			▬▬				
Halley (England)				▬▬▬			
Whiston (England)				▬▬			
Velikovsky (USA)							▬▬

THE ORPHIC TRINITY IN THE SCIENCES

Bruno, 1593

Giordano Bruno (1548–1600) was a heretic of this dogma of the perfect order of the heavens. He said Earth could take a sharp left, and that it had done so at various times in the past. One reason was the influence of comets. People have been afraid of comets for a long time, and this fear has been an important theme in the history of religion. It is an aspect of the USW Problem, for a collision with a comet would knock Earth for a loop! Even a close passage could cause Earth to turn sharply from its customary path.

Bruno visited England in 1588, debating his theory with the schoolmen at Oxford. In 1592, he was imprisoned by the Inquisition. On February 17, 1600, he was burned at the stake in Rome in a public spectacle of terrorism attended by hundreds of thousands of cheering spectators. At the last moment, he was offered reprieve if he would recant his faith in the infinity of the universe. *"I should not say that, so I will not,"* he replied.[3]

THREE CRIMES

The reasons for which Bruno was imprisoned and tortured for eight years, and then burned at the stake, have been debated ever since.[4]

One theory is that Bruno was persecuted because he supported the Copernican model of the heliocentric solar system, which had been condemned by the church. According to another, it was because he insisted on the Copernican theory that the universe is infinite, which had enormous implications for scholastic dogma. (Where could Yahweh reside if not *outside* the celestial sphere?) According to a third theory, Bruno was persecuted because he believed in a theory that Earth had taken a sharp left turn. This aspect of Bruno is important for the USW Problem, and for our story. According to Annie Besant, the English theosophist,

> Giordano Bruno, in his last and greatest work, *Di Imenso,* published just after his imprisonment, made clear the meaning of the assertion of the principle of indifference. He denied the existence of a providential order in nature and hence the stability of the solar system, which is linked with the doctrine of circular movements. He declared that only their imperfect astronomical observations (speaking of earlier astronomers) permitted them to believe that the heavenly bodies moved in circles and in the long run returned to their original position. He pointed out that astronomical movements are bound to be infinitely complex. Belief in the simple and regular motion of the planets, he continued, is a

delusory product of astrological thinking. It is necessary to free mathematical astronomy from Platonic and Pythagorean metaphysical accretions, he said. From the relativity of motion follows the relativity of time. Since no completely regular motion can be discovered, and since we possess no record which can prove that all the heavenly bodies have taken up exactly the same position with regard to Earth as those previously occupied by them, the motions are rigidly regular at best, no absolute measure of time can be found.[5]

In short, Bruno attacked the theological faith in the perfect regularity of Earth's motion.

CHRISTIAN DOGMA

When the Catholic establishment burned Bruno, the eternal stability of the solar system became official church dogma. One advantage of this scholastic dogma of the church is that it provides a certain platform of confidence for the USW Problem— faith that the sun will rise again and again forever. Thus among the rewards for faith is freedom from worry about sunrise. Bruno's attack on the stability dogma diminished the attraction and stability of the church itself, and induced in people the maximum of anxiety and fear. Threatening a sharp left turn of Earth tomorrow is not the most laudable thing a person can do. Newton himself apparently believed that God preserved the celestial order, as the planets left to their own devices would run amok.

Newton himself apparently believed that God preserved the celestial order, as the planets left to their own devices would run amok.

Newton and Whiston

Sir Isaac Newton (1647–1727) is sometimes credited with the greatest contribution to our history ever made by a single individual. His life and works have been the subject of an entire industry of scholarship, especially since 1936, when his secret journals (hidden by his family for two hundred years) finally came to light. Poor Will Whiston, on the other hand, is virtually unknown.[6] We will trace the story of their relationship, decade by decade, from 1640 to 1730. We will outline the careers of both Newton and Whiston, as their relationship illuminates the debate that raged in the seventeenth century over the USW Problem.[7]

Newton's mathematical model, so far as it intends to be a model for the clockwork regularity of the universe, may not have much to do with the real universe. So if the model Earth, in the model solar system, takes a sharp turn, you might still believe that the real Sun is going to rise tomorrow. However, if the real

THE ORPHIC TRINITY IN THE SCIENCES

Earth took a sharp left and departed its traditional orbit, we would see the Sun irregularly, and it would become smaller and weaker each time. Mathematical modeling isn't everything; but since Newton the question of the stability of the solar system has become a mathematical issue of great debate.

Newton was secretive about what he believed.[8] Considering Bruno's fate shortly before Newton's birth, this is hardly surprising. Newton's life work in alchemy remained hidden until recently. His opinions on the stability of the solar system and the role of comets in history may yet be unknown. His mental illness in 1695, following publication of the *Principia,* may have been related to this stability problem. It suggests that Newton believed in chaos in the solar system, repressed by the intervention of a divine god or order, just as Tiamat was defeated by Marduk.

1640s–1660s

Galileo died at the time Newton was born and Descartes flourished in Paris. Leibniz was born around the same time. A civil war raged in England, ushering in a brief Orphic revival that was exemplified by the Diggers, with their alternative lifestyle of peaceful cooperation, and the development of modern harmony in music.[9]

The return of Charles II to the throne ushered in a period of conservative backlash. At age nineteen Newton was at Cambridge, where he saw John Wilkins, the master of his college, along with other nonconformists, dismissed.[10] When Henry Lucas died, leaving a large endowment to Cambridge University for a Chair of Mathematics in Trinity College, William Barrow was appointed the first Lucasian Professor.[11] During the plague years, 1665 and 1666, Newton developed the calculus, the universal theory of gravitation, and his theory of colors.[12] When Barrow resigned, Newton was appointed second Lucasian Professor.[13]

ARIANISM

Arius of Alexandria, in the fourth century A.D., believed that the Father is the One God of the Bible, while the Son and Holy Spirit are divine but secondary. His contemporary, Athanasius, held, on the contrary, that the three are *consubstantial* and *coeternal:* an ensemble, constituting the One God.

Newton studied early Christianity extensively, to prove that Athanasius falsified the Gospels to establish his own view, while spreading scandals about Arius. Early Christianity adopted the Athanasian creed in the first ecumenical council, convened in Nicea by Emperor Constantine I of Byzantium, in 325. The Church of England adopted this Nicene Creed, and Arianism (which Newton called *Primitive Christianity*) was declared a punishable heresy.[14] In this case, we know that Newton hid his beliefs, and why he hid them. Further, the Arian view held by Newton allows a substantial part of the divine realm to be secondary to the power of God, so that the material universe and the solar system need not be eternally perfect.

1670s–1690s

When Newton was elected Fellow of the Royal Society, he had already become an Arian, although he kept these heretical views a closely held secret. Ordination as an Anglican minister was a requirement of his position at Trinity, the "college of the holy and undivided trinity," but he managed to gain an exemption from this requirement, thus keeping his secret without perjury. Meanwhile, he further developed the universal law of gravitation, and proved the laws of Kepler, the second part of his great gift to humanity.[15]

The decade beginning in 1680 witnessed the passage of the Great Comet, later called Halley's Comet. The world actually came close to destruction with its passage.[16] In the same year, Burnet sent Newton his manuscript, *The Sacred Theory of the Earth* (published 1681), which replaced the Mosaic creation myth of Genesis with Descartes' theory of vortices. Newton disapproved.[17]

THE COMET AND THE BOOK

Many people worried that the comet would collide with Earth. Sir Edmund Halley (1656–1742), the Astronomer Royal, concerned with this possibility, tried to prove that the orbit of a comet is an ellipse, which would avoid collision. Newton casually mentioned to Halley one day that he had proved this long ago, but never published it. Halley demanded proof, which led to the writing of Newton's *Principia Mathematica*. Halley saw to its publication in 1687. Here, Newton claimed to prove the stability of the solar system.[18]

WHISTON'S THEORY

William Whiston was born in 1667. Having studied the *Principia*, he arrived in Cambridge and met Newton in 1694, becoming his student in mathematics and in Primitive Christianity. He prepared a book, *A New Theory of the Earth, From Its Original to the Consummation of All Things. Wherein the Creation of the World in Six Days, the Universal Deluge, and the General Conflagration, as Laid Down in the Holy Scriptures, Are Shewn to be Perfectly Agreeable to Reason and Philosophy.* It rebutted Burnet's *Sacred Theory of the Earth,* pleased Newton, and went through six editions.[19] Whiston's theory, like Bruno's a century earlier,

THE ORPHIC TRINITY IN THE SCIENCES

included *the chaotic role of comets in the creation of the solar system.* Newton, since 1680, had shared this view,[20] which interprets Genesis as a creation of Earth from a confused chaos, with comets causing the major transformations.[21] Earth is created by a divine transformation of the orbit of a comet from an eccentric ellipse to a nearly circular one. *Tohu wabohu* refers to the atmosphere of the comet. In fact, "chaos" means "comet," according to Whiston.[22] He wrote:

> The Mosaick Creation is not a Nice and Philosophical account of the Origin of All Things, but an Historical and True Representation of the formation of our single Earth out of a confused Chaos, and of the successive and visible changes thereof each day, till it became the habitation of Mankind.[23]

According to Whiston:

1. Earth began life as a comet, orbiting the Sun eccentrically (chaos).
2. At some point, God decided to make Earth a planet with a circular orbit (order) and a period of 360 days.
3. Eventually, other comets, guided by God, brushed against Earth, causing the Flood, the obliquity (slant) of Earth's axis, the eccentricity of Earth's orbit, and thus the seasons, Earth's daily rotation, and the cycle of days and nights. The solar year changed from 360 to 365 days at this time. The Egyptian calendar is evidence for this. Halley secretly shared this view.[24]

1700–1720s

In 1701, Newton, who was suffering depression, accepted a job as Warden of the Mint, and moved to London.[25] He employed his favorite student, Whiston, to deliver his weekly thirty-minute lectures at Trinity College, Cambridge. After two years, Newton resigned his professorship, and upon his recommendation Whiston replaced him as the third Lucasian Professor of Mathematics. (About this time, Newton maneuvered his friend Edmund Halley into the Savilian Chair of Geometry at Oxford.)[26]

Almost immediately, differences between Newton and Whiston began to grow. Whiston was too radical for Newton, in his public stance at least. Newton turned to a fundamentalist position, publicly supporting a literal interpretation of the Bible in his book *Opticks* in 1704. His argument was based on the similarity of the orbits of all the planets. Meanwhile, Whiston commenced going about the town giving imprudent lectures on Primitive Christianity, sending radical letters to archbishops, and seeking to publish his research on the Arian heresy.[27]

Whiston's obsession with honesty, and the necessity of putting the Anglican church back on the Arian track, provoked the response from the hierarchy that all his friends had anticipated. He was expelled from Trinity College on October 30, 1710, and persecuted in a variety of courts for four years. Newton kept his silence, lest he be expelled as well.[28] Whiston moved to London, where he supported himself with various mathematical odd jobs, including astrological charts and massage. He further elaborated his creation theory in *Primitive Christianity Reviv'd* in 1711, in *Athanasius Convicted of Forgery* in 1712, and in *Astronomical Principles of Religion, Natural and Reveal'd* in 1717. Newton published the second edition of his *Principia* in 1713, with added material in support of the Mosaic creation story of Genesis. Here he argued unsuccessfully for the stability of the solar system as a mathematical proposition, and claimed that God must intervene from time to time, to reset the planets on their proper trajectories.[29] His fear of the discovery of his Arian heresy led him to avoid any association with Whiston.[30]

With Whiston's heresy all but forgotten and Newton's still a well-kept secret, they continued to avoid each other. When Halley nominated Whiston for fellowship in the Royal Society in 1720, Newton threatened to resign as president, and the matter was dropped.[31] Halley at last published his comet theory of the origin of the solar system; Newton published the third edition of his *Principia,* and died. The next year, in 1728, his work *The Chronology of the Ancient Kingdoms Amended* was published posthumously. (This book may have been inspired by *The Chronology of Ancient Nations* of Albiruni, discussed in chapter 7.) Making use of the procession of the equinox, which he had calculated quite accurately, this work was devoted to the refutation of Whiston's theory of comets and chaos. During this time (and earlier), Newton was working regularly at his alchemical furnace, although he and his heirs successfully suppressed this fact for two hundred years.[32]

THE USW PROBLEM AGAIN

Newton was originally attracted to Whiston because of Whiston's theory about the relationship between comets and the chronology of the Bible, especially Genesis. The biblical Flood is a manifestation of chaos, and many have speculated that the Flood was caused by the close passage of a comet. According to Livio Stecchini,

> One of the precursors of Velikovsky as to the general thesis of the catastrophic past of Earth to whom he refers in his work was William Whiston. In 1694, seven years after the first edition of the *Principia,* Whiston, then a fellow of Cambridge University, became a devoted pupil of Newton and two years later submitted to his master the manuscript of a book entitled, *New Theory of the Earth.* The book was intended to replace *Popular Theory of the Earth* by Thomas Burnet and dealt with the theme with which Newton had been concerned for more than a score of years. This book of Whiston's contended that the cataclysm described in the Old Testament as the universal deluge was caused by the impact of a comet at the end of the third millennium B.C. And that up to the deluge, the solar year had the duration of 360 days only, yet the new calendar of 365 days had to wait to be introduced by Nebonassar in 747 B.C. These contentions were based mainly on historical evidence whereas astronomical considerations were the main ground for suggesting that comets may become planets.[33]

As to Newton's views, he was bent on proving that the machinery of the world's perfectly contrived system cannot be the result of mechanical cause, but must be the result of an intelligent and consistent plan. In order to support further the story of Genesis, that the world was created by a single act, he argued also that the world is stable and has remained unchanged since Creation. But he could not prove this point, since he admitted that according to his own theory, the gravitational pull among the several members of the solar system would tend to modify their orbits. Hence he begged the question, and claimed that God in his providence must intervene from time to time to reset the clockwork of the heavens to his original state.

Leibniz observed that Newton cast God not only as a clockmaker, and a poor one at that, but as a clock repairman.

This view of Newton's doctrine is well-known. It was the object of sarcastic comments by Leibniz, Newton's great rival in the mathematical field. Leibniz observed that Newton cast God not only as a clockmaker, and a poor one at that, but as a clock repairman.[34] This is just the tip of an iceberg. The controversy—involving Whiston, Newton, and Leibniz—turned on the same point for which Bruno was burned: the USW Problem and the stability of the solar system.

Summary

The Arianism of Newton, shared with William Whiston and others of a close circle of friends, developed into his obsession with revelations and prophesy. This in turn led to history, or rather chronology, and ultimately, to the Mosaic creation myth of Genesis. At this point, a bifurcation occurred. Newton followed a basic creed of faith in order, including divine intervention to maintain the order of the heavens: *the church dogma of stability.* Meanwhile, Whiston followed the path of chaos, and the divinely guided comets. Newton became Sir Isaac, while Whiston became Poor Will. Bruno's demise may have been a factor in Newton's paranoia and secrecy. These men were, in effect, the last of the Sumerians.[35]

CHAOS, GAIA, AND EROS TODAY

Celestial Chaos

CHAPTER 16

In February 1966 I was working at Princeton University. My research and teaching had to do with the stability of the solar system. A study group there, called Cosmos and Chronos, was interested in the ideas of Immanuel Velikovsky, who happened to be living in Princeton at that time.[1] Like Bruno and Whiston, Velikovsky believed that at some time in the recent past, Earth had taken a sharp turn off its orbit. Some of my graduate students were in this group, and eventually they came to me and asked if this was possible. In this way my first book, called *The Foundations of Mechanics,* turned out to be an extensive essay on the question: Can Earth, in its course around the Sun, take a sharp left, or not?

Twenty-two years later, in February of 1988, I got a phone call from two gentlemen, who introduced themselves as Jeremy Taylor and Thomas Levenson, the producers of a forthcoming documentary program on chaos for the television series *Nova.* They wanted to include me in this program, and had some specific questions. The first question ended the phone call, as they asked something I could not answer:

King Oscar of Sweden, at age sixty, had offered a prize for a mathematician to prove the stability of the solar system in the context of Newton's model. The *Nova* people called me because they read about this prize in my book. They asked: Why did King Oscar offer the prize? I said, Well, probably because people thought it important that the Sun should rise tomorrow. Not satisfied, one of them insisted, Why King Oscar, off there in Stockholm? What's his story? That question sent me off on a long voyage of discovery, and this chapter is the story of the answer.

Classical Analysis

After the time of Newton and Whiston came a century of mathematical developments, including the elaboration of the calculus into the theories of dynamical systems, partial differential equations, and so on; all of which is now known as classical analysis, one of the main branches of mathematics. (See table 16.1 for some biographical data for the people discussed in this chapter; table 16.2 lays out the chronology of "the Oscar.")

LAPLACE, 1796

After Newton, Pierre-Simon Laplace was the person who best and most miraculously developed the application of the calculus to the mathematical model for the solar system. He did this in the context of the so-called *three-body problem,* a Newtonian model that might apply, for example, to the Sun, Earth, and the Moon. He made a great study of the stability problem, using classical analysis in the context of *lunar theory.* Anticipating Husserl, he felt that anxieties about the Sun rising tomorrow, and the pos-

TABLE 16.1
Mathematicians 1500–2000

Dateline	1500	1550	1600	1650	1700	1750	1800	1850	1900	1950	2000
Bruno (Italy)		▬▬▬									
Newton (England)				▬▬▬							
Whiston (England)					▬▬▬						
Laplace (France)							▬▬▬				
Dirichlet (France)								▬▬			
Weierstrass (Germany)								▬▬▬			
Mittag-Leffler (Sweden)									▬▬▬▬		
Kovalefsky (Sweden)									▬▬		
Poincaré (France)									▬▬▬		
Kolmogorov (Russia)										▬▬▬	

✾ THE ORPHIC TRINITY IN THE SCIENCES

TABLE 16.2
Chronology of "the Oscar"

1583	Bruno denies the stability dogma
1687	Newton's *Principia*
1695	Newton's mental illness
1710	Whiston banished
1773	Laplace proposes stability problem in three-body problem
1796	Laplace proposes nebular hypothesis
1846	Dirichlet, inspired by Laplace, studies stability
1858	Dirichlet tells Kronecker (a close friend of Weierstrass) of solution
1859	Dirichlet dies
1873	Weierstrass writes to Kovalevsky about stability, suggests prize
1881	Kovalevsky's prize paper on the spinning top
1882	Kovalevsky meets Poincaré
1883	Kovalevsky arrives in Stockholm, November 11
1884	Kovalevsky meets King Oscar
1886	Kovalevsky to Paris, sees Poincaré
1887	King Oscar (age sixty) offers prize, Kr 2500
1889	Poincaré wins the Oscar, discovery of mathematical chaos
1950	Velikovsky martyred
1954	Kolmogorov's theory
1961	Ueda discovers experimental chaos with analog computer
1966	Cosmos and Chronos study groups at Princeton
1974	AAAS condemns Velikovsky
1988	Wisdom announces chaos in the solar system

sibility of a collision with a comet, were very important in the evolution of society and culture, and wrote extensively about it.

After his death people misunderstood what he wrote. A dogma of stability developed around his name. But he was unable to prove stability as a mathematical result of Newton's model; he accepted it purely as an article of faith. It was wrongly claimed that he had proved the stability of the solar system. Laplace indicated, in his result of 1784 (called *Laplace's theorem on the stability of the solar system*), that the slow oscillations in the planetary orbits do not grow larger and larger. At the same time, he proposed his nebular hypothesis, a theory for the origin of the solar system in a natural process of cosmogenesis.[2]

Laplace became a mythical figure, like Pythagoras.[3] The popular acceptance of this theory eroded belief in the Bible, and paved the way for the triumph of evolution theory in biology. Herbert Spencer wrote an article on the nebular hypothesis in 1858, in which he proposed for the first time a general theory of evolution.[4]

DIRICHLET, 1858

Later, when people reviewed the technical details of Laplace's work having to do with the stability of the solar system model, they tried to extend his equations to prove the model stable. Peter Dirichlet, one of the greatest experts of these technical details, believed he had completed the proof, and told this to Leopold Kronecker, another noted mathematician, who was visiting him at the time. When Dirichlet died without publishing the proof, people went through his papers, but never found his proof that the solar system was stable.

WEIERSTRASS, 1873

Karl Weierstrass was one of the most careful of mathematical analysts, and a colleague of Kronecker, from whom he heard of Dirichlet's claim. He also tried to complete the proof, writing to his former student Sophia Kovalevsky about his efforts. As the mathematical version of the USW Problem now seemed more significant, because of the failure of the greatest mathematicians to solve it, he suggested that this problem deserved a prize competition.

KOVALEVSKY, 1886

Kovalevsky, because of great respect for her teacher, Weierstrass, especially regarded this as an important mathematical problem. Meanwhile, another student of Weierstrass, Mittag-Leffler of Sweden, had been appointed rector of a radically new kind of university in Stockholm. It offered free education for up to three

✸

hundred students from the city, and women were allowed to study there as well as men. Not only was it one of the first coed universities, women were actually sought out to serve on the faculty.

Kovalevsky was one of the best mathematical talents of the time, having won a coveted prize for her work on the spinning top. As one of the few great women in mathematics, and an ardent champion for the rights of women to higher education,[5] she was invited to Stockholm. Having no other offers, and in spite of some reservations about living in the climate and remoteness of Sweden, she accepted. In 1883 Kovalevsky became the first woman professor in a European university since Hypatia was murdered in 415.

In 1883 Kovalevsky became the first woman professor in a European university since Hypatia was murdered in 415.

Since emigrating from Russia, she had developed a strong relationship with Paris, which had become one of the largest and best centers for mathematics. There she associated with the leading mathematicians, including Poincaré, whom she met in 1882.[6] In this way, Poincaré came to know of Dirichlet's claim.

"THE OSCAR"

Sophia Kovalevsky had a close relationship in Stockholm with Mittag-Leffler's sister, Anna Carlotta Leffler, an actress and womens' rights activist.[7] The two of them were very prominent in Swedish social circles, which included the progressive king of Sweden, Oscar II.[8] Then in middle age, Oscar had initiated many social reforms in Sweden, had encouraged the city of Stockholm in the creation of the new university, and was an avid fan of mathematics. He learned of the outstanding problem of mathematics from either Kovalevsky or Mittag-Leffler. Oscar offered the prize of 2,500 Swedish kronor for its solution; this a large sum comparable with a professor's annual salary. The prize was announced in 1889 on the occasion of King Oscar's sixtieth birthday. Poincaré, who was thirty-five, probably learned of the prize from Kovalevsky.[9]

POINCARÉ, 1890

Beginning in 1880, Henri Poincaré had created a new approach to the study of differential equations, now called dynamical systems theory.[10] He managed to win "the Oscar" without actually proving that the solar system was stable.[11] Instead, he found a serious obstruction to the analytical method of Laplace, and in the process created whole new branches of mathematics, including differential topology, global analysis, and qualitative dynamics, along with the theories of chaotic attractors and bifurcations. His prize paper was published in 1890.

Velikovsky, 1950

The mathematical problem of stability rested, after Poincaré, until 1954, when a reincarnation of William Whiston appeared unexpectedly in New Jersey. Immanuel Velikovsky had much in common with both William Whiston and Giordano Bruno.[12] Following a reading of Freud's *Moses and Monotheism* in 1939, which inspired him to analyze the evolution of society, he did extensive historical research in the 1940s, and published his results in 1950 amid great controversy.[13]

The violent opposition to Velikovsky's theory, which continues to this day, began when astronomers heard that this work was in press, and tried to persuade the publisher to drop it.[14] Velikovsky saw what other scholars were unable to see, because he relied on evidence that they had chosen to neglect: the accumulated records of human experience. Natural scientists who scorned these records put themselves in the position of the early astronomers who held that no truly respectable scholar should resort to the telescope. They denied a creative new idea on the grounds of dogma, which they took to be the truth.

In only thirteen years, a number of fundamental discoveries predicted by Velikovsky demonstrated the value of his method. One could have predicted that the academic world would react to his thesis with a most unscholarly fury, even personal vindictiveness. The record shows that astronomers hold rigidly to a peculiar dogma, not much advanced from Laplace's nebular hypothesis or the biblical story of creation: that the solar system has remained essentially unchanged since it was created eons ago. Their assumption has of necessity predetermined the views of geologists and historical biologists. This dogma, basically of theological and not scientific nature, as Galileo and Laplace pointed out, is grounded on fear. The dogma is groundless but the fear is real, and was the principal reason for a prolonged emotional outburst against Velikovsky, in which almost the entire scientific community of the 1950s took part. It was an outburst of what Søren Kierkegaard termed *fear and trembling*.

VELIKOVSKY'S THEORIES

Velikovsky proposed a new revision of human history, with four main principles:

1. Evolution proceeds in discrete jumps, caused by geological catastrophes. (In this he agreed with Plato.)
2. The solar system evolved to its present form only recently, and has suffered catastrophes even within our historical time.
3. The human psyche evolved in reaction to these events.

4. Our current chronology of the ancient kingdoms is largely fictitious. (Here he agreed with Newton.)[15]

We will consider only the second of these theories, in which the planet Venus plays a main role.

One event in the recent evolution of our solar system, according to Velikovsky, was the arrival of the planet Venus in the eighth century B.C., after it left Jupiter in the fifteenth century B.C. and had a brief existence as a comet.[16] The evidence for this was human experience recorded in the myths of many different cultures, much in the spirit of Hamlet's Mill, or the Flood myth of Babylonia and the Bible.

In 1974 the American Association for the Advancement of Science met specifically to condemn Velikovsky. The storm that began with the publication of his book in 1950 had not yet died down, and apparently it was still necessary for scientists to deny Velikovsky's thesis solely on the grounds of the stability dogma. Several books denouncing Velikovsky were published between 1950 and 1977.[17] Famous astronomers, such as Harlow Shapley and Carl Sagan, condemned Velikovsky on the mistaken grounds that Newton's model does not allow chaos: no sharp turns to the left or right. They believed, religiously, in the stability of Newton's mathematical model of the solar system. There are two problems with this stability dogma:

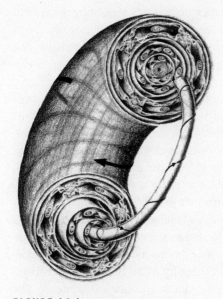

FIGURE 16.1
The Chaotic Attractor of Kolmogorov

Drawing by Christopher Shaw, from Abraham (1978, 1982). Courtesy Addison-Wesley, Reading, Massachusetts. Reprinted with permission.

1. The model may not be stable with respect to perturbation. Thus, if a comet passed, the orbits could be shaken loose, and take a sharp turn. This remains uncontested after a century of mathematical effort.

2. The model is not stable internally. Thus some orbits can turn suddenly after a long period of good behavior, even without an external perturbation such as a comet. This was suspected by Poincaré, and is now firmly established, thanks to the revolutionary work of Andrei Kolmogorov on celestial chaos.[18]

Kolmogorov, 1954

Poincaré discovered a mathematical model for chaos in the three-body problem for the solar system in 1899, now called the *homoclinic tangle*.[19] His great American follower, George David Birkhoff, developed the full theory of these models for chaotic behavior in the 1930s. Kolmogorov, the leading Russian mathematician of this century, discovered the necessity of such tangles in regions of chaos near the regular motions in the solar system model, as shown in figure 16.1. His work provided the reason for the failure of Laplace's method to prove stability, completing the program begun by Poincaré in his prize memoir of 1890.

Perhaps God is playing dice with us, but the dice are strongly loaded in our favor.

In the model, as shown in figure 16.1, there are zones of stability and zones of instability. The size of the unstable zones gives the probability of an unpredictable sharp turn. Fortunately, they are small, and our chances can be computed, so that we may get a little assurance for the future. Perhaps God is playing dice with us, but the dice are strongly loaded in our favor.[20]

According to mathematics alone, there is nothing to rule out a planet's sharp turn to the left. Through mathematics alone, one cannot contradict Velikovsky. The dogma of stability remains just an article of faith.

Comets

Besides this intrinsic chaos, there is the totally independent possibility of a close encounter with a comet. The argument against Bruno, Whiston, and Velikovsky, who believed in this cataclysmic comet theory, cannot be made on the basis of Newton's model for a finite solar system. By now most people are agreed, whether astronomers or not, that there is a significant possibility of Earth getting hit head-on by a comet someday. This is especially true if comets themselves behave chaotically. The Moon is covered with craters, and Earth has many scars as well. One theory for the mass extinctions of dinosaurs that occurred 65 million years ago blames a direct hit by a comet on Earth, raising a massive dust cloud, resulting in a sort of nuclear winter.[21] The asteroid Eros came close to hitting Earth in 1931.[22] And on March 23, 1989, Earth was again nearly struck by an asteroid.[23]

Where Are We?

In Kolmogorov's picture of the solar system model, with its zones of stability and chambers of chaos, we've estimated our chances for the future according to the size of the zones, which may be calculated with some precision. This estimate is made assuming no information as to the actual position, within the map of figure 16.1, of our own solar system configuration. If we threw a dart at the target without taking aim, we'd be more likely to hit the larger zones. But where are we? As the accuracy of our computer calculations increases year-by-year, we get better estimates of our solar system's position in the model. Astronomers have very accurate values for all these numbers: the size and shape of Earth's orbit (semi-major and semi-minor axes), the inclination of the axis of rotation, the velocities, and so on. Putting them in the model and computing for a long time permits an estimate of our proximity to a region of chaos in the model.

This has been worked out only recently by Jack Wisdom, an astronomer at MIT. According to his calculations, we are in a chaotic zone. As reported in the *San Francisco Chronicle* on Thursday, May 19, 1988:

> SCIENTIST DESCRIBES A CHAOTIC SOLAR SYSTEM
> From tumbling moons to planets whose orbits defy prediction, the solar system is riddled with chaos, a scientist said. A new understanding of celestial mechanics coupled with a vigorous new branch of mathematics called chaos theory suggests that in some far eon, Earth itself may adopt a radically different orbit that could destroy present day life. "I wouldn't rule anything out," said Jack Wisdom, associate professor of planetary sciences at MIT during a special session of the American Geophysical Union's spring meeting. His description of moons and planets whose motions are irregular and unpredictable badly undermines traditional views that the laws of physics and the vast spaces between planets allow scientists to calculate where solar system bodies will be billions of years in advance. Wisdom also noted that the discoveries come hot on the heels of revelations that Nancy Reagan influenced the schedule of White House events by consulting astrology, an occult system derived from ancient beliefs in divine clockwork regularity of celestial motions. "The closer we look, the more chaos we find," Wisdom said.

In 1988 Jack Wisdom discovered the chaotic motion of Hyperion, one of the satellites of Saturn. Shortly afterward, around October 1988, he found that the orbit of Pluto was chaotic; not the actual planet Pluto, but the model Pluto in the Newtonian model solar system. He ran the model for 832 million years, longer than the entire Pleistocene epoch. Combining the computation with the theory of Kolmogorov makes a pretty convincing argument that Pluto may not be around forever. Its orbit is extremely eccentric; much more inclined to the average plane of the other planets than anything else except a comet, and it looks very cometlike. It's certainly possible that, once upon a time, it *was* a comet.[24]

Summary

This whole chronology on the stability dogma, whether coming from Christianity or from its successor religion, scientism, is the fundamental context for our interpretation of the Chaos Revolution. Throughout history, this fear has given power to religion, and the persecution of heretics like Bruno, Whiston, and

Velikovsky. Since the wheel, religion has promised order. Previously, TriVia encouraged peaceful coexistence with chaos. What if we were to give up the dogmatic belief in stability because of the discovery of chaos theory? What if chaos theory offers us a view of chaos that itself is highly ordered and really safe? This kind of chaos was recognized and accepted happily by generations and generations of Orphic poets, musicians, troubadours, and spiritual masters. We have to learn about the order in chaos, to make friends with it, to get the basic idea of it, to take it upon ourselves (as Tillich says), in order to understand anything, even the most basic things in the world around us: solar system, biological systems, social systems. The Orphic trinity now rises again.

Gaian Fevers

CHAPTER 17

I grew up in Vermont, where they say there are two seasons: winter and July. To me, this was a perfect climate, as I am an avid skier. They say that the Cro-Magnon people succeeded in Europe after their arrival around 35,000 B.C. because they were so well adapted to the cold weather of that time, deep in the last major Ice Age.

My whole family shares my obsession with skiing. We are Cro-Magnons. Our family reunions take place in ski resorts, where at least three generations meet to revive our spirits in the snow. In winter 1983–84, I rented an apartment in Bill Fiedler's house, under the chair lift at Squaw Valley, California. My son John, a professional skier at age twenty, lived there full time, and I came almost every weekend.

It was a winter to cherish forever. There were several snorkel days, the days of under-snow skiing of which skiers dream. The day we moved out, the first of May, Bill's house was still covered by fifteen feet of snow. We exited through a tunnel cut through the ice.

Climate and History

Metahistorians like Toynbee have pointed out the crucial role of climate variation in the patterns of history.[1] Of the three major bifurcations emphasized in this book—static/agriculture, periodic/dominator, chaotic/partnership—the first two are related to climate shifts. Let us consider the first of these.[2]

Agriculture

Early in the Holocene interglacial, our Mesolithic ancestors mastered agriculture. Global climate warming, as late glacial conditions gave way to Neothermal, was the essential precondition for this development.[3] Following this warming, the ancient Near East was fertile for some thousands of years, before it was overcome by desertification.[4] The early Egyptian civilization depended on the annual flood of the Nile River for irrigation, and the precise prediction of this roughly annual event was required for a good harvest. An accurate record of the river's height was made with observatories called *Nilometers,* described by Herodotus in his world history, written around 450 B.C. (see figure 17.1).[5]

Records of the flooding of the Nile have been kept since 3150 B.C.[6] People have studied this record for thousands of years, seeking some rhythmic pattern with which to predict the climate for the future. The hydropolitics of the Nile are still important in the cultures of the Middle East.[7]

The Pioneers

Weather prediction is useful, perhaps even essential, for human evolution.

Weather prediction is useful, perhaps even essential, for human evolution. Elsworth Huntington was an early advocate of the influence of climate patterns on human history. Traveling in Chinese Turkestan in 1905–6, he observed dwellings abandoned centuries earlier. This led him to propose in his book, *The Pulse of Asia,* published in 1907, pulsations of climate as a cause of population movements. Soon afterward, in 1913, Dr. C. G. Abbott advocated the periodic effects of sunspots and volcanic eruptions on the world's climate. Arnold Toynbee, who studied the effects of climate patterns on history, as described in chapter 3, relied heavily on Huntington's work. Around 1928, C. E. P. Brooks advocated periodic patterns in climate, following Toynbee.[8] A more recent champion of the cycle theory of climate, sea level, salinity, and so on was Rhodes Fairbridge, who traveled up the Nile around 1960.[9]

Dendrochronology

Among the indicators of short-term climate variation, besides the height of the Nile or the ocean, are the widths of rings in trees, such as grapevines (which relate to wine harvests, and thus human happiness and economy),[10] and bristlecone pines (among the oldest living things, providing a continuous record for six thousand years).[11] Dendrochronology, or dendroclimatology, is the study of tree rings and climate, extended over a period of several thousand years. It was founded in 1901 by Andrew Douglas, an astronomer interested in sunspots, who turned an observation that tree rings are thinner in dry years into an important science. Dendrochronology has revised radiocarbon

THE ORPHIC TRINITY IN THE SCIENCES

chronology, and thus our chronology of the ancient kingdoms of Mesopotamia and Egypt in relation to European prehistory.[12] There are many such instances in the history of history in which a new discovery mandates a revision of our view of the past.

Discovery of the Ice Ages

FIGURE 17.1
Nilometer

Drawing by Diane Rigoli, after Maspero (1901), volume 3, Frontispiece.

In the longer view of deep time, the climatic cycles of interest may be hundreds of thousands of years long. Most impressive of these long-scale climate variations are the Ice Ages (shown in table 17.1), the discovery of which brought about a fundamental shift in our view of the past. The clue that led to this shift was the mystery of granite boulders scattered about the Jura, the limestone mountains of Switzerland. Here is the story, in outline form.

In 1787 Bernard Kuhn, a Swiss lawyer, suggested that glaciers had moved the boulders, and his conclusion was supported by James Hutton, the Scottish geologist, in 1795.[14]

In 1818 Jean Pierre Perraudin, an Alpine guide, wrote that the scars on the sides of the valleys were made by vast glaciers, with which they had once been filled. Ignatz Venetz, a Swiss civil engineer, investigated the properties of glaciers in 1829 in order to prove Perraudin's theory. In reaction, Charles Lyell, an English geologist, proposed the following year that the boulders had been frozen in icebergs floating in the biblical Flood.

Reinhard Bernhardi, a German scientist, proposed a theory in 1832 that one massive glacier—the polar icecap—had once reached as far south as Germany.

Jean de Charpentier, director of the salt mines in the resort town of Bex, in Switzerland, presented evidence in support of the theory of Perraudin and Venetz to the Swiss Society of Natural Sciences in 1834. Louis Agassiz, the Swiss-American naturalist was present, but was unimpressed (see figure 17.2). However, when Agassiz spent the summer in Bex, and saw evidence of the glaciers and rocks, he became convinced that Charpentier's theory was correct.

Karl Schimper, a Swiss botanist, contributed the term *Ice Age* to the ongoing debate in 1936, and on July 2, 1937, Agassiz, at age thirty, presented the theory of the ice ages and polar icecap to the Swiss Society of Natural Sciences, of which he was then president, in Neuchâtel. Agassiz published an expanded version of his address at Neuchâtel in a book, *Studies on Glaciers*. The most famous geologists of the time—including the Reverend William Buckland of Oxford, his student Charles Lyell, Roderick

TABLE 17.1

Ice Ages and European Cultures

Time-Scale	Climatic Chronology	Chronology of the Alps	Human Cultures in Europe
	Postglacial		Mesolithic and later
	Last Glaciation	WÜRM$_3$	Mousterian — Upper Paleolithic: Aurignacian, Magdalenian, Solutrian
100,000-		WÜRM$_2$	
		WÜRM$_1$	
	Last Interglacial		
200,000-	Penultimate Glaciation	RISS$_2$	
		RISS$_1$	Levalloisian
300,000-	Penultimate Interglacial	Great Interglacial	Acheulian
400,000-			
	Antepenultimate Glaciation	MINDEL$_2$	Clactonian
		MINDEL$_1$	
500,000-	Antepenultimate Interglacial		Abbevillian or Chellean
	Early Glaciation	GUNZ$_2$	
600,000		GUNZ$_1$	Pre-abbevillian
	Villafranchian		

Murchison, president of the London Geological Society, Archibald Geikie, in England, Alexander von Humboldt of Germany, and Edward Hitchcock and Timothy Conrad in the United States—continued to believe that the Flood had moved the boulders, but their opposition had weakened considerably by the 1860s.[15]

The Theory

What causes *Gaian fevers*, James Lovelock's term for the interglacial periods?

FIGURE 17.2
Louis Agassiz
Swiss-American zoologist Louis Agassiz (1807–73) listens to American mathematician Benjamin Pierce, Harvard University, 1871.

Photo: Culver Pictures, Inc. Reprinted with permission.

FIGURE 17.3

The Orbital Variations[17]

(a) **Stretch**   (b) **Tilt**   (c) **Wobble**

Drawings by Diane Rigoli, © Ralph H. Abraham.

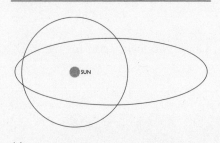

(a)

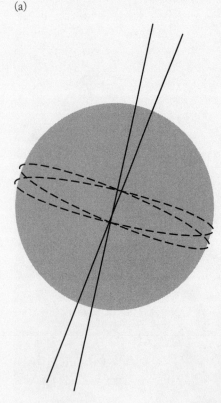

(b)

A century ago, this question had to be posed in the form: What causes ice ages?

Hardly five years had passed after Agassiz's discourse at Neuchâtel before answers were proposed to this question. Again, we shrink the story to a bare outline.[16]

In 1842 Joseph Adhemar, a French mathematician, proposed that *secular variations* in Earth's orbit, thus in the amount of sunlight received annually (Gaia is a solar-powered system), determine the ice ages. He listed two such variations:

- *Wobble:* The ellipticity of Earth's orbit makes the Northern Hemisphere colder or warmer than the Southern Hemisphere; but the cyclic precession of the equinoxes, with a period of about 23,000 years, reverses this bias.
- *Tilt:* The tilt of the polar axis, which varies between 22 and 24 degrees over a period of about 41,000 years, increases the severity of the seasons.

By 1852 Alexander von Humboldt had demonstrated that wobble alone, in Adhemar's theory, could not account for the ice ages. Urbain Leverrier discovered a further variation of Earth's orbit, which he called *stretch*, referring to the eccentricity of the orbit, stretching and relaxing over a period of about 100,000 years (see figure 17.3).

James Croll, the janitor at Andersonian College in Glasgow, had access to the scientific library of the Glasgow Philosophical Society, and in 1864 he began to study the Ice Age problem. Reading of Adhemar's theory, and Leverrier's recent discovery of a further variation of Earth's orbit, he published a paper showing that ice ages should occur in the periods of greatest orbital stretch. His argument used the interconnections between solar power variations, accumulation of the polar ice pack, and reflectivity of the ice. As a result of this paper, he was offered a position at the Geological Survey of Scotland, and elected Fellow of the Royal Society of London.

In 1904 detailed orbit calculations were published by Ludwig Pilgrim, a German mathematician, which enabled Milutan Milankovitch, a Yugoslavian engineer at the University of Belgrade, to carry out extensive calculations on the variation of solar radiation caused by the combination of wobble, tilt, and stretch. In spite of interruptions caused by wars, Milankovitch was able to publish the completed computations in a book, *Mathematical Theory of Heat Phenomena Produced by Solar Radiation,* in 1920.[18]

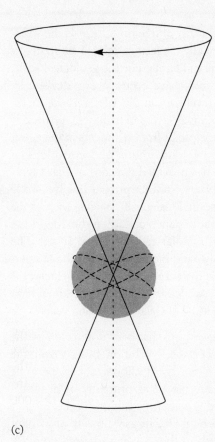

(c)

A German climatologist, Wladimir Koppen, with his son-in-law, Alfred Wegener, compared the Milankovitch radiation data with the recently discovered geological record of European glaciations. Their close correspondence, published in their book, *Climates of the Geological Past,* in 1924, confirmed Milankovitch's theory, and convinced the scientific community of the correlation between the vagaries of Earth's orbit, and the long-term variations in its climate.

In 1972 James Lovelock published his *Gaia Hypothesis,* on the intelligence of the interconnected global system of geosphere, biosphere, atmosphere, and the sun. In 1983 he coauthored, with Andrew Watson, a dynamical model called *Daisy World.*[19] In this fictitious world, the homeostasis of climate (average temperature) is maintained, in spite of a gradual increase in the brightness of the sun, by the cooperation of two species of daisies, one white and the other black.[20] The actual application of this idea on the timescale of the paleoclimatic record may involve the polar icecaps, the ocean, cloud cover, and the biosphere, as modulators of global climate.[21]

Combining climate regulation by the biosphere with climate modulation by orbit variations would be the next step in Gaian modeling. This would require modeling simultaneously the *damping* (the overall constancy [homeostasis] of the average temperature in spite of the powerfully increasing radiation) and the *amplification* (the modulation of this homeostasis by the relatively weak Milankovitch cycle). This is a fair challenge for the tremendous modeling power of the new mathematics, and the technology of the chaotic attractor and its bifurcations brings the right qualifications to the job. While climate models based on chaos theory abound in the great national science institutes of the world, even simple models in which the physical climate variations are tightly coupled to biospheric variables are just beginning to appear. These models require new ideas and new data, and will be intrinsically chaotic. We are thus on the doorstep of an evolution in our knowledge which was impossible before the advent of the Chaos Revolution.

The Record

Climate variations are studied in various timescales: *geological variations,* over thousands or millions of years; *climatic variations,* over centuries; and *secular variations,* over decades. There are historical records of rainfall, temperature, the timing and height of the Nile floods, and other climate indicators, for short-term variations.

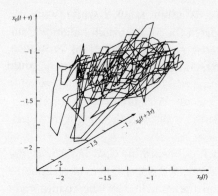

FIGURE 17.4
The Climatic Attractor

From Nicolis and Prigogine (1989). Courtesy of W. H.
Freeman, New York. Reprinted with permission.

Chaos and Gaia

*We know that Earth's orbit is chaotic, with or
without comets, and the near-periods of the
secular variations coincide well with the
paleoclimatic record. The question is, which
is the cause and which the effect?*

Our Coming Ice Age

Dendroclimatology, the study of tree rings, reveals the variation of a combination of two climate factors, rainfall and temperature, over a span of several millennia. For the geological scale, many indicators, called *proxies,* have been cleverly devised by paleoclimatologists. One, developed in the 1940s, is the thickness of *varves,* which are annual layers of sedimentary rock.[22] Another is the oxygen isotope proxy, from sediments in the ocean floor, developed in 1976 by John Imbrie and coworkers at Columbia University. This has provided a record of Gaia's temperature for half a million years.[23] Other proxies involve subtle interconnections between several Gaian subsystems, such as the variations of sea level, the abundance of carbon dioxide in the atmosphere, the variations in solar radiation, and so on. The result shows us a picture of a cold planet, on which the temperate climate we have today is the exception. James Lovelock calls these interglacial periods *Gaian fevers.* The fevers we know have occurred over the whole lifetime of Gaia—4.6 billion years.

The study of this record, since 1976, has been dominated by the periodic paradigm. As the Chaos Revolution sweeps over the Gaia Hypothesis, we begin to regard efforts to find periodic behavior in the paleoclimatic record as primarily of historical interest. The climatic record is chaotic (see figure 17.4).

We know that Earth's orbit is chaotic as well, with or without comets, and the near-periods of the secular variations coincide well with the paleoclimatic record. The question is, which is the cause and which the effect? While the corresponding variation in solar radiation is very small, the variation in climate, snowpack, sea level, biomass, and other indicators is enormous. Somewhere, there must be an amplifying factor.

One proposal for this amplifier is the elasticity of Gaia herself, who is squeezed a bit flat at the poles, under the crushing weight of ice.[24] At this point the full technology of the mathematical theory of complex dynamical systems has been called into service, to simulate the massively complicated system of earth, ocean, ice, atmosphere, and biomass.[25] This is the holistic system described by James Lovelock in the term *Gaian physiology.*[26]

Although the future of our climate cannot be predicted precisely, as chaos theory proves, we know that another Ice Age is inevitable. In spite of the convincing case now made for global climate warming, bifurcation theory and the geological record both suggest that a glaciation could occur very suddenly. We must remember, while we radically alter the atmospheric concentration of greenhouse gases, that the outcome may be sudden, unexpected, and cold.[27] The return of massive glaciers could happen within a century, and would require billions of people to move from the temperate regions to the tropics.[28]

Summary

The discovery of the ice ages, and the theories that have evolved to explain them, may be regarded as an Orphic (Gaian) revival. Belief in the static nature of Earth's climate had to be revised, first to a periodic order, and more recently to a chaotic behavior. The current theory couples the chaos of the solar system (the secular variations in Earth's orbit) with the biography of Gaia; the tightly coupled holarchic system comprising atmosphere, hydrosphere, geosphere, and biosphere of our planet. The advent of the Gaia Hypothesis and associated theories—the physiology of Gaia, biogeography, and so on—completes this revival. Can the concomitance of the Chaos Revolution and the Gaia Hypothesis be coincidental? The climate has been regarded as a driving force in our social evolution by historians from Diodorus to Toynbee.[29] Chaos in the solar system (especially comets, as in Whiston and Velikovsky) is coupled to the phases of Gaia in the biosphere, and thus enters into erodynamics, the rhythms of human society, to which we turn in our last chapter.

Erodynamics

CHAPTER 18

Great mathematicians are raconteurs, and it has been said that the best mathematics is created on the hoof, as these talented performers speak in front of top-notch mathematical audiences. Many years ago, I heard one of the best of these mathematical artists improvise a model for sexual relations. While it made the audience uncomfortable, it also succeeded as an outstanding work of art, reminding me of times when I've had vivid mathematical models in my imagination, while simultaneously trying to negotiate a difficult relationship. Eventually, I found that there is an extensive literature on similar dynamical models for complex relationships, including arms races and emotional codependence.

Social Evolution

Ideas of cycles, linear progress, and spiral advance are fundamental to historiography.[1] Dynamical historiography substitutes a punctuated (dynamic) equilibrium model of time, based on the prerequisites of dynamical models. Previously, we've applied this punctual model to the largest social transformations:

- the Mesolithic bifurcation, from the chaos of the Paleolithic to the stasis of the Neolithic
- the Wheel bifurcation from the Static Epoch to the Periodic, with the birth of civilization, and the rise of patriarchy
- the current Chaos Revolution

The first was enabled by the rising temperatures of the Holocene interglacial. The second was triggered by the desertification of the Near East. The third accompanies the emerging awareness of global climate change caused by our human population. There are numerous smaller bifurcations in history, such as Christianity, the troubadours, and the Renaissance. These are intrinsic bifurcations, triggered by the endogenous evolution of civilization. We now present the recent history of *erodynamics,* the study of social behavior based on dynamical models.

Social Models

Dynamical models may be used as navigational aids for cooperation or conflict resolution in situations where goodwill prevails yet does not suffice.

Complex dynamical systems theory provides a new modeling strategy for social systems, which are usually too complicated to model without a theory that allows for chaos and bifurcation. These new models contribute to the grok circle for evolving social structures, in which mathematical help in understanding may be very welcome, as even the simplest social systems, whether two persons or two nations, tax our intuitive cognitive strategies. Dynamical models may be used as navigational aids for cooperation or conflict resolution in situations where goodwill prevails yet does not suffice. Here we give a few examples of erodynamics, the art of building social models.

First Steps

Newton, soon after his development of the calculus in 1666, became interested in world history and prehistory. He pursued applications of astronomy to the chronology of ancient kingdoms, and probably envisioned dynamical models for cultural evolution.

Our first recorded model for social systems is the Verhulst model for population growth, in 1837. Later, in the context of the Great War, came Lanchester's model for war in 1914, and Richardson's model for the arms race in 1919.

Next came dynamical models for economic systems, with John Maynard Keynes, Joseph Schumpeter, and John von Neumann in the 1930s. Rashevsky, who edited Richardson's papers, invented mathematical sociology during World War II. This sequence accelerated after World War II with the syntheses of general systems theory and cybernetics.

In the mathematical branch of these movements, *systems dynamics,* we have the extensive development of models for factories, cities, nations, the world monetary system, and many other systems. The independent development of dynamical systems theory after Poincaré remained aloof from social applications until recently, and now a reunion of these two branches of mathematics is underway. In the Poincaré lineage came the development of applied singularity theory by René Thom, its extensive application to social systems (as catastrophe theory) by Christopher Zeeman, and new dynamical models for economic systems by Radnor, Smale, and Chichilnisky in the 1970s. Since then, chaos theory has discovered systems with complex structure, and systems dynamics has discovered chaos.

LANCHESTER, 1914

Frederick William Lanchester (1868–1946) was an English engineer and a creative genius. He was interested in economics, physics, military strategy, automobiles, and airplanes, and was one of the first to grasp the military advantage of aircraft. In this context he conceived a dynamical model for armed conflict, in which numerical strength, firepower, strategy, and attitude were all considered.[2]

RICHARDSON, 1919

Lewis Frye Richardson was an English physicist, meteorologist, and Quaker. A conscientious objector in World War I, he served as an ambulance driver on the front lines in France and saw a great deal of death and suffering. After deciding to devote his life to the elimination of war, he developed a *linear model* for the arms race between two nations, in which a spiral of increasing armaments in each nation resulted from mathematical laws, as shown in figure 18.1.

Richardson felt that individual nations caught in this kind of dynamic were innocent victims of an out-of-control global system. He submitted a paper on his model to a scientific journal, fully confident that another war could be averted. The paper was rejected, and World War II began. After this rejection Richardson continued his work, trying to justify the model on the basis of actual armament statistics. In these efforts he founded the field of *politicometrics*. Richardson's life work was published posthumously in 1960.

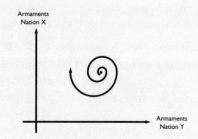

FIGURE 18.1
Richardson's Spiral Process

Drawing by Diane Rigoli, © Ralph H. Abraham.

VON NEUMANN, 1932

The word economics is derived from the Greek oikos nomos, *meaning the management of a household. This is also the source of* oikonomia, *the Christian doctrine of the economy of salvation.*

The word *economics* is derived from the Greek *oikos nomos,* meaning the management of a household. This is also the source of *oikonomia,* the Christian doctrine of the economy of salvation, as described in part 1. In the last century, economics became an important social science. Because it's naturally equipped (since prehistoric times) with numerical data, this was one of the first of the social sciences to receive a mathematical treatment. In 1932 John von Neumann created one of the first dynamical models for an economic system, giving rise to a whole industry of mathematical analyses, computer simulations, and data collection (*econometrics*).[3]

BATESON, 1935

In 1935 Gregory Bateson adapted the Richardson model to the process of the division of a culture into subcultures, analogous to differentiation in biological systems. He called this universal dynamical process for the development of a schism a *Richardsonian process of schismogenesis.*[4] In fact, schismogenesis, a social form of bifurcation, was one of Bateson's main themes.

LEWIN, 1936

Kurt Lewin (1890–1947) was influenced by the hermeneutics of Dilthey, with whom he had contact in Berlin, and Wertheimer, who had developed a field concept in Gestalt psychology as early as 1923. This was extensively developed by Lewin. His *life space* is a sort of psychological field, extending over a group of animals.[5] He modeled social psychological objects by shapes within the life space, or field. He also introduced concepts of dynamics and bifurcations in these shapes, under the name *Topological Psychology.* The rigorous development of Lewin's ideas had to await complex dynamical systems theory, or chaos theory, in the 1960s and 1970s.

RASHEVSKY, 1939

Nicholas Rashevsky (1895–1964) founded mathematical biology at the University of Chicago (see chapter 8). In 1939 he published an early erodynamic paper applying the methods of mathematical biology to sociology. He published a book on this subject in 1947.

THOM, 1972

In the 1960s René Thom developed *catastrophe theory.* He published the theory in 1972, along with a number of ideas for its application in the sciences, linguistics, philosophy, and so on.[6] The final chapter of his book sets out the modern formulation of Erodynamics, in the context of proposed applications to sociology and psychology.

ZEEMAN, 1976

In the 1970s C. A. Isnard and Christopher Zeeman replaced the linear model of Richardson and Bateson with a *nonlinear model:* the cusp catastrophe of Thom's theory, shown in figure 18.2. They applied their model to the original arms race context of Richardson's work, showing how the model fit a situation of schismogenesis, in which the voting population of a democratic nation split into *hawks* and *doves.* Zeeman also adapted the cusp to model *anorexia nervosa,* an emotional disease in which phases of gluttony and fasting alternate.[7]

In 1985, Mark Kushelman (working under the pseudonym Kadyrov due to Soviet anti-Semitism), a systems scientist then in Moscow, put together two of these cusp models into a *double-cusp model* for two nations engaged in an arms race, completing the nonlinear version of Richardson's original model. This model provides a map, in two-dimensional space, of the sensitivities of each nation to armaments of the other. It delineates regions of

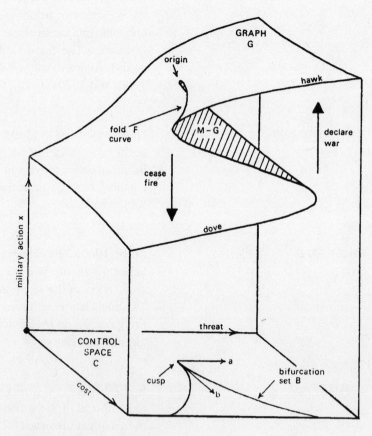

FIGURE 18.2
The Cusp Model
Courtesy of E. C. Zeeman. Reprinted with permission.

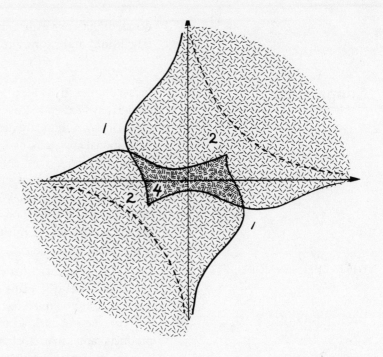

FIGURE 18.3
Kushelman's Map

Drawing by Diane Rigoli, © Ralph H. Abraham.

different behaviors, such as hawks and hawks, hawks and doves, doves and hawks, and doves and doves, as shown in figure 18.3.

Surprisingly, in the northwest and southeast sectors of this map, Kushelman found oscillating behavior, which might be significant in situations of codependence or addictive behavior.[8] A slightly different double-cusp map was used by James Callahan and Jerome Sashin in the treatment of affect-response.[9] Some other nonlinear adaptations of Richardson's model for the arms race have been studied by Gottfried Mayer-Kress and Alvin Saperstein, who found chaotic behavior in their model.[10]

DAY, 1990

Richard Day, a mathematical economist, presented a pathfinding paper in 1990 in which a mathematical model is proposed for the long-run economic dynamics of the human species. This combination of archaeology with economic dynamics and demographics ushers in a new era of erodynamic modeling (see Day, 1990).

Cooperation

In a complex dynamical environment, a complex dynamical model may be used as a navigational aid, to improve the chances of achieving a mutually desired goal. Various examples of this navigational approach, basic to control theory, have been applied to politics (arms races, conflict resolution), medicine (surgical and pharmaceutical intervention), psychiatry (therapeutic strategies), and in other areas. We may consider, as a typical application, the trade cooperation of two nations or multinational corporations, and use the Kushelman model as an example.

THE KUSHELMAN MODEL

In this hypothetical situation, the control parameters in the double cusp model (the plane shown in figure 18.3) would select strategies such as trade restrictions, tariffs, credit limits, and so on. The state of each partner is determined by inventories of products rather than stockpiles of weapons.[11]

The two partners sit down to talk, and each must restrict their agreements according to the supervision of some group of stockholders or voters, which are subject to a process of schismogenesis into two camps, say conservatives and progressives. In the absence of a model, the complex dynamics of these four influence groups overwhelms and frightens the negotiators, and they may wish to risk little, making at best small adjustments in the status quo, waiting to observe results and reactions.[12]

Now let us suppose that a complex dynamical model is at hand—the Kushelman model for example—and that confidence in its application is firmly established in experience. The trading partners then may simply consult their data—quarterly statements, opinion polls, or whatever—and find their positions on the model map. This map applies to them jointly, not individually. They may then cooperate in choosing a strategy, a timed sequence of steps, from among the continuum of choices, with more courage than fear. One possibility is shown in figure 18.4.

It's a short loop, to be traversed in a sequence of steps over a period of time, on a strict schedule. It's roughly a closed loop in the space of strategies. Although it is counterintuitive, it may achieve the mutually desired result with a minimum of cost; by moving with the intrinsic dynamic of the system rather than trying to impose an external order, it leads the joint system from the

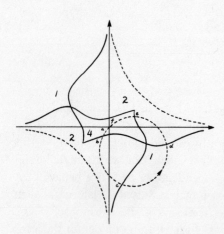

FIGURE 18.4
A Cooperative Strategy

Drawing by Diane Rigoli, © Ralph H. Abraham.

current state to a new state, following a sequence of bifurcations, shown in figure 18.5.

A similar approach has been used by Callahan and Sashin in the treatment of anorexia. It seems unlikely that this phased strategy shift would occur to the partners without a model. The oscillations in the Kushelman model have been avoided as much as possible in this application, as they may be expensive states to maintain. However, if the subjects are lovers rather than trading partners, they may wish to maximize these vibrating states.

Summary

Here we arrive at the present: applications of the dynamical theories of chaos and bifurcation to the social sciences (psychology, sociology, economics). These applications are providing models that are similar in power and style to those in use in the physical and biological sciences. Our understanding of the world economy and emerging planetary society—arms races, political cooperation, and so on—may be improved by the use of mathematical models. Thanks to the Chaos Revolution, the horizon of complexity has receded, and large-scale systems such as the one we live in are no longer beyond our ken. While we may not be able to predict the future with certainty, or at all, we may at least exercise our cognitive processes, with mathematical models and computer graphic simulations that improve our understanding of the present, enhancing our chances of survival in the future.

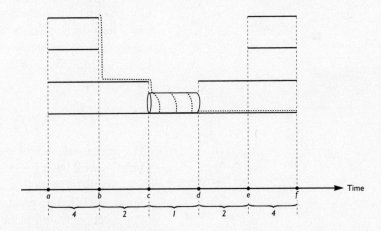

FIGURE 18.5
The Bifurcation Sequence

Drawing by Diane Rigoli, © Ralph H. Abraham.

Summary of Part 3

With a giant paradigm shift still in progress, science must eat humble pie, for Chaos is in once again, and all of the physical sciences are in transition.

Embracing our newfound understanding of complexity, we may face the evolutionary challenges caused by our own success.

The wheel, made manifest in the sciences, provided circular models for most processes. The clock, the calendar, and the motions of the stars and planets were all based on perfect circular models; that is, periodic processes in which Marduk had indeed destroyed Tiamat.

When Orphic revivals threaten, as with Bruno, Whiston, or Velikovsky, terrorist persecution usually discourages them. The Chaos Revolution in the physical sciences, however, has changed this. With a giant paradigm shift still in progress, science must eat humble pie, for Chaos is in once again, and all of the physical sciences are in transition. Here, we've outlined only a single example, that of planetary astronomy. Shifts in the other sciences all follow a similar pattern, as Hesiod knew:

Chaos was born first . . .

Meanwhile, as though by coincidence, the Gaia Hypothesis has taken hold in the biological sciences. The various envelopes of Earth, cooperate in a vast holarchic system:

. . . and after her came Gaia,
the broad-breasted, the firm seat of all . . .

The transformation of the social sciences follows the lead of the physical and biological sciences, and is just getting underway. Our example of erodynamics in group process is just one of many new developments. Similar models for economic systems are coming, along with models which tightly couple the world economy and the global environment. Erodynamics joins Eros with Chaos and Gaia in an evolutionary trinity:

. . . and Eros, the fairest of the deathless gods;

These three sets of exemplary paradigm shifts typify the Orphic revival within science, for so long the temple of Order.

A synthesis of models for the solar system, the Gaian system (atmosphere, hydrosphere, biosphere), and the human system (global economy and planetary society) has now become possible. Thus our understanding of the effects of planetary motions on our climate, the influence of climate on the biosphere and on human society, and the influence of human society and economic activity on the biosphere and climate may now be studied and synthesized to increase our understanding of, and sensitivity to, the whole system in which we live.

We see that the three paradigm shifts currently underway in the sciences—associated with the three cosmic principles of the Orphic trinity, Chaos, Gaia, and Eros—are *linked in a circle:*

1. The chaotic behavior of our solar system (the planets, their satellites, the asteroids and comets) creates chaos in our climate. This is the conclusion of the theory of Croll, Milankovitch, and so on, and the implication of the paleoclimatic data as well.

2. The chaotic behavior of our climate creates chaos in our history. This has been the subject of world histories since Ibn-Khaldûn and Vico.[1] A number of modern texts, for example, address the effect of global climate warming, around 10,000 B.C., on the discovery of agriculture.[2]

   Another exemplary case of this influence of climate on culture is part of the thesis of James Demeo, in which desertification around 4000 B.C. supports the social bifurcation in which the patriarchy overtakes the partnership society of the Goddess TriVia.[3]

   A third exemplary case is the speculation of Carleton Coon that a series of dry years around 2000 B.C. sparked the nomadic incursions leading up to the Urban Revolution.[4]

3. Completing the cycle of the Orphic trinity, human society contributes to the chaos of the solar system through changes to the albedo of the planet Earth, and the launching of solid waste and trash into orbit.

Similarly, human society affects the climate directly (by burning fossil fuels, for example), climate affects the solar system directly through the radiation and reflection of energy, and the planets affect human society directly (by light, tides, and so on).

These influences are subtle. But thanks to the new mathematics of chaos and complex dynamical systems, we now know, as in the butterfly effect, that small causes can have large consequences.

This concludes our case for the third conjecture in our Introduction:

Conjecture 3. The Chaos Revolution currently underway in the sciences, along with the related paradigm shifts associated with the names Gaia and Eros, signal one of the major phase shifts of history.

Here we rest our case. Chaos, the mathematics of complex dynamical systems, is in its infancy, and so are the social sciences.

Joining forces under the banner of Eros, they may aid our future evolution, in harmony with Gaia.

The specific examples we've considered here are just three of many that are currently in progress. Yet these are linked in a particularly suggestive trinity:

Solar system behavior (chaotic orbits of planets and comets) influences Gaian behavior (chaotic variations of climate and chemistry of atmosphere, oceans, soils), which in turn influences social system behavior (chaotic sequence of transformations such as agriculture, civilization/patriarchy, chaos). We are now beginning to perceive the inverse sequence: society influences climate/chemistry influences orbits. Thus all are linked in a cosmic TriVia, and science may be Orphicized at last.

CONCLUSION

The role of gender in the Orphic aspects of the history of consciousness cannot be emphasized enough. The Static Revolution was initiated by women; the Periodic by men; and the Chaotic by both. The peaceful partnership society of our Cro-Magnon ancestors was characterized by the three-way cooperation of three principles, Chaos, Gaia, and Eros, symbolized by the triple-headed goddess TriVia, the Pythagorean Y, and the victory symbol that emerged during World War II, and in the peace movement of the 1960s. The healing of our planetary society from scars of the past six millennia, the Periodic Epoch, will be an Orphic enterprise. We must welcome the Chaotic Epoch. Table C.1 shows the final concordance.

Why Now?

The Chaotic Epoch arrives now, rather than earlier or later, partly because of the computer revolution. Computer graphic visualization of mathematical models has greatly amplified the social transformation we are witnessing, as they've made the models *visible* to the world at large.

Another key to the lock of history may be the weakening of organized Christianity. At the nucleus of this view is the persecution of Giordano Bruno. The question of stability, posed as the USW Problem, is the magnetic center of attraction for many dogmatic religions. From the pyramids of Egypt to those of the Yucatan, the stable, pre-dictable periodicity of the Sun provided the power of the priestly elite. The Judeo-Christian tradition is no exception, although the degree of terrorism and repression applied to heretics in the Christian Inquisition was exceptional. The victory of Marduk over Tiamat, and the violent repression of Chaos by Periodic Order, was reenacted upon Hypatia and Bruno by Christian authorities. Science is heir to the throne of Marduk. Bruno's martyrdom was the fulcrum upon which the church levered the development of science onto its own track, the stability dogma. The intimidation of Galileo, Newton, and others catapulted Marduk, Father Sky, science, and the church to a position of unprecedented dominance, power, authority, and respect.

Another crucial factor in this paradigm shift is the feminist movement. The liberation of women from patriarchal views of nature and society is encouraging the revival of pagan, and especially goddess, traditions, such as that of Inanna and Tiamat. The improving partnership between the genders creates a social ecology favorable to Orphism, the philosophical heritage of the Paleolithic partnership culture.

Mathematics and the computer revolution, the weakening of the authority of Christianity and science, and the growth of feminism are three factors in the success of the Orphic revival now taking place within the sciences. Chaos, Gaia, and Eros are rising from their long rest in the underworld of the collective unconscious. The long line of Orphism seems to be reappearing, renewing the partnership of Father Sky and Mother Earth.

A Word of Warning

One last word of warning. I'm not suggesting the inevitability of the Orphic revival and the salvation of humankind and the biosphere. The anti-Orphic dominator structure of society is in a powerful defensive phase. We have much to accomplish against massive odds to facilitate a transformation, and in this book I've tried to suggest some supportive strategies.

If Petrie's theory is correct, then current events in the mathematical world are crucial. While we do not know the microstructure of social transformations that took place in the past, we can certainly observe the one progressing in our lifetime. We see the conservative forces at work to protect the dominator paradigm. The cooption of chaos theory is underway, as it's used to control systems and preserve the familiar order. It's quite possible that the image I've presented—a major transformation from patriarchy/order to partnership/chaos —is simply a wish-fulfillment dream, projected onto a harsher reality: a chaotic interlude presaging the apocalypse, the end of history for the human race.[1]

Paul Tillich has identified these two human tendencies—the anxious, conservative attraction to the past and the courageous, revolutionary attraction to the future—as the fundamental dynamic of history, and the realization of the divine. *The creativity of Chaos stands between these forces, of the past and of the future.*

The long line of the Orphic trinity connects our past and future life in harmony with earth and sky, through the present moment of creation. In fact, this triadic aspect of the long line of Orphism, placing the present moment between an ideal past and a created future, is the archetype of all utopian literature.[2] This is our Orphic utopia in action.

TABLE C.1
Final Concordance

I	Trinity	Gaia	Eros	Chaos
II	Epochs	Static	Periodic	Chaotic
III	Sciences	Physical	Biological	Social
Conclusion	Genders	Female	Male	Both

N O T E S

INTRODUCTION: THE ORPHIC REVIVAL

1. See Smale, 1980.
2. See the pathfinding paper of Ruelle, 1971.
3. See the highly instructive Shaw, 1984.
4. This connection first occurred in Li and Yorke, 1975.

CHAPTER 1. THE WORLD ACCORDING TO GROK

1. See Heinlein, 1961, 1968, 1987, p. 6: "Back even before the healing which had followed first grokking that he was not as his nestling brothers . . . back to the nest itself."
2. I use the word *hermeneutics* so frequently in this chapter that it would have been convenient to shorten it to "herm," like "math" for mathematics. But then it might have been confused with *hermetics,* the magical tradition from ancient Egypt. Both words, hermetics and hermeneutics, are derived from Thrice Greatest Hermes, the divine who gave writing to the Egyptians. To avoid confusion I will use the word *grok* in place of "hermeneutical understanding." For background on hermeneutics, see Palmer, 1969; Lee, 1988; and Fowden, 1986.
3. To see the world according to grok, you might start with Lee, 1988; Berman, 1981; Bateson, 1979; Palmer, 1969; and Rickman, 1967. More theoretical treatment may be found in Hoy, 1978, and the references therein to the works of Derrida, Habermas, Gadamer, and so on.
4. See Capra, 1987; Abraham, 1986; Tillich, 1961; Bateson, 1979; Bateson, 1984; and White, 1967.
5. Actually, there are three categories of bifurcation in dynamical systems theory: catastrophic, subtle, and explosive. See Abraham and Shaw, 1992, for full details. The catastrophic bifurcation is the type that corresponds to metamorphosis.
6. See Merchant, 1980, p. xix.
7. On the symbols, see Leroi-Gourhan, 1968; and Gimbutas, 1982. For the evolution from the constellations, see Moran, 1953, 1969.
8. Alexandria was founded by Alexander the Great in 331 B.C. He died in Persia eight years later, without seeing his new capital. One of his generals, Ptolemy Soter, took charge of Egypt and its capital, Alexandria, creating its two great institutions, the Palace and the Museion. The latter, modeled on Aristotle's library in Athens, was richly endowed, and became one of the first universities. Its first library, the Mother, housed half a million books. Another, the Daughter, at the Temple of Serapis (a made-up god combining Osiris, Apis, Dionysus, Zeus, and Plato), contained even more volumes. After the rise of Christianity to dominance around A.D. 300, the monks persecuted the pagans. The Serapis temple was destroyed by a Christian mob in 391. With it, the Daughter library was lost. The Mother and all the rest disintegrated after the Arab conquest of 641. For a thrilling account in full detail and great style, see Forster, 1961. More details may be found in Parsons, 1952; and Canfora, 1989.
9. See Yates, 1982b.
10. The events of the sixteenth century leading up to this basic split are extensively documented in Merchant, 1980. See also Kuhn, 1977; Berman, 1981; Yates, 1964; and Davis, 1986.
11. For an extensive account, see Sheldrake, 1988.
12. Carefully documented in Lee, 1988.
13. According to Paul Lee, 1988, Goethe (1749–1832) was the watershed on this line.
14. On organicism, see Haraway, 1976; for general systems, see Davidson, 1983; and for general evolution theory, see Jantsch, 1980; and Laszlo, 1987. According to Haraway, Paul Weiss (one of the founders of organicism) had contact with the

hermeneutical tradition of Dilthey in Berlin. According to Davidson, so did von Bertalanffy, before moving to Canada, where he founded general systems theory.

15. See Palmer, 1969; Lee, 1988; and Sheldrake, 1988.
16. On action research, see Lewin, 1948; and Bateson, 1979.
17. See Berman, 1981; and Thompson, 1981, p. 4.
18. For morphic resonance, see Sheldrake, 1988.
19. This model is called an *excitable medium* by mathematical biologists. See Abraham, 1987b; and Kuhn, 1977.
20. See, for example, Abraham, Mayer-Kress, Keith, and Koebbe, 1991; and Abraham, Corliss, and Dorband, 1991; and the references therein.
21. See Chardin, 1965.
22. This is the Continental school; see Radnitzky, 1973.
23. See Sanford, 1970.
24. Here are some important essays: Kuhn, 1962; Auerbach, 1944; Boltzmann, 1902; Hesse, 1961; Pepper 1961; Black, 1962; Hesse, 1966; Achinstein, 1968; Kordig, 1971; Hein, 1971; Leatherdale, 1974; Haraway, 1976; Maclagan, 1977, p. 66; Rosenblueth and Wiener, 1965; and Lilienfeld, 1978, p. 18.
25. See Dobbs, 1975; and Yates, 1984.
26. See Radnitzky, 1973.

CHAPTER 2. COGNITIVE MAPS AND MYTHOGENESIS

1. See Artigiani, 1987a; Artigiani, 1987b; Artigiani, 1988; and Artigiani, Masulli, Csanyi, and Laszlo, 1989.
2. From Thompson, 1978, pp. 107–8.
3. "Cognitive map" was coined by Tolman in 1946. The extension to "cultural cognitive map" naturally followed. See, for example, Wallace, 1961, 1970, p. 18; Artigiani, 1987a and 1987b; Artigiani, 1988; and Artigiani, 1991a and 1991b.
4. This summary is abstracted from Hilgard, 1953, 1979, ch. 8.
5. For example, Kohler refers to Driesch in Kohler, 1924, p. 66, and to Dilthey in Kohler, 1929, 1970; while Wertheimer discusses vitalism explicitly in Wertheimer, 1924, 1938, p. 7.
6. The field concept occurs already in Wertheimer, 1923, 1938.
7. See Lewin, 1936.
8. For more information, consult the basic books: Koffka, 1924, 1928; Koffka, 1935; Kohler, 1925, 1927; Kohler, 1929, 1970; Kohler, 1940, 1960; Wertheimer, 1945, 1982; Ellis, 1950; Henle, 1961; and Lewin, 1935.
9. This story is from Tolman, 1948, who refers to Lashley, 1964, in which we have found a story very similar to this, on p. 137. Many thanks to my brother, Fred Abraham, for locating this page. He says: "I speculate that the two rats came first, and their story was orally transmitted from Lashley to Tolman. Later, Lashley rigged this experiment to document and replicate the observation."
10. For what the two rats learned about the cognitive maps or about rat men such as Tolman, see "Mazes" in Le Guin, 1988, pp. 61–66.
11. See Tolman, 1948, and the references therein.
12. See Tolman, 1948, p. 207.
13. See, for example, Hebb, 1949; and O'Keefe, 1978.
14. His early work with the Trobriand Islanders is reported in Malinowski, 1922. See also Firth, 1957.
15. For much fun and profit, read Gladwin, 1970.
16. See Malinowski, 1922, and Young, 1979, for this work; and Ellen, Gellner, Kubica, and Mucha, 1988, for an appreciation of his life work. The early development of social anthropology by Malinowski and Radcliffe-Brown is described in Kuper, 1973, 1983. For another view on culture, see Renfrew, 1972.
17. From the Introduction by Margaret Mead to Benedict, 1934, 1959, p. vii; and Firth, 1957, p. 16. Regarding the split between Malinowski and Radcliffe-Brown, see Kuper, 1973, 1983, p. 68.
18. See Benedict, 1934, 1959, p. 78.
19. See Abraham, 1989a.
20. See Bateson, 1972, p. 68.
21. See Bateson, 1936, 1958, 1966, p. 118; and Benedict, 1934, 1959, p. 89.
22. See Richardson, 1939. Also, his posthumous work, Richardson, 1960a, 1960b.
23. See Bateson, 1972, p. 109.
24. See Lilienfeld, 1978, p. 222, for some dissenting discussion.
25. See Davidson, 1983.
26. See Abraham, 1990b.
27. See Boulding, 1956, p. 64.
28. See Artigiani, 1987a.
29. See Artigiani, 1987a, p. 100.
30. See Artigiani, 1987a, 1987b; Artigiani, 1988; and Artigiani, Masulli, Csanyi, and Laszlo, 1989.
31. Graves, 1957.
32. Arthur O. Lovejoy was a later advocate of this approach, subsequently criticized by Quentin Skinner. See Kumar, 1991, p. 44.
33. See Campbell, 1990.

CHAPTER 3. THE HISTORY OF HISTORY

1. See the first volume of *Order and History*, Voegelin, 1956, p. ix.
2. See Glen, 1982.
3. See Gould, 1987.
4. One of the great champions of this view is Voegelin. See Voegelin, 1956. See also Lowith, 1949, especially p. 182; and Cairns, 1962, especially p. 244.
5. See Burke, 1985, p. 55.
6. See Bury, 1958.
7. Socrates, 424A, quoted from Brumbaugh, 1954, p. 87.
8. See Collingwood, 1965, p. 57.
9. From Oldfather, 1963, p. 1.
10. See Berry, 1990, p. xii.
11. See Lowith, 1949, p. 160; and Cairns, 1962, p. 251.
12. See Nisbet, 1969, p. 211.
13. See Cairns, 1962, p. 254.
14. In West, 1975, vol. 1, see the Introduction by Delno West, and ch. B of section 1, by M. Bloomfield; and Lowith, 1949, ch. 8.
15. See Mahdis, 1957, 1964.
16. Quoted from Parsons, 1952, p. 388.
17. See Ibn-Khaldûn, 1958. There is also an abridgement in one volume, Ibn-Khaldûn, 1967. A brief summary may be found in Cairns, 1962, p. 322.
18. For more details on Ibn-Khaldûn's cyclical pattern, see Cairns, 1962, p. 322 and the references therein.
19. See Cassirer, 1963, p. 42.
20. The magisterial source for all this material is Manuel, 1979. For a concise summary, see Kumar, 1991.
21. See Flint, 1874, p. 68; and Wade, 1971, p. 111.
22. See Daly, 1978, pp. 182–97.
23. Leibniz's version of the great chain of being is discussed in Wiener, 1951, Introduction; and Lovejoy, 1936, ch. 5. He also wrote about biological evolution in 1700. See Gooch, 1913, 1959, p. 9.
24. From Gooch, 1913, 1959, p. 9.
25. See Wade, 1971, p. 448.
26. Not only is there no evidence to suggest an awareness of Ibn-Khaldûn, but Vico remarks in his *Autobiography* that, being born in Italy and not in Morocco, he became a scholar. (He describes his sources in part A.) Ibn-Khaldûn was born in Tunis, studied in Córdoba, and wrote his *Prolegomena* in Oran, Algeria.
27. See Gooch, 1913, 1959, p. 9.
28. See Burke, 1985, p. 68; and White, 1978, 1985, p. 202.
29. See Manuel, 1979, p. 456.
30. For more details on Vico's cyclical pattern, see Cairns, 1962, p. 337 and the references therein. See also Gooch, 1913, 1959, p. 9; and Wallace, 1961, 1970, p. 179.
31. Vico was inspired by Herodotus. See Burke, 1985, pp. 55, 71. But the Egyptian cycle of three ages was followed by a period of chaos. See Thompson, 1978, p. 163; Thompson, 1985, p. 53; and Cairns, 1962, p. 233. Polybius (203–120 B.C.) had a cyclical model of development for nations: monarchy, aristocracy, and democracy. See Burke, 1985, p. 57.
32. See Burke, 1985, pp. 4, 7; and Auerbach, 1959, p. 188.
33. See Burke, 1985, p. 7 and the references therein.
34. See White, 1978, 1985, p. 203.
35. See Manuel, 1979, p. 461.
36. See Braudel, 1980, p. 177.
37. See Lovejoy's "Herder and the Philosophy of History," in Lovejoy, 1948, p. 169.
38. See Auerbach, 1959, p. 185.
39. See Auerbach, 1959, p. 188; and Burke, 1985, p. 4.
40. For further details on Herder's universal historical theory, see Manuel, 1979; Herder, 1968; and Gooch, 1913, 1959, p. 9.
41. Translation by J. Sibree, Hegel, 1905. A third edition, by Georg Lasson, appeared in 1921.
42. Translated by H. B. Nisbet, Hegel, 1975, it is highly recommended. Other translations exist.
43. See Cairns, 1962, p. 281, for an excellent summary.
44. See Sheldrake, 1988, p. 44.
45. See Fukuyama, 1992, p. xii.
46. See Flint, 1874, p. 259.
47. See Marx, 1977, p. 13.
48. See Marx, 1977, p. 20.
49. For background on this period in the evolution of evolution theory, see Spencer, 1967, p. ix; and Sheldrake, 1988, p. 45.
50. See Sheldrake, 1988, p. 243.
51. See Harding, 1960 for a very readable account.
52. Quoted from Spencer, 1967, p. xviii.
53. See Spencer, 1967, p. xvii.
54. Spencer's social evolution should not be confused with the notorious *social Darwinism* of the same period.
55. For more details on Burckhardt's view of history, see Gooch, 1913, 1959, p. 529; and Löwith, 1949, p. 20 and the references therein.
56. See Tylor, 1958, p. xi.
57. See Spender, 1983, p. 144.
58. See Dilthey, 1961, 1962, ch. 1.
59. The story is well told in Petrie, 1903, and in Drower, 1985.

60. Katherine Hayles (Hayles, 1990) has recently argued that social transformations begin in the liberal arts.

61. See Petrie, 1911. For a critical appraisal, see Collingwood, 1965, p. 80.

62. For the general history of this revolution, see Gardner, 1985; and Lilienfeld, 1978. For vitalism and organicism, see Haraway, 1976. Regarding holism, see Koestler, 1979.

63. For more details on Spengler's view of history, see Cairns, 1962, p. 353 and the references therein, especially to the 1917 original or its two-volume translation into English (Spengler, 1926a), or the abridged (Spengler, 1926b). Further, in a chapter of Braudel, 1980, entitled "The History of Civilizations: The Past Explains the Present," Braudel discusses the entire history of culture and civilization, including Voltaire (1756), Guizot (1828), Burckhardt (1860), Spengler (1918), Toynbee (1934), Weber (1935), and Bagby (1958). See Frankfort, 1959, pp. 17 and 20, for a critique of Spengler.

64. See Cairns, 1962, ch. 7.

65. See Smith, 1990.

66. For more details on Toynbee's cyclical view of history, see Cairns, 1962, p. 403 and the references therein; as well as Toynbee and Caplan, 1972; and Toynbee, 1958, especially the summary by D. C. Somervell.

67. See Cairns, 1962, pp. 278–79.

68. See Frankfort, 1959, p. 15, for a critique of Toynbee's method.

69. See Thompson, 1981, p. 5.

70. For more details on Sorokin's view of history, see Cairns, 1962, p. 379 and the references therein; as well as the original Sorokin, 1925; Sorokin, 1937, 1962; and Sorokin, 1957.

71. See for yourself, in Rosenstock-Huessy, 1938, 1964.

72. See Gebser, 1949, 1953, 1985, 1986, as well as Feuerstein, 1987; and Wilber, 1981.

73. See Cairns, 1962, ch. 6.

74. The volumes of (Voegelin, 1956–57).

75. See Voegelin, 1956, vol. 1, pp. 126, 172.

76. See Turner, 1980, p. 43, for additional discussion and references on sacred history.

77. See Tillich 1951, 1957, 1963, p. 326.

78. See Bertalanffy, 1968, p. 168.

79. See the recollections of Karreman, 1990.

80. See Rashevsky, 1968, p. 119.

81. See McKenna and McKenna, 1975, part 2. A more extensive account may be found in McKenna, 1987.

82. In particular, we may recommend the works of Robert Artigiani, Morris Berman, Ferdinand Braudel, Eric Chaisson, Riane Eisler, Erich Jantsch, Ervin Laszlo, Carolyn Merchant, Eugen Rosenstock-Huessy, Rupert Sheldrake, William Irwin Thompson, Hayden White, and William Strauss and Neil Howe, listed in the bibliography.

CHAPTER 4. THE AGES OF THE WORLD

1. See Settegast, 1986, p. 266.

2. This number occurs in Iceland and Babylonia also. See Campbell, 1974, p. 72.

3. See the entry by H. J. Jacobi, vol. I, p. 200 in Hastings, 1955.

4. From Daniélou, 1985, 1987, p. 197. See also Cairns, 1962, pp. 28–29, where the antiquity of this theory is discussed.

5. See the entry by A. Jeremias, vol. I, p. 183 in Hastings, 1955. See also Cairns, 1962, p. 10.

6. See Thompson, 1981, pp. 4–7; and Cairns, 1962, p. 233. The Myth of Ages may go back to Sumer. See West, 1978.

7. From Lattimore, 1959.

8. See the entry by K. F. Smith, vol. I, p. 192 in Hastings, 1955 and Cairns, 1962, p. 196.

9. See Maury, 1955.

10. See Guthrie, 1966, p. 197.

11. For the full story of the development of deep time, see Gould, 1987.

12. See Daniel, 1988.

13. Darwin's *The Origin of Species* appeared in 1859. Enuma Elish came to the attention of the public in 1873. See Heidel, 1942, p. 2, for the details. These two events eroded confidence in the Old Testament and the Genesis cosmogony and gave rise to paleontology. See Anderson, 1984, p. 1, for details.

14. For an account of the Big Bang cosmogony of modern science, see Hawking, 1988, or Chaisson, 1989. On the derivation from Babylonia, see Sheldrake, 1988, p. 257.

15. This point is well made in Sarna, 1966, 1970, p. 18.

16. See Sheldrake, 1988 for a full history.

17. See Heidel, 1942, p. 2.

18. From Singer, 1954, 1967, p. l.

19. From Singer, 1954, 1967, p. li.

20. For the pattern of agriculture, for example, see Renfrew, 1989.

21. See Lee, 1988.

CHAPTER 5. THE THREE DYNAMICAL EPOCHS

1. His papers on this subject are collected in his terrific book. See Zeeman, 1977.

2. My papers on this subject are collected in Abraham, 1985.

3. One of the pioneers of this dynamical model of history is Colin Renfrew, who has used systems dynamics and catastrophe theory in his description of prehistorical transformations such as the urban and agricultural revolutions. See, for example, Daniel, 1988, and Renfrew and Poston, 1979. Riane Eisler, a more recent pioneer, has written extensively about social transformations such as the patriarchal takeover in dynamical systems terms, in Eisler, 1987b. See also Abraham, 1986 and Abraham, 1987a.
4. See Abraham and Shaw, 1992, parts 1 and 2.
5. See Abraham and Shaw, 1992, part 1.
6. See Abraham and Shaw, 1992, part 3.
7. See Lorenz, 1963.
8. For a pictorial introduction to all of these technical concepts, see Abraham and Shaw, 1992.
9. Christopher Zeeman, personal communication. This theory is compatible with Sheldrake's Hypothesis of Formative Causation and theory of morphic resonance. See Sheldrake, 1988.
10. Adapted from Chorlton, 1983.
11. See Auel, 1980 for a fantasy on the intelligence of *Homo erectus*.
12. This revolution occurred at different times in different places. According to one theory, it spread in waves of diffusion from various centers. See Renfrew, 1989 for a review.
13. Regarding the space-time patterns of this transformation, see Renfrew, 1989; and Gamkrelidze, 1990.
14. See Marshack, 1972; Thompson, 1989, p. 158; and Thompson, 1985, p. 94.
15. See Thompson, 1985, p. 94.
16. See Singer, 1954, 1967, pp. 195, 211, 716. See also Frankfort, 1959, p. 20, where the ancient Egyptian worldview is described as static and unchanging.
17. See Ueda, 1992; and Gleick, 1988.
18. Another division of history according to dynamical concepts may be found in Thompson, 1967, 1972, ch. 4, in which five "emergences" are described in the past 200,000 years: Culture, Society, Civilization, Industrialization, and Planetization. Leaving out Culture (200,000 B.C.) and Industrialization (A.D. 1950), the remaining events correspond very closely with our three bifurcations. This correspondence challenges us for a dynamical model for the Industrial Revolution. See also Eliade, 1949, 1959.
19. See Lovelock, 1988, 1990.
20. See Lumley, 1969; and Solecki, 1971.
21. See Shaw, 1988. Also see part 3 of this book.
22. The chaotic behavior of the solar system, still controversial, is the subject of recent work. See Peterson, 1993; see also part 3 of this book.
23. According to Marija Gimbutas. See Eisler, 1987, p. 250.
24. The General Evolution Research Group (GERG) is devoted to the midwifery of this transformation. See works by its members and *World Futures: The Journal of General Evolution.*

CHAPTER 6. THE EVOLUTION OF CONSCIOUSNESS

1. See Abraham and Shaw, 1992, part 4.
2. See Koestler, 1979.
3. See Lamarck, 1792, 1984, part 3.
4. See Lotka, 1925, ch. 30, and Vernadsky, 1944, p. 10.
5. See Chardin, 1965, pp. 13, 180–84.
6. See Chardin, 1965, pp. 148, 139, 181.
7. See Smuts, 1926.
8. The French version is Vernadsky, 1944.
9. See Koestler, 1979, pp. 23, 37.
10. For an introduction to the modern theory, see the conference proceedings edited by Jantsch or Yates, and the works referenced therein (Jantsch, 1981) and (Yates, 1989).
11. See Snyder, 1985; and Lovelock, 1988, 1990. A concise introduction to the new subject of biospherics is given in Snyder's *The Biospherics Catalogue,* along with an excellent bibliography.
12. See Abraham, 1976; Bateson, 1972; and Sheldrake, 1988.
13. See Bateson, 1979, pp. 8–12.
14. See Abraham, 1989b and the references therein.
15. See Tillich, 1971, p. 140.
16. See Chardin, 1965, pp. 257–64.
17. See Chardin, 1965, pp. 257–64.
18. See Chardin, 1965, pp. 268–72.
19. See Ferguson, 1980.
20. See Argüelles, 1987.
21. See Metzner, 1986, pp. 1–3.
22. See Abraham, 1989a.
23. See Argüelles, 1984.

PART 2. THE ORPHIC TRINITY IN MYTH

1. Among the best books on these shifts are Mellaart, 1978; Eisler, 1987b; Gimbutas, 1982; and Thompson, 1981.
2. See Eisler, 1987, for the whole story. See also Settegast, 1986.
3. See Briffault, 1965.
4. See Eisler, 1987, p. 139.

5. A recent Ph.D. thesis develops this connection in abundant detail. See Eglash, 1991.

CHAPTER 7. THE GODDESS TRIVIA

1. See Anthony, 1991.
2. This is just one of many possible evolution scenarios. For another, see Renfrew, 1972.
3. Chuang Tzu lived at roughly the same time as Pythagoras. This quotation is found in Chuang Tzu, 1964, p. 38.
4. See Tillich, 1951, 1957, 1963, p. 128.
5. For a discussion of the Mesolithic, or transitional, period, see Clark, 1980, Introduction.
6. A number of recent books are devoted to the reconstruction of this religion. See, for example, Stone, 1976; Eisler, 1987; Gimbutas, 1982; Johnson, 1988; Gadon, 1989; Briffault, 1927; Settegast, 1986; and Getty, 1991.
7. This is not firmly established before Catal Huyuk, but is indicated by backward extrapolation from the historical cultures of Egypt, Mesopotamia, Crete, India, and Greece, as well as mythological evidence from various other regions. See McLean, 1989.
8. See Getty, 1991, p. 12; see also Walker, 1985b.
9. See Walker, 1985b, p. 21, as well as George, 1992.
10. In the Middle Ages, after Boethius, the Latin form *Trivium* came to mean the lower division of the seven-part liberal arts curriculum: grammar, logic, and rhetoric. Hence the words *trivia* and *trivial*. The other four parts of the curriculum comprise the *Quadrivium*: algebra, geometry, music, and astronomy. For more information on the goddess TriVia, see Daly, 1978, pp. 75–79. Also, see Harrison, 1955, pp. 286–92; James, 1959, ch. 1; McLean, 1958; Gadon, 1989; Sjöo, 1987; and Walker, 1985b.
11. This is the title of a book by one of the greatest Sumerian scholars. See Kramer, 1956, 1988.
12. Chronology from Kramer, 1989, p. 11. Compare Dalley, 1989, p. xxi.
13. See Hooke, 1963, p. 15.
14. See Kramer, 1961, p. 93; Kramer, 1989, pp. 2, 3, and 82; and Hooke, 1963, p. 15.
15. Eventually, Ninhursag was replaced by Inanna as the Mother goddess. Inanna also belonged to a secondary triad, with her young consort, Dumuzi, and her older sister, Erishkegal.
16. See Thompson, 1981, ch. 3; and Getty, 1991, p. 18.
17. See Kramer, 1989, pp. 19, 20. This is a prime example of the shift from the Chalice to the Blade, in the theory of Riane Eisler, 1987.
18. See James, 1957, p. 213.
19. See Hooke, 1963, p. 18.
20. See Sayce, 1979, p. 313; and Hooke, 1963, p. 20.
21. See Stone, 1979, vol. 1, p. 105.
22. Regarding the Persian analogue, Ahuramazda, Mithras, and Anahita, see Voegelin, 1956, p. 49.
23. See Hooke, 1963, pp. 21, 22, and 31.
24. See Hornung, 1971, 1972, p. 66.
25. See Sayce, 1979, pp. 90, 143. Also, three results from the addition of a child to divine couple. See Hornung, 1971, 1972, p. 218. Compare Tillich, 1910, 1974, p. 85, which proposes an evolution from the triad Isis/Osiris/Horus to one trinitarian god, Osiris, and hence monotheism.
26. See Aldred, 1961, 1984, p. 100.
27. See Voegelin, 1956, pp. 88–95, on the evolution to Horus; or Tillich, 1910, 1974, p. 85, on the evolution to Osiris.
28. See Hooke, 1963, p. 24.
29. See Lamy, 1981, pp. 20, 50; and Huxley, 1979, p. 8.
30. See Green, 1990, pp. 408–12; and Legge, 1950, vol. 1, ch. 2.
31. See Aldred, 1961, 1984, p. 36, for the skeleton Osirian legend; and essay 2 by A. M. Blackman in Hooke, 1933, for a fuller account, including details of the spring festivals of Osiris. The earliest and most complete version of the Osiris legend, due to Plutarch, a priest in the temple at Delphi in the first century A.D., may be found in Legge, 1950, vol. 1, ch. 2, pp. 33–35.
32. See Daniélou, 1979, 1984, p. 22.
33. See James, 1957, pp. 162, 196; and James, 1965, p. 54.
34. See Daniélou, 1979, 1984, p. 35; and Basham, 1975, p. 14.
35. See Levy, 1963, p. 213.
36. A complete account may be found in Eisler, 1987. A controversial point in this version of prehistory is the association of the patriarchal, dominator society with the proto-Indo-Europeans. For the various sides of this debate, see Renfrew, 1987; Renfrew, 1989; Gamkrelidze and Ivanov, 1990; Mallory, 1989; Gimbutas, 1989; Skomal and Palome, 1987; and Johnson, 1988.
37. See Daniélou, 1979, 1984, p. 36.
38. See Settegast, 1986, p. 144.
39. See Nilsson, 1925, 1949, p. 18; and Nilsson, 1950, 1968, part 1.
40. See Daniélou, 1979, 1984, p. 25.
41. See Willetts, 1962, pp. xi, 44, and 50.
42. See Nilsson, 1950, 1968, ch. 15.
43. See James, 1965, p. 63.
44. See Levy, 1963.
45. See MacDonell, 1971, p. 2.
46. See Daniélou, 1985, 1987, p. 9.
47. See Santillana and von Deschend, 1969.

48. According to Barbara Walker (1985b), p. 22, there was an explicit attempt by the Brahman priesthood to replace an original feminine trinity, TriVia, by this masculine trinity.
49. See Daly, 1984, p. 89.
50. See Loye, 1989.
51. See Nilsson, 1932, 1963, p. 21.
52. See also McLean, 1989, for more triads.
53. See Daniélou, 1979, 1984. On the migration of Osiris/Isis/Horus into Serapis/Isis/Harpocrates, see Green, 1990.
54. See Settegast, 1986, p. 167.
55. See West, 1983, p. 16.
56. See Harrison, 1955, p. 286. See also Jung and Kerényi, 1949, 1963, p. 19.
57. See Graves, 1948, 1952, ch. 22. See also Wind, 1958, 1968, appendix 2, part 3, on the tripod of Apollo, the three faces of Diana, the three Graces of the Roman goddess Venus, and a host of other pagan trinities, all vestiges of TriVia.
58. See Tillich, 1910, 1974, p. 65.
59. See Graves, 1948, 1952, p. 387.
60. See Walker, 1985b, p. 24.
61. See Graves, 1957, ch. 24.
62. See Sandmel, 1979, p. 95; and Matthews, 1991, p. 94.
63. See Begg, 1985, p. 76.
64. See Chadwick, 1967, 1986, chapters 4, 5; and Legge, 1950, vol. 1, ch. 2. The development of the Christian trinity throughout the Christian Era is told in full detail in LaCugna, 1991.
65. See, for example, Panikkar, 1973.
66. For the meaning of the Christian trinities, see Tillich, 1951, 1957, 1963, vol. 3, part 4, ch. 4.
67. For the definitive discussion of the soul of the world, see Plato, *Timeus,* section 6.
68. For the story of his discovery, see Jung, 1960, 1969, p. 202.
69. See Jung, 1953, 1968, pp. 25–26.
70. For a fascinating reconstruction of this period, see Settegast, 1986. A thorough reconstruction of the gender transformation from goddesses to gods may be found in Getty, 1991.
71. The benefits of the trinitarian way are extolled uniquely in Sabelli, 1989, along with path-breaking modern applications to personal, institutional, and international therapy.

CHAPTER 8. NEW YEAR FESTIVALS

1. Written from 1900 to 1910, the second edition appeared in 1927 (Whitehead and Russell, 1927, 1960).
2. Process is epitomized in the numerical process of Chuang Tzu. See Chuang Tzu, 1964, p. 53.
3. See Gordon, 1968, p. 79.
4. See his autobiography (Kramer, 1986). His obituary appeared in the *San Francisco Chronicle* (and other papers) on November 27, 1990.
5. See Kramer, 1963, pp. 147, 281, for this theory; and McClain, 1978, for mathematical support of it. An alternative explanation of Sumerian origins is given in Sitchin, 1978.
6. The existence of the Sumerians was rediscovered by Jules Oppert in 1869. See Sitchin, 1978, p. 22.
7. See Hooke, 1963, ch. 3.
8. Actually, Herodotus wrote that the king chose any woman he wanted. See Patai, 1947, 1967, p. 88.
9. For the original dates, see Kramer, 1969, pp. 49, 63. See also Qualls-Corbett, 1988, p. 24.
10. See James, 1965, p. 197.
11. See Willetts, 1962, pp. 51, 110.
12. See Hawkes, 1968, p. 283.
13. A brief summary of Sumerian lore is given in Kramer, 1969. Longer versions of the myths may be found in Kramer, 1956, 1988, and Hooke, 1963. An excellent discussion of the significance of the Inanna cycle, very compatible with our own views, may be found in Gadon, 1989, ch. 9.
14. See Wakeman, 1973, p. 7.
15. See Langdon, 1923, p. 32; as well as Santillana and von Deschend, 1969, ch. 15.
16. See Voegelin, 1956, p. 34; and Eliade, 1949, 1959, p. 55.
17. See Hole, 1965, 1969, ch. 1.
18. See Gordon, 1968, pp. 55–60.
19. See Sitchin, 1978, p. 14.
20. See Waterfield, 1963, 1968.
21. See Thompson, 1929.
22. For more details, see Smith, 1988, pp. 29–31 and the references therein, esp. Smith's own book, Smith, 1876, 1977.
23. See Gordon, 1968, p. 116.
24. See Heidel, 1942, which is devoted to Enuma Elish and other Babylonian creation stories.
25. See Langdon, 1923, pp. 10, 16.
26. See Smith, 1876, 1977 for his own version.
27. See Cairns, 1962, p. 18.
28. See Hooke, 1963, p. 53.
29. See James, 1957, p. 191. See also Eliade, 1963, 1975, p. 48; Eliade, 1949, 1959, p. 55; and Voegelin, 1956, p. 41.
30. See Langdon, 1923, p. 20.
31. See Hooke, 1933, p. 9.
32. See Hooke, 1938, pp. 10, 12, 18.
33. For many more details, see James, 1965, p. 139; Hooke, 1963, p. 44.

34. See Oates, 1979, 1986, pp. 175–76. See also Willetts, 1962, p. 107–8, and James, 1965, pp. 141–46, as well as pp. 47–48 of essay 3 by C. J. Gadd in Hooke, 1933, which is the most detailed account of the festival, and of the creation myth as well. See also Hooke, 1963, p. 53. An alternative interpretation is argued extensively in Sitchin, 1978.

35. See Kramer, 1969; and Qualls-Corbett, 1988.

36. See essay 1, in Hooke, 1933.

37. See Frankfort, Frankfort, Wilson, and Jacobsen, 1946, 1963, p. 34; Bleeker, 1967, pp. 35–87; and Lamy, 1981, pp. 50, 86.

38. Sukkot, the Feast of Tabernacles, occurs for seven days in Tishri (October). It is part of the major festival season, with Passover and Shavuot. Passover is the festival commemorating the Exodus, while Shavuot celebrates the sacred marriage of God and Israel, the giving of the Torah. Sukkot, now the least well known of the three festivals, was, in biblical times, the most important. See Strassfeld, 1985, p. 126. See also essay 6, by W. E. O. Westerley, and essay 8, by T. H. Robinson, in Hooke, 1933; and Hooke, 1938, p. 47.

39. Primary authors on this theme are F. Legge, Henri Frankfort, and S. O. Henry. See Legge, 1950, vol. 1, ch. 2; and Frankfort, 1948, ch. 22. For a superb synthesis and further references, see Voegelin, 1956, ch. 9, sections 4 and 5. The Sukkot festival is a late form of an earlier festival of divine kingship, enthronement, and the New Year, deduced from the Enthronement Psalms by Mowinkel and other Old Testament scholars. See Voegelin, 1956, p. 287; and Eliade, 1949, 1959, p. 60.

40. See Frankfort, 1959, p. 58.

CHAPTER 9. THE LONG LINE OF ORPHISM

1. See Willetts, 1962, pp. 241–43, for details of this sacred cave.

2. The recognition of this long tradition, and its relationship to Greek Orphism, occurs in the work of G. R. S. Mead, one of the greatest scholars of the Theosophical tradition. See Mead, 1960, p. 42.

3. See Settegast, 1986, pp. 144, 250.

4. These Kurgan waves may have also brought the proto-Indo-European language to Europe. For several sides to this controversial question, see Skomal and Palome, 1987; Renfrew, 1989; Skomal and Palome, 1987; and Mallory, 1989.

5. See Michell, 1988, p. 29.

6. The case is presented in Daniélou, 1979, 1984. For example, the Cretan language has affinities with Dravidian, p. 22. Further, Samuel Noah Kramer observed the affinities of the Sumerian pantheon and the Harappan, as noted in ch. 2.

7. See the entry on Jainism by Hermann Jacobi, in Hastings, 1955, pp. 465–74.

8. See Daniélou, 1979, 1984, ch. 1, "Origins," where the Cretan Dionysus is seen as an import from India. See also Wilder's comments, Taylor, 1791, 1875, pp. 125, 158. The fact that the Sanskrit literature was unknown in Taylor's time is partly responsible for the fact that this connection is not well known today.

9. See Kerényi, 1975, ch. 1, for the etymology of the word Zeus.

10. See Settegast, 1986, p. 186.

11. For parallel versions of this myth, such as Adonis and Atys, see Legge, 1950, p. 37. Later, Zeus and Zagreus are confused.

12. See Burkert, 1977, 1985, p. 162; and Kerényi, 1976.

13. See Rohde, 1925, 1950, ch. 8, who sees Thrace as the origin of this belief; and Kerényi, 1976.

14. See Otto, 1933, 1965, ch. 2; and also Nilsson, 1950, 1968.

15. See Daniélou, 1979, 1984. The Chalcolithic period begins in different times in different places (see table 4.3).

16. See Meyer, 1987, p. 64.

17. See "Famous Orpheus" by Emmet Robbins, in Warden, 1982, pp. 3–24, for the classical references to Orpheus.

18. See Fowden, 1986, p. 29; and Warden, 1982, p. 11.

19. See Sitchin, 1978, p. 45.

20. See Eliade, 1961; and Settegast, 1986, p. 176.

21. For a full account of the early Greek evolution of these legends, see Guthrie, 1966, ch. 3.

22. See Eisler, 1920, 1991, p. 12. Eisler believed that the word Orpheus means fisher.

23. See Daniélou, 1985, 1987, p. 26, for an extensive concordance of Greek and Hindu myth. He notes that Pythagoras founded his community and Gautama became a monk in the same year, 530 B.C. On Pythagorianism, see Burkert, 1987; and Bamford's chapter in Thompson, 1987. Especially, Bamford points out (p. 11) that Osiris and Horus became Dionysus and Apollo, according to Plutarch, and Orpheus mediates between these two.

24. A recent translation is found on p. 126 of Guthrie, 1987.

25. See Guthrie, 1966, p. 16; and West, 1983, p. 16.

26. Quoted from Guthrie, 1966, p. 111.

27. See Harrison, 1955, p. xi, and ch. 9.

28. For a compact account of the Osiris/Isis/Horus cycle, see Hooke, 1963, 1988, pp. 66–70. For Orpheus, see Nilsson, 1935; or Warden, 1982.

29. See Hooke, 1933, ch. 4, p. 71, as well as Legge, 1950, p. 38.

30. See Guthrie, 1966.

31. See Hooke, 1963, p. 29. An early Sumerian version (Inanna and Dumuzi) in English translation may be found in Wolkstein and Kramer, 1983, while the Akkadian story (Ishtar and Tammuz) is translated in Dalley, 1989.

32. Cotton was not yet in common use at this time. These cults abstained from using wool. For more details, see Legge, 1950, vol. 1, ch. 4, p. 127. On the relationships of Bacchism, Orphism, and Pythagoreanism, see Burkert, 1977, 1985, section 2.3.

33. See Guthrie, 1966; and the discussion in Settegast, 1986, p. 199. Also, see Mckenna, 1992, pp. 124–37, for a discussion of the intoxicants used.

34. See Guthrie, 1966, p. 69.

35. See Cross, 1976, p. 329.

36. See Warden, 1982, p. ix, based on Guthrie's translation.

37. See Nilsson, 1935, p. 198.

38. The Orphic Hymns that have come down to us probably date from the early Christian period, when they were used in mystic Dionysiac ceremonies associated with Demeter. See Athanassakis, 1977, introduction.

39. See Daniélou, 1979, 1984, p. 28. This is consistent with Kramer's opinion that the Sumerian pantheon derived from the Indus River civilizations.

40. Diodorus explains this in great detail in the first volume of his world history, Oldfather, 1963. For modern commentary, see Burkert, 1987; and Meyer, 1987.

41. See Harrison, 1955, p. xi and ch. 10.

42. See Meyer, 1987, p. 20, and the discussion in Settegast, 1986, p. 157, where this legend is compared to the myth of Isis in Egypt.

43. See the inspired discussion in Tillich, 1910, 1974, p. 90.

44. See Taylor, 1791, 1875, including the introduction by Wilder.

45. See Wasson, 1978, ch. 1, and also ch. 3, for a description of the mysteries.

46. For an excellent survey of Greek Orphism, see Mead, 1960, pp. 36–57.

47. See Curtius, 1948, 1953, p. 106.

48. See Godwin, 1981, p. 132.

49. The definitive text on this concordance is Eisler, 1920, 1991.

50. See Meyer, 1987, p. 159.

51. From Reinach, 1935, p. v.

52. See Evans, 1988.

CHAPTER 10. CREATION MYTHS

1. For the original graphics, see Ueda, 1992; and Lorenz, 1963. See Abraham and Shaw, 1992, part 2, for details and further references.

2. See Ruelle and Takens, 1971. This paper was rejected on its first submission.

3. See May, 1976.

4. See Shaw, 1988; Saperstein, 1984; and Langs, 1987.

5. See Liddell, 1978, p. 446. See also Santillana and von Deschend, 1969, p. 46.

6. See Hastings, 1955, p. 125.

7. See Sheldrake, 1988, pp. 255–58, for an account of the role of myth in general evolution theory.

8. See McKechnie, 1979

9. See Voegelin, 1956, p. 14.

10. See Hastings, 1955, pp. 125–76.

11. See Eisler, 1987, ch. 4, for a study of this transformation. See also Getty, 1991, p. 17.

12. Riane Eisler, private communication. See also Stone, 1979, vol. 1, pp. 99–130.

13. See Langdon, 1923, pp. 17–20.

14. From Eisler, 1987, pp. 21, 64; also Campbell, 1974, pp. 77, 157; and Stone, 1979, p. 82. Nammu may also denote chaos.

15. From Stone, 1979, vol. 1, p. 107.

16. See Sayce, 1979, pp. 376, 377; and Heidel, 1942, p. 61.

17. See Frankfort, Frankfort, Wilson, and Jacobsen, 1946, 1963, p. 184; Walker, 1985, p. 27; and Eliade, 1949, 1959, p. 15.

18. In the celestial interpretation of Santillana and von Deschend, 1969, Apsu and Tiamat represent the celestial equator and the ecliptic (see p. 153). Alternatively, Tiamat is the Milky Way (see p. 262). In the climatic interpretation of Claiborne, 1970, Tiamat rules the chaotic schedule of floods of the Tigris and Euphrates rivers, which flow into the Red Sea (see p. 281). Among the Arabs, the Red Sea is called Tiamat; see Getty, 1991, p. 18. According to Neumann, a student of Jung (Neumann, 1955), Apsu represented the waxing patriarchal, and Tiamat the waning matriarchal, aspects of society (see footnote 8 on p. 213). Also (p. 213), they represent the male and female aspects of the *uroboros*, that is, the fundamental dichotomy. They are identical (p. 213) to *Tohu* and *Bohu* of Genesis. Tiamat is older and more fundamental than Apsu. She is the irrational power of the

collective unconscious (p. 214). She holds the tables of fate, the astrological constellations (p. 226).

19. See Sayce, 1979, p. 377.
20. See Roberts, 1972, p. 16.
21. See Santillana and von Deschend, 1969, p. 262.
22. This theory is developed in Thompson, 1978, pp. 46–48.
23. See Roberts, 1972, p. 45.
24. From the entry by Sayce, in Hastings, 1955, vol. II, pp. 128–29.
25. See Heidel, 1942, p. 14; and Dalley, 1989, p. 228.
26. See Graves, 1957, p. 35.
27. Circa 3500 B.C. (Eisler, 1987), ch. 4.
28. See the entry by Sayce, in Hastings, 1955, vol. II, p. 128.
29. See p. 387 in Sayce, 1979.
30. From Frankfort, Frankfort, Wilson, and Jacobsen, 1946, 1963, p. 184. See also Dalley, 1989, p. 233.
31. See Huxley, 1979, p. 20, for an excellent summary of the whole story. He associates Enkidu with the constellation Orion, Marduk with Pegasus, and Anu with the celestial equator.
32. Recall that these older gods are more than gods, they are theogonic principles, as defined by Frank Cross (Cross, 1976).
33. See Langdon, 1923, p. 15.
34. From Langdon, 1923, pp. 12–16, 147.
35. See the entry by Sayce, in Hastings, 1955, vol. II, p. 129, and Heidel, 1942, p. 75. Also Langdon, 1923, pp. 66–67, explains that Mummu is the Logos, the creative principle and messenger of Apsu. Mummu is translated as *chaos* by Sayce (Sayce, 1903, p. 388), while Damascius has identified this with the intelligible world of Plato's ideas.
36. Compare also the Hindu cosmogony from Buhler, 1886, 1969, pp. 1–14.
37. See Sayce, 1903, p. 238.
38. See Aldred, 1961, 1984, pp. 72, 84, 100.
39. See Voegelin, 1956, pp. 77–91.
40. See Bleeker, 1967, p. 39; and Frankfort, Frankfort, Wilson, and Jacobsen, 1946, pp. 30–32.
41. See Claiborne, 1974, p. 120.
42. More details may be found in Hooke, 1963, ch. 3.
43. See Hawkes, 1968.
44. See the entry by Burns, in Hastings, 1955, vol. II, p. 146.
45. See Athanassakis, 1983, p. 16.
46. See, for example, Athanassakis, 1983, p. 7.
47. See Kirk, 1957, p. 26.
48. See Kirk, 1957, p. 26. See also Cornford, 1952.
49. See Athanassakis, 1983, p. 41.
50. See Cary, 1949, p. 183.
51. See Morris, 1978.
52. See Kirk, 1957, p. 27. However, the connection between Chaos and Tiamat may have been observed by Hesiod. See Gomperz, 1929–39, p. 41.

53. For example, see Brown, 1953, p. 56.
54. See Brown, 1953, p. 15.
55. See Hastings, 1955, p. 146. See also Harrison, 1955, ch. 12; and Gomperz, 1929–39, p. 89.
56. It's usually said that the adaptation of the word *cosmos* to indicate the order of the universe originated about this time with Pythagoras. See MacLagan, 1977, p. 20. However, it's more likely that this usage originated with Heraclitus or Parmenides, circa 500 B.C. See Hahn, 1985, appendix 1.
57. For discussion of the astral interpretation of Cronos, see Santillana and von Deschend, 1969, p. 189.
58. See Sandmel, 1979, pp. 95–96; and Matthews, 1991, p. 94. Another connection between Chaos and Sophia is made in the Hekhalot literature of early Jewish mysticism. See Gruenwald, 1980, p. 112.
59. It is in the P hand; see Hastings, 1955, p. 151, and compare with Genesis 2, in the J hand, discussed in Hooke, 1963, p. 105.
60. See Chamberlin, 1950, p. 17.
61. See p. 213 of Neumann, 1955.
62. See Gunkel, 1964, for a full discussion of this concordance. Also, p. 176 of Hooke, 1933.
63. See Wolff, 1951, p. 389. Also, there is an entire chapter on *Tohu wabohu,* beginning on p. 75.
64. See also Anderson, 1984, p. 26.
65. For all this and more, see Gorg, 1980.
66. See Graves, 1964, p. 21.
67. See Niditch, 1985, p. 12.
68. See Voegelin, 1956, p. 289; and Eliade 1949, 1959, p. 60.
69. See Eliade, 1963, 1975, p. 48, and the references and discussion therein. Also, see Voegelin, 1956, p. 307.
70. See Patai, 1947, 1967, p. 33.
71. See ch. 8 by A. M. Hocart, in Hooke, 1935; and Wakeman, 1973, p. 9.
72. See de Santillana, 1969, pp. 78–80, 162–63.
73. See Daniélou, 1979, 1984; Daniélou, 1985, 1987; and Buhler, 1886, 1969.
74. See Girardot, 1983.
75. See Girardot, 1983, p. 49, which also discusses the importance of ch. 42 in this connection.
76. See Girardot, 1983, p. 81.
77. Compare the Sanskrit Rig Veda, Hymn 190 of Mandala X, where there is no contest: *Universal form and harmony were born of cosmic will, . . .*

CHAPTER 11. CHAOS AND COSMOS

1. For extensive discussion of this conflict in the Babylonian context, see Frankfort, Frankfort, Wilson,

and Jacobsen, 1946, 1963, p. 187. Gunkel referred to this battle theme as the *Chaoskampf*. See Anderson, 1984, introduction, for extensive discussion of this.

2. See Santillana and von Deschend, 1969, p. 188, for the celestial interpretations.
3. See p. 298 of Voegelin, 1956.
4. See Getty, 1991, pp. 20, 23.
5. See Kirk, 1957, p. 68. Besides Marduk and Tiamat in Enuma Elish, there is the victory of the storm god over the dragon in the Hurrian-Hittite story Illuyanka; and the daily struggle of the Egyptian Sun god Re with the dragon Apophis.
6. Chaos meant disorder for Anaximander. For details, see Hahn, 1985.
7. See Eisler, 1987, pp. 86–87. Note that there are different kinds of creation: creation from nothing, creation from within, creation from without. See Eisler, 1987, p. 28, for a similar distinction between *actualization power* and *domination power*.
8. See James, 1965, p. 63.
9. See Gunkel, 1964, p. 26; and Hooke, 1963, p. 119. A more complete discussion is given in Heidel, 1942, pp. 98–101.
10. See Sarna, 1966, 1970, ch. 1.
11. See Sarna, 1966, 1970, p. 21. See also Heidel, 1942, pp. 102–14; Gunkel, 1895; and Hooke, 1933, pp. 9, 85, which claims that the battle of Yahweh and the dragon is derived from that of Marduk and Tiamat.
12. See Campbell, 1983.
13. See Thompson, 1985, p. 42.
14. Fragment 118 (Wheelwright, 1959, pp. 102–3).
15. Revelation 12:7–9, from Chamberlin, 1950.
16. In Revelation 20:2–3. See the discussion in Wolff, 1951, p. 183.
17. This is mentioned in Hooke, 1933, p. 85, and there is an extensive analysis by Hermann Gunkel in Anderson, 1984, ch. 1 (originally written in 1895).
18. See Wright, 1957, p. 101. Also, a comparison of a dozen or so Near Eastern cosmic battle myths may be found in Wakeman, 1973.
19. From section 4, *The motive for creation: the world a unique copy of a unique, perfect and eternal model,* of the *Timeaus.* See also section 21, *Description of the primitive chaos.*
20. See Gomperz, 1929–39, p. 213.
21. See Stone, 1980, p. 101.
22. See p. 105 in Scholem, 1960, 1965, 1969, p. 105.
23. A modern interpretation of the basic opposition of chaos to cosmos, in thermodynamic terms, is given in Thompson, 1985, p. 42.
24. See Glass, 1979.
25. The idea of a fall from an ideal society in the past is utopian. See Tillich, 1971, p. 125, in which a tri-

adic utopian process is described: the original utopian state, the fall into the present condition, and the yearning for a restoration.
26. See Eisler, 1987, p. 137. This sequence could also be interpreted as a chaotic transient between static attractors. Chaotic transients are typical of bifurcations, and are neither good nor bad.
27. For another very interesting theory of social transformation and chaos, see Turner, 1977.
28. See Voegelin, 1956, p. 34.
29. For the entire myth, see Wolkstein, 1983. For additional feminist interpretation, see Perera, 1981.
30. For details and a complete analysis, see Warden, 1982.
31. See Langs, 1987, for details on the structure of the unconscious system.
32. See Thompson, 1985, pp. 42, 98.
33. Abraham, quoted in Gleick, 1988, p. 52.
34. For other, closely related reenchantment proposals, see Berman, 1981; and Sheldrake, 1991.

CHAPTER 12. GAIA AND EROS

1. For discussion of this quaternity, see Frankfort, Frankfort, Wilson, and Jacobsen, 1946, 1963, p. 150.
2. See Nilsson 1925, 1949, p. 74.
3. See James, 1957, pp. 162–65.
4. For more detail, see Carson, 1986; and Jung and Kerényi, 1949, 1963, p. 53.
5. See Athanassakis, 1983, p. 42.
6. See Hayles, 1990, p. 20.
7. See Harrison, 1963, p. 68; and Spretnak, 1978, 1984, p. 45.
8. See Duerr, 1978, 1985, p. 27.
9. See Duerr, 1978, 1985, p. 21.
10. See Thompson, 1985, p. 164; and Ashe, 1976, 1988, p. 10.
11. See Cassirer, 1932, 1953, p. 10.
12. See Anderson, 1984, p. 25; and Bamford, 1993, p. 289.
13. See Thompson, 1987, p. 16.
14. See Duerr, 1978, 1985, p. 209.
15. See Harrison, 1955, pp. 657–58.
16. See Ulansey, 1989, p. 120.
17. Taken from Burkert, 1977, 1985, p. 152.
18. See Qualls-Corbett, 1988, p. 17.
19. See May, 1969, p. 94; and Curtius, 1948, 1953, p. 122.
20. See Cassirer, 1963, p. 131.
21. See Warden, 1982, p. 208.
22. See Warden, 1982, p. 208. Also, on Eros in the Renaissance Neoplatonism of Ficino, Pico, and

Bruno, see Yates, 1964; and Cassirer, 1932, 1953, p. 10. On Eros in the Middle Ages, see Bamford, 1993.

CHAPTER 13. THE WHEEL

1. From Johnson, 1988, p. 50.
2. See Gladwin, 1970.
3. See Solecki, 1971; Pfeiffer, 1982, ch. 6; and Lumley, 1969.
4. See Solecki, 1971; and also Pfeiffer, 1982, ch. 7.
5. See Leroi-Gourhan, 1968; and Pfeiffer, 1982, ch. 7.
6. See Marshack, 1972.
7. See Santillana and von Deschend, 1969.
8. This may be the explanation of the fact that the Mayans had developed toys with wheels, yet did not have actual pottery wheels. See Brunowski, 1973, p. 194; and Gladwin, 1947, p. 356.
9. See Leroi-Gourhan, 1968.
10. See Gimbutas, 1989, p. 165.
11. This partnership is basic to Taoism also. See Hoff, 1983.
12. See Michell, 1990, pp. 42, 62.
13. A theory of three nuclei has been suggested in Renfrew, 1989; and Gamkrelidze, 1990.
14. See Settegast, 1986, pp. 225, 228.
15. See, for example, Lockyer, 1897; or Santillana and von Deschend, 1969.
16. See Gordon, 1968, ch. 2.
17. See Harris, 1986; and Derringer, 1968.
18. See Mayer, 1977.
19. See Moran, 1953, 1969.
20. See Eisler, 1987, p. 43; and compare Settegast, 1986.
21. See Lamy, 1981, p. 71.
22. See Settegast, 1986, p. 234.
23. See Singer, 1954, 1967, ch. 9, Rotary Motion, by V. Gordon Childe, especially pp. 202–4.
24. See Claiborne, 1970, p. 365.
25. See Wainwright, 1989.
26. See Hawkins, 1965, p. vi.
27. Charles Piazzi Smyth (1819–1900) had arrived in 1865 to measure the Great Pyramid. His results were published in his books of 1867, 1870, and 1884. The first of these had inspired Sir Flinders Petrie, who arrived at the pyramid in 1880, as described in ch. 9.
28. According to Bruno's theory, described in a later chapter, the Egyptian calendar was correct, it was Earth's orbit that changed.
29. Isaac Newton was obsessed with the history of the armillary sphere, which he called the *primitive sphere*. For details on the importance of this astro-

nomical device for the Odyssey of the Argonauts, see Manuel, 1963.
30. For details of the Antikythera device, see Price, 1974.

CHAPTER 14. ORPHEUS REVISITED

1. Since published as Abraham, McKenna, and Sheldrake, 1992.
2. See Apollodorus, 1976, p. 21; and Hogart, 1993, pp. 20–22.
3. Found in Virgil, 1990, Book 4.
4. See Warden, 1982, p. 13.
5. For a line-by-line comparison of the Virgil and Ovid versions, see W. S. Anderson's essay, in Warden, 1982.
6. For an excellent synthesis of this mythogenesis, see Getty, 1991.
7. See Warden, 1982, p. 4.
8. See Eisler, 1987, p. xx.
9. See Curtius, 1948, 1953, p. 107.
10. In the *Symposium*. See the chapter by Robbins, in Warden, 1982, p. 17.
11. See Strauss, 1971, p. 18 and the references therein.
12. Found in Cocteau, 1970, p. 76.
13. For additional discussion of Orphogenesis, see Segal, 1989, chapter 7.

CHAPTER 15. CELESTIAL ORDER

1. For discussion and extension of this basic question on the stability of the universe, and the related assumption *I can always do it again,* see Schutz, 1973, p. 7. Here are found also the references to USW in Husserl.
2. The first (1967) edition of my mechanics text (Abraham and Marsden, 1978, 1982) is devoted to this problem. Also, Derrida argues that USW is the essence of mathematical idealization in general, in Derrida, 1962, 1978, 1989, p. 135.
3. Actually, there were seven charges against Bruno by the Inquisition. For a full and careful version of Bruno's trial, see Manuel, 1979, ch. 8.
4. See Manuel, 1979, p. 240. Even recently, new theories were proposed for the burning of Bruno and the imprisonment of Galileo (Lerner, 1986).
5. Quoted from Besant, 1913.
6. See Manuel, 1963, p. 177.
7. See McLachlan, 1941, 1972, p. 117, for more details and analysis.

8. See McLachlan, 1941, 1972, p. 124.
9. See Winstanley, 1941, 1965.
10. See Schwartz, 1992, p. 18.
11. On the relationship between Barrow and Newton, see Westfall, 1980, p. 99.
12. See Hall, 1963, 1981, p. 278.
13. For many further details, read Westfall, 1980, p. 206.
14. Read Westfall, 1980, p. 310, for more about this subject; and Force, 1985, p. 108.
15. See Hall, 1963, 1981, p. 278.
16. See Manuel, 1963, p. 8.
17. See Fauvel, 1988, p. 175.
18. See Force, 1985, pp. 101, 34, 138; and Westfall, 1980, p. 390.
19. See Force, 1985, pp. 50, 52.
20. For evidence of Newton's approval, see Force, 1985, p. 49.
21. See Force, 1985, p. 41.
22. See Force, 1985, pp. 44, 45.
23. See Manuel, 1963, p. 144.
24. See Stecchini, 1973, p. 23; Fauvel, 1988, p. 175; and Force, 1985, pp. 52, 53. For criticism of Whiston's theories, see Manuel and Manuel, 1979, p. 454.
25. For additional details, see Force, 1985, pp. 34, 138; and Westfall, 1980, p. 390.
26. See Fauvel, 1988, p. 161.
27. See Stecchini, 1973, p. 23; and Force, 1985, p. 18.
28. See McLachlan, 1941, 1972, pp. 129, 147; and Manuel, 1963, p. 172.
29. This was one of the main topics in the Newton-Leibniz debates. See Merchant, 1980.
30. See Force, 1985, pp. 18, 22, 108, 112, 113; Stecchini, 1973, p. 23; Whiston, 1749, pp. 227, 293, 294; Westfall, 1980, p. 834; and McLachlan, 1941, 1972, pp. 161, 162.
31. For Whiston's view of this, see McLachlan, 1941, 1972, p. 162.
32. For Newton and Whiston, see Force, 1985, p. 23; Stecchini, 1973, p. 24; and Whiston, 1749, p. 292. For further analysis of the chronology, see Manuel, 1963. Regarding Newton's alchemy, see Dobbs, 1975, as well as Rattansi, 1972; and Westfall, 1972.
33. See Stecchini, 1973.
34. See Stecchini, 1973; and Merchant, 1980, p. 281.
35. See Santillana and von Deschend, 1969, p. 9.

CHAPTER 16. CELESTIAL CHAOS

1. See Bauer, 1984, p. 69.
2. See Numbers, 1977, for the history of this theory from its origin in 1796 to its demise around 1900.
3. For a more complete version of this story with technical details, see Moser, 1973, especially the historical details on p. 8; Abraham and Marsden, 1978, 1982; and Arnold, 1990, p. 71.
4. For discussion of this point, see Spencer, 1967, p. xxi. A compact technical summary of the stability question, as of 1831, may be found in Somerville, 1831, ch. 6, especially p. 288.
5. See Kennedy, 1983, p. 83.
6. See Kovalevskaya, 1978, p. 221.
7. See Kennedy, 1983, p. 221; and Kovalevskaya, 1978, p. 227.
8. See Kovalevskaya, 1978, p. 228. See Oakley, 1966, p. 215, for background on King Oscar II.
9. See Dantzig, 1954, 1968, p. 5.
10. See Bell, 1945, p. 416, for a compact summary of this innovation, and the entry on Poincaré by Dieudonne in Gillispie, 1970, for a more technical history.
11. Originally, Poincaré thought he had proved stability, but an error was discovered, and the prize manuscript had to be revised several times.
12. He acknowledged his debt to Whiston. See Force, 1985, p. 169.
13. The main publications are Velikovsky, 1950, republished in paperback in 1977 (Velikovsky, 1952–77), and Velikovsky, 1955.
14. See Mage, 1978, p. 2.
15. This formulation is adapted from Mage, 1978.
16. See Velikovsky, 1977, p. 7, for the definitive statement in Velikovsky's own words.
17. See Mage, 1978; Bauer, 1984; Grazia, 1966; and Goldsmith, 1977.
18. For a lengthy discussion of these two problems, see Abraham and Marsden, 1978, 1982, introduction and conclusion of the first edition.
19. See Abraham and Shaw, 1992, part 3, Global Behavior.
20. See Stewart, 1989. In the language of the algorithmic information theory of Gregory Chaitin, data of this kind (of natural chaos) is called *deep data*. This notion is originally due to C. H. Bennett. See Chaitin, 1977.
21. See Lovelock, 1988, 1990, p. 43; and Levenson, 1989, p. 30.
22. See Dyson, 1992, p. viii.
23. Particularly good on this crucial bifurcation is Westfall, 1980, around p. 319. About the close call by a comet in March 1989, see Peterson, 1993. For the close approach of 1991BA in January 1991, see Shaw, 1994.
24. See Stewart, 1989, p. 260; and Peterson, 1993.

CHAPTER 17. GAIAN FEVERS

1. Many books are devoted to this theme. One of the most readable, though now dated, is Claiborne, 1970. See also Tetsuro, 1961, 1988; and Tickell, 1977, 1986.
2. For the other, Carlton Coon has proposed that a period of drought inspired the incursions by nomads, which resulted in the birth of civilization in Sumer. See Turner, 1980, p. 38; and Demeo, 1991. The beginnings of horseback riding may also have been involved in this complex social bifurcation.
3. See Clark, 1980, pp. 39–40.
4. See Frankfort, 1959, p. 34.
5. See Oldfather, 1963, p. 125, for a discussion of Herodotus and other early historians on this subject. Diodorus describes a Niloscope at Memphis.
6. See Rampino, 1987, ch. 1; and Lamb, 1982, p. 83.
7. See Waterbury, 1979.
8. See Pearson, 1978, p. 23.
9. See Rampino, 1987, p. 23.
10. See Ladurie, 1967, 1988.
11. See Fritts, 1976; and in Ladurie, 1967, 1988, the bibliography at p. 397.
12. See Daniel, 1988, p. 178; and Ladurie, 1967, 1988, p. 403.
13. From Singer, 1954, 1967, p. ii. See also Pearson, 1978, p. 104.
14. Hutton (1726–97), who studied alchemy, chemistry, and mathematics under MacLauren, was the founder of modern geology. He understood rhythm in evolution of Earth over geological time, as set forth in his works of 1785, 1788, 1794, and 1795. See Hutton, 1973. See also Lovelock, 1988, 1990, p. 10.
15. For more details of this tale, see Chorlton, 1983; and Imbrie, 1986.
16. The full account may be found in Chorlton, 1983; and Imbrie, 1986.
17. See also Chorlton, 1983, p. 107.
18. See Cornwall, 1970, p. 140; Claiborne, 1970, p. 120; and Levenson, 1989, p. 37.
19. For the history and synopsis of these events, see Lovelock, 1988, 1990), pp. 8, 35.
20. See Lovelock, 1988, 1990, ch. 3.
21. For details on this model, and many other novel and important ones, see Lovelock, 1991.
22. See Donovan, 1968, p. 80.
23. See Levenson, 1989, p. 38.
24. See Ghil, 1983.
25. For an analysis of the paleoclimatic record in the context of chaos theory, see Nicolis, 1989, appendix.
26. See Lovelock, 1988, 1990.
27. This point is made very convincingly by English mathematician David Rand, in the 1989 British television documentary *Chaos, the New Science.*
28. For a detailed scenario, see Ephron, 1988; and Chorlton, 1983, ch. 5.
29. See Pearson, 1978, ch. 11, for a modern summary; and Demeo, 1991, for the current frontier of this idea.

CHAPTER 18. ERODYNAMICS

1. For a concise summary of evolution theory, see Sheldrake, 1988, p. 243.
2. The original articles of 1914 were reprinted in a book in 1916, and again in Newman, 1956, vol. 4, pp. 2136–57.
3. See Goodwin, 1991.
4. See Bateson, 1972, p. 68.
5. See Lewin, 1936.
6. See Thom, 1972, or the English translation, Thom, 1975.
7. For all of these cusp models, see Zeeman, 1977. For other psychological applications, see Postle, 1980.
8. See Abraham, Mayer-Kress, Keith, and Koebbe, 1991, for a description of this relatively inaccessible paper.
9. See Callahan, 1987.
10. See Saperstein and Mayer-Kress, 1988.
11. The inspiration for this model is Morito, 1986. Can this be love?
12. This is the classical prisoner's dilemma; see Axelrod, 1984.

SUMMARY OF PART 3

1. See, for example, Tickell, 1977, 1986; and Tetsuro, 1961, 1988.
2. See Clark, 1980, p. 57.
3. See Demeo, 1991. See also Sears, 1960.
4. See Turner, 1980, p. 38.

CONCLUSION

1. I want to thank Paul Lee, Harry Bunham, Dharshi Bopegedra, and Terence McKenna for making me add these warnings.
2. See Tillich, 1971, p. 134.

GLOSSARY

Academe: Plato's school in Athens; the first university in the European tradition.

agriculture: Revolutionary new life strategy discovered around 10,000 B.C.

Alexandrian library: The library of the Museion in Alexandria, Egypt.

Alexandrian Museion: The third university in the European tradition; founded around 300 B.C. in Alexandria, Egypt.

Anatolia: Early centers of civilization, such as Catal Huyuk, now in Turkey.

androcracy: Type of social organization in which one gender or class dominates another.

archaeology: Study of prehistoric human life.

attractor: Region in the domain of a dynamical system that attracts all nearby states.

Bacchus: Roman name for Dionysos, primary god of Crete and ancient Greece.

basin: The set of all initial states that share one attractor as final destination.

bifurcation: Significant change in the portrait of attractors and basins of a dynamical system, as its rules are changed.

bifurcation, catastrophic: Type of bifurcation in which an attractor suddenly appears or disappears.

bifurcation, explosive: Type of bifurcation in which the size of an attractor suddenly changes.

bifurcation, subtle: Type of bifurcation in which an attractor subtly changes its character. For example, a periodic attractor becomes subtly chaotic.

Chalcolithic: Historic period characterized by the working of bronze; the Bronze Age.

chaos: In Hesiod, the gap between heaven and earth; one of the fundamental forces of the Orphic trinity; in ordinary parlance since classical Greece, a state of disorder; in chaos theory, a dynamical system that is neither static nor periodic.

Chaos Revolution: Series of paradigm shifts affecting the sciences since around 1970.

chaos theory: Pop name for dynamical systems theory, a branch of mathematics.

chaotic behavior: In chaos theory, dynamical behavior that is neither static nor periodic.

Christian trinity: The three principles of God the Father, the Son, and the Holy Spirit.

chronology: Listing of events in temporal sequence.

cognitive map: Mental image empowering thinking, for an individual (the individual cognitive map, or ICM) or for a culture (the cultural cognitive map, or CCM).

comets: Planetoids on very eccentric elliptic (or even hyperbolic) orbits around the Sun.

complex dynamical system: A dynamical system consisting of a number of component dynamical systems connected in a network.

cosmogony: Creation myth describing how the cosmos is created.

cosmos: The ordered universe; also, the patriarchal order of society.

Cro-Magnon: Human species following *Homo erectus,* from which our species, *Homo sapiens,* is thought to have evolved.

cultural anthropology: Study of cultures, and their history and evolution.

culture: Social system that is taught and learned by successive generations.

cybernetics: Way of thinking created during World War II by a group of novel intellectuals, including Gregory Bateson and Norbert Weiner.

cyclic behavior: Dynamical behavior in which a cycle of states reoccur over and over, each cycle taking the same time, the period of the cycle; also called periodic behavior.

Dionysos: One of the primary gods of ancient Crete, Mycenae, and Greece; consort of Semele, the Earth goddess.

dischaos: State of inadequate chaos, the result of an obsession with order.

disorder: State of inadequate order, the result of an obsession with chaos.

dynamical historiography: Theory of history in which dynamical concepts are used to conceptualize the metapatterns of history and prehistory.

dynamical system: Mathematical model in which states of a natural system are modeled by points in a geometrical space, and movement is specified by unchanging rules that are attached to the points in the space.

Eleusinian mysteries: Orphic rituals performed at rare intervals at Eleusis in ancient Greece.

Eleusis: Location near Athens, center of the Orphic religion in ancient times.

epoch: Divisions of history on the largest scale.

epoch, chaotic: Historical epoch beginning with the Chaos Revolution in the 1970s.

epoch, periodic: Historical epoch from the Wheel Revolution (ca. 3500 B.C.) up to the Chaos Revolution (ca. 1970).

epoch, static: Historical epoch from the Agricultural Revolution (ca. 10,000 B.C.) until the Wheel Revolution (ca. 3500 B.C.).

erodynamics: New style in the social sciences, characterized by dynamical models, computer simulation, and the methods of chaos theory.

Eros: In Hesiod, the creative principle connecting Chaos and Gaia, one of the fundamental forces of the Orphic trinity; later in the ancient world, a god of love; in Christianity, *agape,* divine love; eventually, the attraction of sex or romance.

etiology: Creation theory.

evolution: Modern form of the myth of progress, in which things somehow keep growing and improving without death.

Gaia: In Hesiod, the material universe, space and time, matter and energy; one of the fundamental forces of the Orphic trinity.

Gaia Hypothesis: Theory due to James Lovelock and Lynn Margulis, in which all systems of the planet Earth are interconnected in a single intelligent system.

Gaian fever: A term introduced by James Lovelock as a synonym for interglacial, the brief periods between Ice Ages.

general evolution theory: Variant form of general systems theory, in which evolution is seen as a universal pattern observed in all natural systems.

general systems theory: Theory, created by von Bertalanffy, in which complex systems are viewed holistically, as amounting to more than the sum of the parts.

GR wave: gylanic resurgence wave, a conception of Riane Eisler, in which the gylanic (gender partnership, cooperative, peace-loving) culture violently repressed by the androcracy around 3500 B.C. wells up from the racial unconsciousness in a brief renaissance.

grok: Synonym for hermeneutic.

gylany: Term introduced by Riane Eisler for a partnership society, such as that of the goddess culture of the late Paleolithic.

harmony of the spheres: Pythagorean cosmology in which the universe is seen as a system of concentric spheres, vibrating in harmony.

hermeneutics: Dualistic cognitive theory, in which the observer and the observed are locked in a tight embrace of interaction; the science of interpretation.

hermeticism: Style of philosophy traditionally ascribed to Thrice Greatest Hermes, the divine who gave writing to the ancient Egyptians; the world is seen as a complex of living intelligences, connected by forces beyond our ken; magic and astrology are derived from this tradition, popular in the Hellenistic world (especially Alexandria) and in the Florentine Renaissance.

Hesiod: Early Greek poet (seventh century B.C.), author of *Theogony* and *Works and Days.*

historiography: Theory of history.

history: Story of human societies; written story of human societies.

Homo erectus: Grandparent of our human species; the "cave people" who colonized the entire planet; skilled in sailing, stone tools and industries, celestial navigation, archaeoastronomy, and archaeomathematics.

Ice Age: The state of Earth's climate, most of the time, about five degrees Fahrenheit colder than the present; large sheets of ice cover all but the tropics; ocean level hundreds of feet lower than now.

interglacial: See *Gaian fever.*

Interglacial, Holocene: The official name for the Gaian fever we live in, which made the agricultural revolution possible.

Lykeion: Aristotle left Plato's Academe and founded this competing institution; the second university in the European tradition.

matriarchy: Dominator form of society (androcracy) in which women are the dominant gender.

Megalithic: Meaning, "with very large rocks"; for example, a Megalithic monument such as Stonehenge, or a Megalithic society such as ancient Egypt.

Memphis trinity: The three divines of Memphis, ancient Egypt: Osiris, his mate Isis, and their child, Horus.

Mesolithic: A middle age between the late Paleolithic and the early Neolithic.

metahistory: The history of history; a theory of history; the pattern that connects all of history.

morphogenesis: The process of pattern formation.

mythogenesis: The evolutionary process, within the cultural field or cognitive map of a society, in which myths are created, transformed, and maintained.

mythography: The study and mapping of mythogenesis.

Neanderthal: Species of human following *Homo erectus,* named after the valley of the Neander river in Germany, where remains were first found.

Neolithic, early: The period from 10,000 B.C. to 4000 B.C.

Neolithic revolution: Beginning of the Neolithic period, or New Stone Age; coincides roughly with the discovery of agriculture.

Neoplatonism: Revival of Platonic philosophy, beginning in Alexandria in the second century A.D.

Neopythagorean: Revival of Pythagorean philosophy, beginning in Athens in the fourth century B.C.

noogenesis: Term coined by Teilhard de Chardin for the evolution of the mental field of the human species.

order: Antithesis of chaos, according to the conventional patriarchal view; dischaos.

Orphic revival: Sporadic emergence of Orphic cultural values from a state of repression; examples include the Florentine Renaissance, the hippies of the 1960s.

Orphic tradition: The tradition of the prehistoric goddess and her male devotees, such as Hermes, Osiris, Dionysos, Bacchus, Orpheus, Pythagoras, Plato, and so on.

Orphic trinity: The three divine or cosmic principles of Chaos, Gaia, and Eros, introduced by Hesiod.

Orphism: The most important religion of ancient Greece, including the Eleusinian mysteries; the longer tradition, of which Greek Orphism is an integral part.

Orphism, long line of: The tradition of the goddess TriVia, from Paleolithic prehistory to the present, including the Greek Orphic form, in which the sacred trinity manifest as Chaos, Gaia, and Eros.

pagan: Pre-Christian; an epithet used by early Christians to describe outsiders.

Paleolithic: Old Stone Age; preceded the Neolithic.

Paleolithic, late: From 25,000 to 10,000 B.C.

paleontology: Study of early life forms, especially through collection of fossils.

partnership: Synonym of gylany, Riane Eisler's word for the prehistoric goddess culture, characterized by cooperation of the genders.

patriarchal takeover: Social transformation in which the partnership form was replaced by a dominator form, in which men dominated women, around 4000 B.C..

patriarchy: Dominator form of society (androcracy) in which men are the dominant gender.

phase shift: Bifurcation; paradigm shift; catastrophic transformation.

prehistory: Before writing, and written records of human events.

Pythagoras: Mythical or historical Greek philosopher; one of the line of mythical culture heroes or *Prisci Theologi,* after Hermes, Moses, and Orpheus; proponent of the cosmical model of the harmony of the spheres, and the relationship between number and harmony.

renaissance: Major social transformation, for example, the Florentine Renaissance of the fifteenth century.

sacred marriage: Basic feature of the New Year Festival of Sumer and Babylonia, Egypt and Canaan, in which the god (represented by the king) and the goddess (represented by a priestess of her temple) are married, and the dowry of fertility and good fortune is bestowed on the people.

schismogenesis: Model process, in the theory of Gregory Bateson, for the development of a division and conflict.

sociogenesis: Process of creation and change of social structures.

stability dogma: Dogmatic belief in the stability of the solar system, the biosphere, or the social system.

static behavior: Situation of a point attractor, in which all nearby states tend to rest; compare with periodic or chaotic behavior.

theogony: Type of creation myth in which the goddesses and gods come into existence.

trinity: Triple of cosmic principles, goddesses, or gods; also, a form of religious structure characterized by a triple, as opposed to a pair or single, principle.

TriVia: The three-in-one goddess of the late Paleolithic.

USW Problem: The *und so weiter* problem of Husserl; the question of the stability of the world of appearances, especially the question, Will the sun rise tomorrow morning?

wheel: The mathematical wheel, or cycle, or periodic attractor; the material wheel, used in models of the solar system, for making pots, and for propelling vehicles; the paradigm shift of 3500 B.C. or so, in which material wheels arrived along with the dominator culture they propelled.

Abraham, Ralph H. "Vibrations and the Realization of Form." In *Evolution in the Human World,* edited by Erich Jantsch and Conrad Waddington, Reading, MA: Addison-Wesley, 1976, 134–49.

———. *On Morphodynamics.* Santa Cruz, CA: Aerial Press, 1985.

———. "Mathematics and Evolution: A Manifesto." *IS Journal* 1, no. 3 (1986): 14–23.

———. "Complex Dynamics and the Social Sciences." *J. World Futures* 23 (1987a): 1–10.

———. "Mathematics and Evolution: A Proposal." *International Synergy* 2, no. 2 (1987b): 27–45.

———. "Mechanics of Resonance." *Revision* 10, no. 1 (1987c): 13–19.

———. "Social and International Synergy." *International Synergy* 7/8 (1989a): 18–26.

———. "The New Mathematics." *Dynamics Newsletter* 3, no. 5 (1989b): 3.

———. *Complex Dynamics.* Santa Cruz, CA: Aerial Press, 1990a.

———. "Erodynamics." *International Synergy* 9 (July 1990b): 2.

———. "Phase Regulation of Coupled Oscillators and Chaos." In *A Chaotic Hierarchy,* edited by Gerold Baier and Michael Klein, Singapore: World Scientific, 1991, 49–78.

Abraham, Ralph H., John B. Corliss, and John E. Dorband, "Order and Chaos in the Toral Logistic Lattice." *Int. J. Bifurcations and Chaos* 1, no. 1 (1991): 227–34.

Abraham, Ralph H. and Jerrold E. Marsden. *Foundations of Mechanics,* 2d ed. Reading, MA: Addison-Wesley, 1978, 1982.

Abraham, Ralph H., Gottfried Mayer-Kress, Alexander Keith, and Matthew Koebbe. "Double Cusp Models, Public Opinion, and International Security." *Int. J. Bifurcations and Chaos* 1, no. 2 (1991): 417–30.

Abraham, Ralph H., Terence McKenna, and Rupert Sheldrake. *Trialogues at the Edge of the West.* Santa Fe, NM: Bear, 1992.

Abraham, Ralph H. and Joel Robbin. *Transversal Mappings and Flows.* New York: Benjamin, 1967.

Abraham, Ralph H. and Christopher D. Shaw. *Dynamics, the Geometry of Behavior,* 2d ed. Reading, MA: Addison-Wesley, 1992.

Achinstein, Peter. *Concepts of Science, a Philosophical Analysis.* Baltimore: Johns Hopkins, 1968.

Al-Daffa', Ali Abdullah. *The Muslim Contribution to Mathematics.* Atlantic Highlands, NJ: Humanities Press, 1977.

Aldred, Cyril. *The Egyptians.* London: Thames and Hudson, 1961, 1984.

Anderson, Bernhard W. *Creation in the Old Testament.* Philadelphia: Fortress Press, 1984.

Anthony, David, Dimitri Y. Telegin, and Dorcas Brown. "The Origin of Horseback Riding." *Scientific American* (December 1991): 94–100.

Apollodorus. *Gods and Heroes of the Greeks.* Amherst: University of Massachusetts, 1976.

Argüelles, José. *Earth Ascending, an Illustrated Treatise on the Law Governing Whole Systems.* Boulder, CO: Shambhala, 1984.

———. *The Mayan Factor: Path Beyond Technology.* Santa Fe, NM: Bear, 1987.

Arnold, Vladimir Igorevich. *Huygens and Barrow, Newton and Hooke, Pioneers in Mathematical Analysis and Catastrophe Theory from Evolvents to Quasicrystals.* Basel: Birkhauser Verlag, 1990.

Artigiani, Robert. "Cultural Evolution." *World Futures* 23 (1987a): 93–121.

———. "Revolution and Evolution: Applying Prigogine's Dissipative Structures Model." *J. Social Biol. Struct.* 10 (1987b): 249–64.

———. "Scientific Revolution and the Evolution of Consciousness." *World Futures* 25 (1988): 237–81.

———. "Social Evolution: A Nonequilibrium Systems Model." In *The New Evolution Paradigm,* edited by Ervin Laszlo. New York: Gordon and Breach, 1991a, 93–129.

———. "Post-Modernism and Social Evolution: An Inquiry." *World Futures* 30 (1991b): 149–61.

Artigiani, Robert, Ignazio Masulli, Vilmos Csanyi, and Ervin Laszlo. *Cognitive Maps.* Vienna: Vienna Academy, May 1989.

Ashe, Geoffrey. *The Virgin, Mary's Cult and the Re-emergence of the Goddess.* London: Arkana, 1976, 1988.

Athanassakis, Apostolos N. *The Orphic Hymns, Text, Translation and Notes.* Missoula, MT: Scholars Press, 1977.

———. *Hesiod, Theogony, Works and Days, Shield: Introduction, Translation, and Notes.* Baltimore: Johns Hopkins University Press, 1983.

Auel, Jean M. *The Clan of the Cave Bear: A Novel.* New York: Crown, 1980.

Auerbach, Erich. "Figura (1944)." In *Scenes from the Drama of European Literature, Six Essays,* translated by Ralph Manheim. New York: Meridian Books, 1959, 11–76.

Axelrod, B. *The Evolution of Cooperation.* New York: Basic Books, 1984.

Badiner, Allan Hunt. *Dharma Gaia: A harvest of essays in Buddhism and Ecology.* Berkeley: Parallax Press, 1990.

Bamford, Christopher. "The Magic of Romance: The cultivation of Eros from Sappho to the Troubadors." *Alexandria* 2 (1993): 287–310.

Basham, A. L. *A Cultural History of India.* Delhi: Oxford University Press, 1975.

Bateson, Gregory. *Naven.* Cambridge: Cambridge University Press, 1936, 1958, 1966.

———. *Steps to an Ecology of Mind.* New York: Ballantine Books, 1972.

———. *Mind and Nature, a Necessary Unity.* New York: Bantam, 1979.

Bateson, Mary Catherine. *With a Daughter's Eye, a Memoir of Margaret Mead and Gregory Bateson.* New York: Morrow, 1984.

Bauer, Henry H. *Beyond Velikovsky.* Urbana: University of Illinois Press, 1984.

Begg, Ean. *The Cult of the Black Virgin.* London: Arkana, 1985.

Bell, E. T. *The Development of Mathematics.* New York: McGraw-Hill, 1945.

Benedict, Ruth. *Patterns of Culture.* New York: Houghton-Mifflin, 1934, 1959.

Berman, Morris. *The Reenchantment of the World.* Ithaca: Cornell University Press, 1981.

Berry, Thomas. *The Dream of the Earth.* San Francisco: Sierra Club, 1990.

Bertalanffy, Ludwig von. *General System Theory: A New Approach to Unity of Science.* Baltimore: Johns Hopkins Press, 1951.

———. *General System Theory: Foundations, Development, Applications.* New York: George Braziller, 1968.

Besant, Annie. *Giordano Bruno: Theosophy's Apostle in the Sixteenth Century,* a lecture delivered in the Sorbonne at Paris, on June 15, 1911, and *The Story of Giordano Bruno,* Adyar: Theosophist Office, 1913.

Black, Max. *Models and Metaphors: Studies in Language and Philosophy.* Ithaca: Cornell University Press, 1962.

Bleeker, C. J. *Egyptian Festivals: Enactments of Religious Renewal.* Leiden: E. J. Brill, 1967.

Boltzmann, Ludwig. "Model (1902)." In *Theoretical Physics and Philosophical Problems,* edited by Ludwig Boltzmann. Dordrecht: D. Reidel, 1974.

Boulding, Kenneth E. *The Image.* Ann Arbor, MI: University of Michigan Press, 1956.

Braudel, Fernand. *On History.* Chicago: University of Chicago Press, 1980.

Briffault, Robert. *The Mothers: A Study of the Origins of Sentiments and Institutions.* London: Allen, 1927.

———. *The Troubadors.* Bloomington: Indiana University Press, 1965.

Brown, Norman O. *Hesiod's Theogony.* Indianapolis: Bobbs-Merrill, 1953.

Brumbaugh, Robert S. *Plato's Mathematical Imagination: The Mathematical Passages in the Dialogues and Their Interpretation.* Bloomington: Indiana University Press, 1954.

Brunowski, J. *The Ascent of Man.* New York: Little, Brown, 1973.

Buhler, Georg. *The Laws of Manu.* New York: Dover, 1886, 1969.

Burckhardt, Jacob. *The Civilization of the Renaissance in Italy.* New York: Penguin Books, 1860, 1990.

Burke, Peter. *Vico.* Oxford: Oxford University Press, 1985.

Burkert, Walter. *Lore and Science in Ancient Pythagoreanism.* Cambridge: Harvard University Press, 1972.

———. *Greek Religion, Archaic and Classical,* translated by John Raffan. Oxford: Basil Blackwell, 1977, 1985.

———. *Ancient Mystery Cults.* Cambridge: Harvard University Press, 1987.

Bury, J. B. *The Ancient Greek Historians.* New York: Dover, 1908, 1958.

Cairns, Grace E. *Philosophies of History: Meeting of East and West in Cycle-Pattern Theories of History.* New York: Philosophical Library, 1962.

Callahan, James. "A Geometric Model of Anorexia and Its Treatment." *Behavioral Science* 27 (1982): 140–54.

Callahan, James and Jerome I. Sashin. "Models of Affect-Response and Anorexia Nervosa." In *Perspectives in Biological Dynamics and Theoretical Medicine,* edited by S. H. Koslow, A. J. Mandell, and M. F. Shlesinger. New York: New York Academy of Sciences, 1987, 241–59.

Campbell, Joseph. *The Mythic Image.* Princeton: Princeton University Press, 1974.

———. *The Way of the Animal Powers, Volume 1: Historical Atlas of World Mythology.* San Francisco: Harper & Row, 1983.

———. Campbell, Joseph. *Transformations of Myth through Time.* New York: Harper & Row, 1990.

Campbell, Joseph and Bill Moyers. *The Power of Myth.* New York: Doubleday, 1988.

Canfora, Luciano. *The Vanished Library,* translated by Martin Ryle. Berkeley: University of California Press, 1989.

Capra, Fritjof. *The Role of Physics in the Current Change of Paradigms.* Preprint, 1987.

Carson, Anne. *Eros, the Bittersweet, an Essay.* Princeton: Princeton University Press, 1986.

Cary, M. *The Oxford Classical Dictionary.* Oxford: Oxford University Press, 1949.

Cassirer, Ernst. *The Platonic Renaissance in England.* Austin: University of Texas Press, 1932, 1953.

———. *Rousseau, Kant, Goethe: Two Essays.* Princeton: Princeton University Press, 1945, 1970.

———. *The Individual and the Cosmos in Renaissance Philosophy.* New York: Harper & Row, 1963.

Ceruti, M. and E. Laszlo. *Physis: abitare la terra.* Milano: Feltrinelli, 1988.

Chadwick, Henry. *The Early Church.* New York: Dorset Press, 1967, 1986.

Chaisson, Eric. *The Life Era: Cosmic Selection and Conscious Evolution.* New York: Atlantic Monthly Press, 1989.

Chaitin, G. J. "Algorithmic Information Theory." *IBM J. Research and Development* 21 (1977): 350–59.

Chamberlin, Roy B. and Herman Feldman. *The Dartmouth Bible.* Boston: Houghton Mifflin, 1950.

Chardin, Teilhard de. *The Phenomenon of Man.* New York: Harper, 1965.

Chorlton, Windsor. *Ice Ages.* Alexandria, VA: Time-Life Books, 1983.

Chuang Tzu. *Basic Writings,* translated by Burton Watson. New York: Columbia University Press, 1964.

Claiborne, Robert. *Climate, Man, and History.* New York: Norton, 1970.

———. *The Birth of Writing.* New York: Time-Life Books, 1974.

Clark, Grahame. *Mesolithic Prelude: The Paleolithic-Neolithic Transition in Old World Prehistory.* Edinburgh: Edinburgh University Press, 1980.

Cocteau, Jean. *Two Screen Plays.* London: Calder & Boyars, 1970.

Collingwood, R. G. *The Idea of History.* Oxford: Clarendon Press, 1946.

———. *Essays in the Philosophy of History.* Austin: University of Texas Press, 1965.

Combs, Allan. *Cooperation: Beyond the Age of Competition.* Philadelphia: Gordon and Breach, 1990.

Cornford, F. M. *Greek Religious Thought from Homer to the Age of Alexander.* New York: AMS Press, 1923, 1969.

———. *Before and After Socrates.* Cambridge: Cambridge University Press, 1932, 1979.

———. *The Unwritten Philosophy and Other Essays.* Cambridge: Cambridge University Press, 1950, 1967.

———. *Principium Sapientiae.* Cambridge: Cambridge University Press, 1952.

Cornwall, Ian. *Ice Ages: Their Nature and Effects.* London: John Baker, 1970.

Creuzer, Georg Frederic. *Religions de l'antiquite.* 1825.

Critchlow, Keith. *Islamic Patterns.* New York: Schocken Books, 1976.

Cross, Frank Moore. "The 'Olden Gods' in Ancient Near Eastern Creation Myths." In Magnalia Dei, *The Mighty Acts of God: Essays of the Bible and Archaeology in Memory of G. Ernest Wright,* edited by Frank Moore Cross, Werner E. Lemke, and Patrick D. Miller, Jr. New York: Doubleday, 1976, 329–38.

Curtius, E. R. *European Literature and the Latin Middle Ages.* Princeton: Princeton University Press, 1948, 1953.

Dalley, Stephanie. *Myths from Mesopotamia: Creation, the Flood, Gilgamesh, and Others.* Oxford: Oxford University Press, 1989.

Daly, Mary. *Gyn/Ecology, the Metaethics of Radical Feminism.* Boston: Beacon Press, 1978.

———. *Pure Lust, Elemental Feminist Philosophy.* Boston: Beacon Press, 1984.

Daniel, Glyn and Colin Renfrew. *The Idea of Prehistory.* Edinburgh: Edinburgh University Press, 1988.

Daniélou, Alain. *Shiva and Dionysus, The Religion of Nature and Eros,* translated by K. F. Hurry. New York: Inner Traditions International, 1979/1984.

———. *While the Gods Play: Shaiva Oracles and Predictions on the Cycles of History and the Destiny of Mankind.* Rochester, VT: Inner Traditions, 1985, 1987.

Dantzig, Tobias. *Henri Poincaré, Critic of Crisis: Reflections on His Universe of Discourse.* New York: Greenwood Press, 1954, 1968.

Davidson, Mark. *Uncommon Sense: The Life and Thought of Ludwig von Bertalanffy (1901–1972), Father of General Systems Theory.* Los Angeles: J. P. Tarcher, 1983.

Davis, Philip J. and Reuben Hersh. *Descartes' Dream: The World According to Mathematics.* New York: Harcourt, Brace, Jovanovich, 1986.

Demeo, James. "The Origins and Diffusion of Patrism in Saharasia, c. 4000 B.C.E.: Evidence for a Worldwide, Climate-Linked Geographical Pattern in Human Behavior." *World Futures* 30 (1991): 247–71.

Derrida, Jacques. *Edmund Husserl's Origin of Geometry.* Lincoln: University of Nebraska Press, 1962, 1978, 1989.

Derringer, David. *The Alphabet: A Key to the History of Mankind.* London: Hutchinson, 1968.

Dilthey, Wilhelm. *Pattern and Meaning in History: Thoughts on History and Society.* New York: Harper, 1961, 1962.

Dobbs, Betty Jo Teeter. *The Foundations of Newton's Alchemy, or "The Hunting of the Greene Lyon."* Cambridge: Cambridge University Press, 1975.

Donovan, D. T. *Stratigraphy.* Chicago: Rand McNally, 1968.

Drower, Margaret S. *Flinders Petrie: A Life in Archaeology.* London: Gollancz, 1985.

Duerr, Hans Peter. *Dreamtime: Concerning the Boundary Between Wilderness and Civilization.* Oxford: Basil Blackwell, 1978, 1985.

Dyson, Freeman. *From Eros to Gaia.* New York: Pantheon, 1992.

Eglash, Ron. *The Cybernetics of Chaos.* Ph.D. thesis. Santa Cruz: University of California, 1991.

Eisler, Riane. "Woman, Man, and the Evolution of Social Structure." *World Futures* 23 (1987a): 79–92.

———. *The Chalice and the Blade: Our History, Our Future.* New York: Harper & Row, 1987b.

———. "Technology, Gender, and History: Toward a Non-linear model." *World Futures* 32 (1991): 207–25.

Eisler, Robert. *Orpheus, the Fisher: Comparative Studies in Orphic and Early Christian Cult Symbolism.* Kila, MT: Kessinger Publishing, 1920, 1991.

Eliade, Mircea. *Cosmos and History: The Myth of the Eternal Return,* translated by Willard R. Trask. New York: Harper & Row, 1949, 1959.

———. *Myths, Dreams, and Mysteries.* New York: Harper, 1960, 1975.

———. *Images and Symbols.* New York: Sheed and Ward, 1961.

———. *Myth and Reality.* New York: Harper, 1963, 1975.

Ellen, Roy, Ernest Gellner, Grazyna Kubica, and Janusz Mucha. *Malinowski Between Two Worlds: The Polish Roots of an Anthropological Tradition.* Cambridge: Cambridge University Press, 1988.

Ellis, Willis D. *A Source Book of Gestalt Psychology.* New York: The Humanities Press, 1950.

Engnell, Ivan. *Studies in Divine Kingship in the Ancient Near East.* Oxford: Basil Blackwell, 1967.

Ephron, Larry. *The End: The Immanent Ice Age and How We Can Stop It.* Berkeley: Celestial Arts, 1988.

Evans, Arthur. *The God of Ecstasy, Sex Roles and the Madness of Dionysos.* New York: St. Martin's Press, 1988.

Fauvel, John. *Let Newton Be.* Oxford: Oxford University Press, 1988.

Ferguson, Marilyn. *The Aquarian Conspiracy.* Los Angeles: J. P. Tarcher, 1980.

Ferguson, Wallace K. *The Renaissance.* New York: H. Holt, 1940.

———. *The Renaissance in Historical Thought.* New York: AMS Press, 1948/1981.

Feuerstein, Georg. *Structures of Consciousness: The Genius of Jean Gebser.* Lower Lake, CA: Integral Publishing, 1987.

Firth, Raymond. *Man and Culture: An Evaluation of the Work of Bronislaw Malinowski.* London: Routledge and Kegan Paul, 1957.

Fisch, Max Harold and Thomas Goddard Bergin, tr. See Vico, Giambattista.

Fishwick, Paul A. and Paul A. Luker. *Qualitative Simulation Modeling and Analysis.* New York: Springer-Verlag, 1991.

Flint, Robert. *The Philosophy of History in France and Germany.* London: William Blackwood, 1874.

Force, James E. *William Whiston, Honest Newtonian.* Cambridge: Cambridge University Press, 1985.

Forster, E. M. *Alexandria: A History and a Guide.* Garden City, NY: Anchor Books, 1961.

Fowden, Garth. *The Egyptian Hermes.* Cambridge: Cambridge University Press, 1986.

Frankfort, Henri. *Kingship and the Gods.* Chicago: University of Chicago Press, 1948.

———. *Ancient Egyptian Religion, An Interpretation.* New York: Harper, 1948, 1961.

———. *The Birth of Civilization in the Near East.* Bloomington: Indiana University Press, 1959.

Frankfort, H., H. A. Frankfort, John A. Wilson, and Thorkild Jacobsen. *Before Philosophy: The Intellectual Adventure of Man.* Baltimore: Penguin Books, 1946, 1963.

Fritts, H. C. *Tree Rings and Climate.* New York: Academic Press, 1976.

Fukuyama, Francis. *The End of History and the Last Man.* New York: Free Press, 1992.

Gadon, Elinor W. *The Once and Future Goddess: A Symbol for Our Time.* San Francisco: Harper & Row, 1989.

Gamkrelidze, Thomas V. and V. V. Ivanov. "The Early History of Indo-European Languages." *Scientific American* 259 (March 1990): 110–16.

Gardner, Howard. *The Mind's New Science: A History of the Cognitive Revolution.* New York: Basic Books, 1985.

Gebser, Jean and Noel Barsted. *The Ever-present Origin,* translated by Algis Mickunas. Athens: Ohio University Press, 1949, 1953, 1985, 1986.

George, Demetra. *Mysteries of the Dark Moon: The Healing Power of the Dark Goddess.* San Francisco: HarperSanFrancisco, 1992.

Getty, Adele. *Goddess.* London: Thames and Hudson, 1991.

Ghil, M. and J. Tavantzis. "Global Hopf Bifurcation in a Simple Climate Model." *SIAM J. Appl. Math.* 43 (1983): 1019–41.

Gillispie, Charles Coulton. *Dictionary of Scientific Biography.* New York: Scribners, 1970.

Gimbutas, Marija. *The Goddesses and Gods of Old Europe, 6500–3500 B.C.: Myths and Cult Images.* New York: Thames and Hudson, 1982.

———. *The Language of the Goddess.* San Francisco: Harper & Row, 1989.

Girardot, N. J. *Myth and Meaning in Early Taoism: The Theme of Chaos (Hun-Tun).* Berkeley: University of California Press, 1983.

Gladwin, Harold Sterling. *Men Out of Asia.* New York: McGraw-Hill, 1947.

Gladwin, Thomas. *East Is a Big Bird: Navigation and Logic on Puluwat Atoll.* Cambridge: Harvard University Press, 1970.

Glass, Leon and Michael C. Mackey. "A Simple Model for Phase Locking of Biological Oscillators." *J. Math. Biology* 7 (1979): 339–52.

Gleick, James. *Chaos: The Making of a New Science.* New York: Viking, 1988.

Glen, William. *The Road to Jaromillo: Critical Years of the Revolution in Earth Science.* Stanford: Stanford University Press, 1982.

Godwin, Joscelyn. *Mystery Religions in the Ancient World.* London: Thames and Hudson, 1981.

Goldsmith, Donald. *Scientists Confront Velikovsky.* Ithaca: Cornell University Press, 1977.

Gomperz, Theodor. *Greek Thinkers, a History of Ancient Philosophy.* London: Murray, 1929–39.

Gooch, G. P. *History and Historians in the Nineteenth Century.* Boston: Beacon Press, 1913/1959.

Goodwin, Richard. *Chaotic Economic Dynamics.* Cambridge: Cambridge University Press, 1991.

Gordon, Cyrus H. *Forgotten Scripts: Their Ongoing Discovery and Decipherment.* New York: Dorset Press, 1968.

Gorg, Manfred. "Tohu Wabohu." *Zeitschrift fur die alttestamentliche wissenchaft* 92 (1980): 431–34.

Gould, Stephen Jay. *Time's Arrow, Time's Cycle: Myth and Metaphor in the Discovery of Geological Time.* Cambridge: Cambridge University Press, 1987.

Graves, Robert. *The White Goddess: A Historical Grammar of Poetic Myth,* 3d ed. London: Faber and Faber, 1948, 1952.

———. *The Greek Myths,* volume 1. New York: George Braziller, 1957.

Graves, Robert and Raphael Patai. *Hebrew Myths: The Book of Genesis.* Garden City, NY: Doubleday, 1964.

Grazia, Alfred de, Ralph E. Juergens, and Livio C. Stecchini. *The Velikovsky Affair.* New Hyde Park, NY: University Books, 1966.

Green, Peter. *Alexander to Actium.* Los Angeles: University of California Press, 1990.

Gruenwald, Ithamar. *Apocalyptic and Merkavah Mysticism.* Leiden: E. J. Brill, 1980.

Gunkel, Hermann. *Schopfung und Chaos in Urzeit und Endzeit.* Gottingen: Van denhoeck und Ruprecht, 1895.

———. *The Legends of Genesis.* New York: Schocken, 1964.

Guthrie, Kenneth Sylvan. *The Pythagorean Sourcebook and Library.* Grand Rapids, MI: Phanes, 1987.

Guthrie, W. K. C. "Early Greek Religion in the Light of the Decipherment of Linear B." *Bull. of the Inst. of Classical Studies* 6 (1959): 35–46.

———. *Orpheus and Greek Religion, A Study of the Orphic Movement.* New York: W. W. Norton, 1966.

Hahn, Charles H. *Anaximander and the Origins of Greek Cosmology.* Philadelphia: Centrum, 1985.

Hall, A. Rupert. *From Galileo to Newton.* New York: Dover Publications, 1963, 1981.

Haraway, Donna Jeanne. *Crystals, Fabrics, and Fields: Metaphors of Organicism in Twentieth-Century Developmental Biology.* New Haven: Yale University Press, 1976.

Harding, Esther M. *Women's Mysteries Ancient and Modern.* New York: Bantam Books, 1971.

Harding, Thomas G. *Evolution and Culture.* Ann Arbor: University of Michigan Press, 1960.

Harris, Roy. *The Origin of Writing.* London: Duckworth, 1986.

Harris, T. G. "About Ruth Benedict and Her Lost Manuscript." *Psychology Today* 4 (1970): 51–52.

Harrison, Jane Ellen. *Prolegomena to the Study of Greek Religion.* New York: Meridian, 1955.

———. *Mythology.* New York: Cooper Square Publishers, 1963.

Hastings, James. *Encyclopedia of Religion and Ethics.* New York: Scribner, 1955.

Hawkes, Jacquetta. *Dawn of the Gods.* New York: Random House, 1968.

Hawking, Stephen. *A Brief History of Time: From the Big Bang to Black Holes.* New York: Bantam Books, 1988.

Hawkins, Gerald S., with John B. White. *Stonehenge Decoded.* New York: Dell Publishing, 1965.

Hayles, N. Katherine. *Chaos Bound: Orderly Disorder in Contemporary Literature and Science.* Ithaca: Cornell University Press, 1990.

Hebb, Donald O. *The Organization of Behavior.* New York: Wiley, 1949.

Hegel, G. W. F. *Philosophy of History,* translated by J. Sibree. New York: P. F. Collier, 1905.

———. *Lectures on the Philosophy of World History; Introduction: Reason in History,* translated by H. B. Nisbet. Cambridge: Cambridge University Press, 1975.

Heidel, Alexander. *The Babylonian Genesis: The Story of Creation.* Chicago: University of Chicago Press, 1942.

Hein, Hilda S. *On the Nature and Origin of Life.* New York: McGraw-Hill, 1971.

Heinlein, Robert A. *Stranger in a Strange Land.* New York: Ace Books, 1961, 1968, 1987.

Henle, Mary. *Documents of Gestalt Psychology.* Berkeley: University of California Press, 1961.

Herder, Johann Gottfried von. *Reflections on the Philosophy of the History of Mankind,* edited by Frank E. Manuel. Chicago: University of Chicago Press, 1968.

————. *J. G. Herder on Social and Political Culture,* edited by F. M. Barnard. Cambridge: Cambridge University Press, 1969.

Hesse, Mary B. *Forces and Fields, the Concept of Action at a Distance in the History of Physics.* London: Thomas Nelson, 1961.

————. *Models and Analogies in Science.* Notre Dame, IN: University of Notre Dame, 1966.

Hilgard, E. R. *Introduction to Psychology.* New York: Harcourt Brace Jovanovich, 1953, 1979.

Hilgard, Ernest R. and Gordon L. Bower. *Theories of Learning,* 3d ed. New York: Appleton-Century-Crofts, 1948, 1956, 1966.

Hoff, Benjamin. *The Tao of Pooh.* New York: Penguin Books, 1983.

Hogart, R. C. *The Hymns of Orpheus: Mutations.* Grand Rapids, MI: Phanes, 1993.

Hole, Frank and Robert F. Heizer. *An Introduction to Prehistoric Archaeology,* 2d ed. New York: Holt, Rinehart and Winston, 1965, 1969.

Hooke, S. H. *Myth and Ritual: Essays on the Myth and Ritual of the Hebrews in Relation to the Culture Pattern of the Ancient East.* London: Oxford University Press, 1933.

————. *The Labyrinth: Further Studies in the Relation Between Myth and Ritual in the Ancient World.* London: Society for Promoting Christian Knowledge, 1935.

————. *The Origins of Early Semitic Ritual.* Oxford: Oxford University Press, 1938.

————. *Myth, Ritual, and Kingship: Essays on the Theory and Practice of Kingship in the Ancient Near East and in Israel.* Oxford: Clarendon Press, 1958, 1960.

————. *Babylonian and Assyrian Religion.* Norman: University of Oklahoma Press, 1963.

————. *Middle Eastern Mythology.* New York: Penguin Books, 1963, 1988.

Hornung, Erik. *Conceptions of God in Ancient Egypt: The One and the Many.* Ithaca: Cornell University Press, 1971, 1972.

Hoy, David Couzens. *The Critical Circle: Literature, History, and Philosophical Hermeneutics.* Berkeley: University of California Press, 1978.

Hutton, James. *James Hutton's Theory of the Earth, 1785.* New York: Hafner Press, 1973.

Huxley, Francis. *The Dragon: Nature of Spirit, Spirit of Nature.* London: Thames and Hudson, 1979.

Ibn-Khaldūn. *An Arab Philosophy of History: Selections from the Prolegomena of Ibn-Khaldūn of Tunis (1332–1406),* edited by Charles Issawi. London: John Murray, London, 1950.

————. *The Muqaddimah: An Introduction to History,* 3 volumes, translated by Franz Rosenthal. Princeton: Princeton University Press, 1958.

————. *The Muqaddimah: An Introduction to History (abridged),* translated by Franz Rosenthal and edited by N. J. Dawood. Princeton: Princeton University Press, 1967.

Imbrie, John and Katherine Palmer Imbrie. *Ice Ages: Solving the Mystery.* Cambridge: Harvard University Press, 1986.

Jacobsen, Thorkild. "Formative Tendencies in Sumerian Religion." In *The Bible and the Ancient Near East,* edited by G. Ernest Wright. New York: Doubleday, 1961, 1965, 267–78.

James, E. O. *Prehistoric Religion, A Study in Prehistoric Archaeology.* New York: Barnes & Noble, 1957.

————. *The Cult of the Mother-Goddess, An Archaeological and Documentary Study.* New York: Frederick A. Praeger, 1959.

————. *From Cave to Cathedral: Temples and Shrines of Prehistoric, Classical, and Early Christian Times.* New York: Praeger, 1965.

————. *Creation and Cosmology: A Historical and Comparative Inquiry.* Leiden: E. J. Brill, 1969.

Jantsch, Erich. *Design for Evolution: Self-organization and Planning in the Life of Human Systems.* New York: Braziller, 1975.

————. *The Self-Organizing Universe: Scientific and Human Implications of the Emerging Paradigm of Evolution.* New York: Pergamon, 1980.

————. *The Evolutionary Vision: Toward a Unifying Paradigm of Physical, Biological, and Sociocultural Evolution.* AAAS Selected Symposia 61. Boulder, CO: Westview, 1981.

Johnson, Buffie. *Lady of the Beasts: Ancient Images of the Goddess and Her Sacred Animals.* San Francisco: Harper & Row, 1988.

Jonas, Hans. *The Gnostic Religion: The Message of the Alien God and the Beginnings of Christianity.* Boston: Beacon Press, 1958, 1963.

Jung, C. G. *Psychology and Alchemy,* 2d ed. The Collected Works of C. J. Jung. Princeton: Princeton University Press, 1953/1968.

————. *The Structure and Dynamics of the Psyche,* 2d ed. The Collected Works of C. J. Jung. Princeton: Princeton University Press, 1960, 1969.

————. *Man and His Symbols.* New York: Doubleday, 1964.

————. *Alchemical Studies.* The Collected Works of C. J. Jung. Princeton: Princeton University Press, 1967.

Jung, C. G. and C. Kerényi. *Essays on a Science of Mythology: The Myths of the Divine Child and the Divine Maiden*. New York: Harper & Row, 1949, 1963.

Karreman, George. "Memories of Rashevsky." *Dynamics Newsletter* 4, nos. 1, 2, 3 (1990): 3–4.

Kennedy, Don H. *Little Sparrow: A Portrait of Sophia Kovalevsky*. Athens, OH: Ohio University Press, 1983.

Kerényi, Carl. *The Gods of the Greeks,* translated by Norman Cameron. London: Thames and Hudson, 1951, 1979.

———. *Eleusis: Archetypal Image of Mother and Daughter,* translated by Ralph Manheim. Princeton: Princeton University Press, 1967.

———. *Zeus and Hera: Archetypal Image of Father, Husband, and Wife,* translated by Christopher Holme. Princeton: Princeton University Press, 1975.

———. *Dionysos: Archetypal Image of Indestructible Life,* translated by Ralph Manheim. Princeton: Princeton University Press, 1976.

King, L. W. and R. C. Thompson. *The Sculptures and Inscription of Darius the Great on the Rock of Behistun in Persia: A New Collation of the Persian, Susian, and Babylonian Texts, with English Translations, Etc.* London: British Museum, 1907.

Kirk, G. S. and J. E. Raven. *The Presocratic Philosophers.* Cambridge: Cambridge University Press, 1957.

Koestler, Arthur. *Janus: A Summing Up.* New York: Vintage, 1979.

Koffka, Kurt. *The Growth of the Mind; an Introduction to Child Psychology.* New York: Harcourt, Brace, 1924, 1928.

———. *Principles of Gestalt Psychology.* New York: Harcourt, Brace, 1935.

Kohler, Wolfgang. "Some Gestalt Problems (1924)." In *Source Book of Gestalt Psychology,* edited by Willis D. Ellis. London: Routledge & Kegan Paul, 1938, 55–70.

———. *The Mentality of Apes.* London: Routledge and Kegan Paul, 1925, 1973.

———. *Gestalt Psychology.* New York: Liveright, 1929, 1970.

———. *Dynamics in Psychology.* New York: Grove Press, 1940, 1960.

Kordig, Karl R. "The Theory-ladenness of Observation." *Rev. Metaphys.* 24 (1971): 448–84.

Kovalevskaya, Sofya. *A Russian Childhood.* Berlin: Springer-Verlag, 1978.

Kovalevsky, Sonya, Anna Carlotta Leffler, Ellen Key, and Lily Wolffsohn. *Sonya Kovalevsky, Her Recollections from Childhood, with a Biography by Anna Carlotta Leffler, and a Biographical Note by Lily Wolffsohn.* New York: The Century Co., 1895.

Kramer, Samuel Noah. *Sumerian Mythology.* Philadelphia: University of Pennsylvania Press, 1944, 1972.

———. *History Begins at Sumer: Thirty-Nine Firsts in Man's Recorded History.* Philadelphia: University of Pennsylvania Press, 1956, 1988.

———. *Mythologies of the Ancient World.* New York: Doubleday, 1961.

———. *The Sumerians: Their History, Culture, and Character.* Chicago: University of Chicago Press, 1963.

———. *The Sacred Marriage Rite.* Bloomington: Indiana University Press, 1969.

———. *In the World of Sumer: An Autobiography.* Detroit: Wayne State University Press, 1986.

Kramer, Samuel Noah and John Maier. *Myths of Enki, the Crafty God.* Oxford: Oxford University Press, 1989.

Kuhn, Thomas S. *The Copernican Revolution, Planetary Astronomy in the Development of Western Thought.* Cambridge: Harvard University Press, 1957, 1959, 1985.

———. *The Structure of Scientific Revolutions.* Chicago: University of Chicago Press, 1962.

———. *The Essential Tension: Selected Studies in Scientific Tradition and Change.* Chicago: University of Chicago Press, 1977.

Kumar, Krishnan. *Utopianism.* Buckingham: Open University Press, 1991.

Kuper, Adam. *Anthropology and Anthropologists.* London: Routledge & Kegan Paul, 1973, 1983.

Kushelman, M. N. (Kadyrov). "A Mathematical Model of the Relations Between Two States." *Global Development Processes* 3. Moscow: Institute for Systems Studies, 1984.

LaCugna, Catherine Mowry. *God for Us: The Trinity and Christian Life.* San Francisco: HarperSanFrancisco, 1991.

Ladurie, Emmanuel Le Roy. *Times of Feast, Times of Famine: A History of Climate Since the Year 1000.* New York: Noonday, 1967, 1988.

Lamarck, J. B. *Zoological Philosophy.* Chicago: University of Chicago Press, 1792, 1984.

Lamb, H. H. *Climate, History and the Modern World.* London: Methuen, 1982.

Lamy, Lucy. *Egyptian Mysteries.* New York: Crossroad, 1981.

Langdon, S. *The Babylonian Epic of Creation: Restored from Recently Recovered Tablets of Assur; Transcription, Translation, and Commentary.* Oxford: Clarendon Press, 1923.

Langs, Robert. "Clarifying a New Model of the Mind." *Contemporary Psychoanalysis* 23 (1987): 162–80.

Lashley, K. S. *Brain Mechanisms and Intelligence: A Quantitive Study of Injuries to the Brain.* New York: Hafner, 1964.

Laszlo, Ervin. *Evolution: The Grand Synthesis.* Boston: Shambhala, 1987.

Lattimore, Richmond. *Hesiod.* Ann Arbor: University of Michigan Press, 1959.

Leatherdale, W. H. *The Role of Analogy, Model and Metaphor in Science.* Amsterdam: North-Holland, 1974.

Lee, Paul. "Hermeneutics and Vitalism." *ReVision* 10, no. 3 (Winter, 1988): 3–14.

Legge, F. *Forerunners and Rivals of Christianity.* New York: Peter Smith, 1950.

Le Guin, Ursula K. *Buffalo Gals and Other Animal Presences.* New York: Penguin, 1988.

Lerner, Lawrence S. and Edward A. Gosselin. "Galileo and the Specter of Bruno." *Scientific American* 255 (1986): 126–33.

Leroi-Gourhan, Andre. "The Evolution of Paleolithic Art." *Scientific American* 5 (February 1968): 58–69.

———. *The Dawn of European Art: An Introduction to Paleolithic Cave Painting.* Cambridge: Cambridge University Press, 1982.

Levenson, Thomas. *Ice Time: Climate, Science, and Life on Earth.* New York: Harper & Row, 1989.

Levy, Gertrude Rachel. *The Gate of Horn, A Study of the Religious Conceptions of the Stone Age, and Their Influence upon European Thought.* London: Faber and Faber, 1963.

Lewin, Kurt. *A Dynamic Theory of Personality: Selected Papers of Kurt Lewin.* New York: McGraw-Hill, 1935.

———. *Principles of Topological Psychology.* New York: McGraw-Hill, 1936.

———. *Resolving Social Conflicts.* New York: Harper, 1948.

———. *Field Theory in Social Science: Selected Theoretical Papers.* Westport, CN: Greenwood Press, 1951, 1975.

Li, T. Y. and J. A. Yorke. "Period Three Implies Chaos." *Am. Math. Monthly* 82 (1975): 985.

Liddell, H. G. *An Intermediate Greek-English Lexicon.* Oxford: Oxford University Press, 1978.

Lilienfeld, Robert. *The Rise of Systems Theory.* New York: Wiley, 1978.

Lockyer, J. Norman. *The Dawn of Astronomy: A Study of Temple-Worship and Mythology of the Ancient Egyptians.* New York: The Macmillan Company, 1897.

Lorenz, Edward. "T." *J. of Atmos. Sci.* 20 (1963): 130–41.

Lotka, Alfred J. *Elements of Physical Biology.* Baltimore: Williams and Watkins, 1925.

Lovejoy, Arthur O. *The Great Chain of Being.* Cambridge, MA: Harvard University Press, 1936/1964.

———. *Essays in the History of Ideas.* Baltimore: Johns Hopkins Press, 1948.

Lovelock, James. *The Ages of Gaia: A Biography of Our Living Earth.* New York: Bantam Books, 1988, 1990.

———. *Healing Gaia: Practical Medicine for the Planet.* New York: Harmony Books, 1991.

Lowith, Karl. *Meaning in History.* Chicago: University of Chicago Press, 1949.

Loye, David. *The Healing of a Nation.* New York: Dell Books, 1972.

———. *Moral Sensitivity and the Evolution of Higher Mind.* Preprint, 1989.

Lumley, Henry de. "A Paleolithic Camp at Nice." *Scientific American* 5 (May 1969): 42–50.

MacDonell, Arthur A. *A History of Sanskrit Literature.* Delhi: Motilal Banarsidass, 1971.

Maclagan, David. *Creation Myths: Man's Introduction to the World.* London: Thames and Hudson, 1977.

Macqueen, James G. *Babylon.* London: R. Hale, 1964.

Mage, Shane. *Velikovsky and His Critics.* Grand Haven, MI: Cornelius Press, 1978.

Mahdi, Muhsin. *Ibn Khaldun's Philosophy of History.* Chicago: University of Chicago Press, 1957, 1964.

Malinowski, Bronislaw. *Argonauts of the Western Pacific: An Account of Native Enterprise and Adventure in the Archipelagoes of Melanesian New Guinea.* London: George Routledge, 1922.

———. *Myth in Primitive Psychology.* New York: Norton, 1926.

Mallory, J. P. *In Search of the Indo-Europeans: Language, Archaeology and Myth.* London: Thames and Hudson, 1989.

Manuel, Frank E. *The Eighteenth Century Confronts the Gods.* Cambridge: Harvard University Press, 1959.

———. *Isaac Newton, Historian.* Cambridge: Harvard University Press, 1963.

———. *Shapes of Philosophical History.* Stanford: Stanford University Press, 1965.

———. *A Portrait of Isaac Newton.* Cambridge: Harvard University Press, 1968.

———. *The Religion of Isaac Newton: The Freemantle Lectures, 1973.* Oxford: Clarendon Press, 1974.

Manuel, Frank E. and Fritzie P. Manuel. *Utopian Thought in the Western World.* Cambridge: Harvard University Press, 1979.

Markey, T. L. and John A. C. Greppin. *When Worlds Collide: Indo-Europeans and Pre-Indo-Europeans, The Bellagio Papers.* Ann Arbor, MI: Karoma Publishers, 1990.

Marshack, Alexander. *The Roots of Civilization: The Cognitive Beginnings of Man's First Art, Symbol and Notation.* New York: McGraw-Hill, 1972.

Marx, Karl. *On History and People,* edited by Saul K. Padover. The Karl Marx Library, volume 7. New York: McGraw-Hill, 1977.

Maspero, Gaston. *A History of Egypt, Chaldea, Syria, Babylonia, and Assyria,* 13 volumes. London: Grolier Society, 1901.

Matthews, Caitlin. *Sophia, Goddess of Wisdom: The Divine Feminine from Black Goddess to World Soul.* London: Mandala, 1991.

Maury, G. Bonet. "Ages of the World (Christian)." In *Encyclopedia of Religion and Ethics*, volume 1, edited by James Hastings. New York: Scribner, 1955.

May, Robert. "Simple Mathematical Models with Very Complicated Dynamics." *Nature* 261 (1976): 459–67.

May, Rollo. *Love and Will*. New York: Norton, 1969.

Mayer, Dorothy. "Star-Patterns in Great Basin Petroglyphs." In *Archeoastronomy in Pre-Colombian America*, edited by Anthony F. Aveni. Austin: University of Texas Press, 1977, 110–30.

McClain, Ernest G. *The Myth of Invariance: The Origin of the Gods, Mathematics and Music from the Rg Veda to Plato*. Boulder, CO: Shambhala, 1978.

McKechnie, Jean L. *Webster's Deluxe Unabridged Dictionary*, 2d ed. New York: Simon and Schuster, 1979.

McKenna, Terence. "Temporal Resonance." *Revision* 10, no. 1 (Summer 1987): 25–30.

————. *Food of the Gods: The Search for the Original Tree of Knowledge*. New York: Bantam Books, 1992.

McKenna, Terence and Dennis McKenna. *The Invisible Landscape: Mind, Hallucinogens and the I Ching*. New York: Seabury Press, 1975.

McLachlan, Herbert. *The Religious Opinions of Milton, Locke, and Newton*. New York: Russell & Russell, 1941, 1972.

McLean, Adam. *Triple Goddess: An Exploration of the Archetypal Feminine*. Grand Rapids, MI: Phanes, 1989.

Mead, G. R. S. *Fragments of a Faith Forgotten*. New York: University Books, 1960.

Mead, Margaret. *Cooperation and Competition Among Primitive Peoples*. New York: McGraw-Hill, 1937, 1961.

————. *An Anthropologist at Work: Writings of Ruth Benedict*. Boston: Houghton-Mifflin, 1959, 1966.

Mellaart, James. *The Archaeology of Ancient Turkey*. Totowa, NJ: Rowman and Littlefield, 1978.

Merchant, Carolyn. *The Death of Nature: Women, Ecology, and the Scientific Revolution*, San Francisco: Harper & Row, 1980.

Metzner, Ralph. *The Transformation of Human Nature and Consciousness*. Los Angeles: Tarcher, 1986.

Meyer, Marvin W. *The Ancient Mysteries, A Sourcebook; Sacred Texts of the Mystery Religions of the Ancient Mediterranean World*. San Francisco: Harper & Row, 1987.

Michell, John. *The Dimensions of Paradise*. San Francisco: Harper & Row, 1988.

————. *New Light on Glastonbury*. Glastonbury: Graven Image, 1990.

Moran, Hugh A. and David H. Kelley. *The Alphabet and the Ancient Calendar Signs*, 2d ed. Stanford: Daily Press, 1953, 1969.

Morito, Akio. *Made in Japan*. New York: NAL Penguin, 1986.

Morris, William. *American Heritage Dictionary of the English Language*. New York: Houghton Mifflin, 1978.

Moser, Jurgen. *Stable and Random Motions in Dynamical Systems, with Special Emphasis on Celestial Mechanics*. Princeton: Princeton University Press, 1973.

Neumann, Erich. *The Great Mother: An Analysis of the Archetype*. Princeton: Princeton University Press, 1955.

Newman, James R. *The World of Mathematics*. New York: Simon and Schuster, 1956.

Nicolis, Gregoire and Ilya Prigogine. *Exploring Complexity: An Introduction*. New York: W. H. Freeman, 1989.

Niditch, Susan. *Chaos to Cosmos: Studies in Biblical Patterns of Creation*. Chico, CA: Scholars Press, 1985.

Nilsson, Martin P., *Primitive Time-Reckoning: A Study in the Origins and First Development of the Art of Counting Time Among the Primitive and Early Culture Peoples*. Lund: Gleerup, 1920.

————. *A History of Greek Religion*. Oxford: Clarendon Press, 1925, 1949.

————. *The Mycenaean Origin of Greek Mythology*. New York: W. W. Norton, 1932, 1963.

————. "Early Orphism and Kindred Religious Movements." *The Harvard Theological Review* 28, no. 3 (July 1935): 181–230.

————. *Greek Folk Religion*. New York: Harper, 1940, 1961.

————. *Minoan-Mycenaean Religion and Its Survival in Greek Religion*, 2d rev. ed. Lund: Gleerup, 1950, 1968.

Nisbet, Robert A. *Social Change and History: Aspects of the Western Theory of Development*. Oxford: Oxford University Press, 1969.

Numbers, Ronald L. *Creation by Natural Law: Laplace's Nebular Hypothesis in American Thought*. Seattle: University of Washington Press, 1977.

Oakley, Stewart. *A Short History of Sweden*. New York: Praeger, 1966.

Oates, Joan. *Babylon*. London: Thames and Hudson, 1979, 1986.

O'Keefe, John and Lynn Nadel. *The Hippocampus as a Cognitive Map*. Oxford: Oxford University Press, 1978.

Oldfather, C. H. *Diodorus of Sicily in Twelve Volumes*. Cambridge: Harvard University Press, 1963.

Osen, Lynn M. *Women in Mathematics*. Cambridge: MIT Press, 1974.

Otto, Walter F. *Dionysus, Myth and Cult*, translated by Robert B. Palmer. Bloomington: Indiana University Press, 1933, 1965.

Palmer, Richard E. *Hermeneutics: Interpretation Theory in Schleiermacher, Dilthey, Heidegger, and Gadamer*. Evanston, IL: Northwestern University Press, 1969.

Panikkar, Raimundo. *The Trinity and the Religious Experience of Man: Icon-Person-Myth.* New York: Orbis, 1973.

Parsons, Edward Alexander. *The Alexandrian Library; Glory of the Hellenic World.* New York: Elsevier, 1952.

Patai, Raphael. *Man and Temple: In Ancient Jewish Myth and Ritual.* New York: Ktav, 1947, 1967.

Pearson, Ronald. *Climate and Evolution.* New York: Academic Press, 1978.

Pendlebury, J. D. S. *The Archaeology of Crete: An Introduction.* New York: Biblo and Tannen, 1963.

Pepper, Stephen C. *World Hypotheses, a Study in Evidence.* Los Angeles: University of California Press, 1961.

Perera, Sylvia Brinton. *Descent to the Goddess: A Way of Initiation for Women.* Toronto: Inner City Books, 1981.

Peterson, Ivars. *Newton's Clock.* New York: Freeman, 1993.

Petrie, Sir William Matthews Flinders. *A History of Egypt, From the Earliest Kings to the XVIth Dynasty.* London: Methuen, 1903.

———. *The Revolutions of Civilizations.* London: Harper, 1911, 1922.

———. *Seventy Years in Archaeology.* London: Sampson Low, Marston, 1931.

Pfeiffer, John E. *The Creative Explosion: An Inquiry into the Origins of Art and Religion.* Ithaca: Cornell University Press, 1982.

Pfeiffer, Rudolph. *History of Classical Scholarship from 1300 to 1850.* London: Clarendon Press, 1976.

Platon, Nicolas. *Crete.* Geneva: Nagel Publishers, 1966.

Postle, Denis. *Catastrophe Theory.* London: Fontana, 1980.

Price, Derek John de Solla. *Gears from the Greeks: The Antikythera Mechanism, a Calendar Computer from ca. 80 B.C.* Philadelphia: American Philosophical Society, 1974.

Qualls-Corbett, Nancy. *The Sacred Prostitute: Eternal Aspect of the Feminine.* Toronto: Inner City Books, 1988.

Radnitzky, Gerard. *Contemporary Schools of Metascience.* Chicago: Henry Regnery, 1973.

Rampino, Michael R., John E. Sanders, Walter S. Newman, and L. K. Königsson. *Climate: History, Periodicity, and Predictability.* New York: Van Nostrand Reinhold, 1987.

Rashevsky, Nicolas. *Looking at History Through Mathematics.* Cambridge: MIT Press, 1968.

Rattansi, P. M. "Newton's Alchemical Studies." In *Science, Medicine and Society in the Renaissance,* volume 2, edited by Allen G. Debus. New York: Science History Publications, 1972, 167–82.

Reik, Theodor. *Pagan Rites in Judaism.* New York: Farrar, Straus, 1964.

Reinach, Salomon. *Orpheus: A History of Religions.* New York: Liveright, 1935.

Renfrew, Colin. *The Emergence of Civilization: The Cyclades and the Aegean in the Third Millennium* B.C. London: Methuen, 1972.

———. *Archaeology and Language: The Puzzle of Indo-European Origins.* London: Jonathan Cape, 1987.

———. "The Origins of Indo-European Languages." *Scientific American* 261, no. 4 (October 1989): 106–14.

Renfrew, Colin and Timothy Poston. "Villages." In *Transformations: Mathematical Approaches to Culture Change,* edited by A. C. Renfrew and K. L. Cooke. New York: Academic Press, 1979, 437–61.

Richardson, Lewis Frye. "Generalized Foreign Politics." *British J. Psychology,* monograph supplement 23 (1939).

———. *Arms and Insecurities; a Mathematical Study of the Causes and Origins of War.* Pittsburgh: Boxwood Press, 1960a.

———. *Statistics of Deadly Quarrels.* Pittsburgh: Boxwood Press, 1960b.

Rickman, Hans Peter. *Understanding and the Human Studies.* London: Heinemann, 1967.

Roberts, J. J. M. *The Earliest Semitic Pantheon: A Study of the Semitic Deities Attested in Mesopotamia before Ur III.* Baltimore: Johns Hopkins University Press, 1972.

Rohde, Erwin. *Psyche, The Cult of Souls and Belief in Immortality among the Greeks,* translated by W. B. Hillis. London: Routledge & Kegan Paul, 1925, 1950.

Rose, H. J. *A Handbook of Greek Mythology, Including Its Extension to Rome.* London: Methuen, 1928, 1960.

Rosenblueth, Arturo and Norbert Wiener. "Role of Models in Science." In *Collected Works,* volume 4. Cambridge: MIT Press, 1965, 446–51.

Rosenstock-Huessy, Eugen. *Out of Revolution.* New York: Four Wells, 1938, 1964.

Ruelle, David and Floris Takens. "On the Nature of Turbulence." *Commun. Math. Phys.* 82 (1971): 167–92.

Sabelli, Hector. *Union of Opposites.* Lawrenceville, VA: Brunswick Publications, 1989.

Sackett, Hugh and Sandy MacGillivray. "Boyhood of a God: Two Unique Objects Found in Eastern Crete Strongly Suggest a Minoan Link to the Zeus of Classical Mythology." *Archaeology* 42, no. 5 (September/October 1989): 26–31.

Sandmel, Samuel. *Philo of Alexandria, an Introduction.* Oxford: Oxford University Press, 1979.

Sanford, N. "What Ever Happened to Action Research?" *J. of Social Issues* 26, no. 4 (1970): 3–23.

Santillana, Giorgio de and Hertha von Deschend. *Hamlet's Mill: An Essay on Myth and the Frame of Time.* Boston: Gambit, 1969.

Saperstein, Alvin. "Chaos—a Model for the Outbreak of War." *Nature* 309 (1984): 303–5.

Saperstein, Alvin M. and Gottfried Mayer-Kress. *A Systematic Procedure for Evaluating the Impact of New Security Policies Upon the Maintenance of Peace: S.D.I. vs. Star Wars*. Los Alamos, NM: Los Alamos National Laboratory, 1986.
———. "A Nonlinear Dynamical Model of the Impact of SDI on the Arms Race." *J. of Conflict Resolution* 32 (1988): 636–70.
Sarna, Nahum M. *Understanding Genesis*. New York: Schocken Books, 1966, 1970.
Sayce, A. H. *The Religions of Ancient Egypt and Babylonia: The Gifford Lectures on the Ancient Egyptian and Babylonian Conception of the Divine, Delivered in Aberdeen*. New York: AMS Press, 1979.
Scholem, Gershom. *On the Kabbalah and Its Symbolism*. New York: Schocken Books, 1960, 1965, 1969.
Schure, Edouard. *The Great Initiates: A Study of the Secret History of Religions*. West Nyack, NY: St. George Books, 1961.
Schutz, Alfred and Thomas Luchman. *The Structures of the Life-World*. Evanston, IL: Northwestern University Press, 1973.
Schwartz, Joseph. *The Creative Moment: How Science Made Itself*. New York: HarperCollins, 1992.
Sears, Paul B. "Climate and Civilization," in *Climate Change*, edited by Harlow Shapley. Cambridge: Harvard University Press, 1960, 35–50.
Segal, Charles. *Orpheus: The Myth of the Poet*. Baltimore, MD: John Hopkins, 1989.
Settegast, Mary. *Plato Prehistorian: 10,000 to 5000 B.C. in Myth and Archaeology*. Cambridge, MA: The Rotenberg Press, 1986.
Seznec, Jean. *The Survival of the Pagan Gods; the Mythological Tradition and Its Place in Renaissance Humanism and Art,* translated by Barbara F. Sessions. New York: Pantheon, 1953.
Shapiro, Stewart. "Mathematics and Reality." *Philosophy of Science* 50 (1983): 523–48.
Shaw, Herbert. "T." *Eos* 5 (1987): 1651–1665.
Shaw, Herbert R. *A Celestial Reference Frame for Terrestrial Processes*. Stanford: Stanford University Press, 1994.
Shaw, Robert. *The Dripping Faucet as a Model Chaotic System*. Santa Cruz, CA: Aerial Press, 1984.
Sheldrake, Rupert. *A New Science of Life, the Hypothesis of Formative Causation*. London: Blond, 1981.
———. *The Presence of the Past*. New York: Times Books, 1988.
———. *The Rebirth of Nature: The Greening of Science and God*. New York: Bantam, 1991.
Singer, Charles, E. J. Holmyard, and A. R. Hall. *A History of Technology,* volume 1. Oxford: Oxford University Press, 1954, 1967.
Sitchin, Zecharia. *The 12th Planet*. New York: Avon Books, 1978.

Sizemore, Chris Costner. *A Mind of My Own*. New York: William Morrow, 1989.
Sjöö, Monica and Barbara Mor. *The Great Cosmic Mother: Rediscovering the Religion of the Earth*. San Francisco: Harper & Row, 1987.
Skomal, Susan Nacev and Edgar C. Palome. *Proto-Indo-European: The Archaeology of a Linguistic Problem: Studies in Honor of Marija Gimbutas*. Washington, DC: Institute for the Study of Man, 1987.
Smale, Steven. "Global Analysis and Economics I, Pareto optimum and a Generalization of Morse Theory." In *Salvador Symposium on Dynamical Systems,* Mauricio M. Peixoto, ed. New York: Academic Press, 1973.
———. *The Mathematics of Time: Essays on Dynamical Systems, Economic Processes, and Related Topics*. Berlin: Springer-Verlag, 1980.
Smith, George. *Assyrian Discoveries*. London: S. Low, Marston, Low, & Searle, 1875.
———. *The Chaldean Account of Genesis*. Minneapolis: Wizards Book Shelf, 1876, 1977.
———. "The Chaldean Account of the Flood," in *The Flood Myth,* edited by Alan Dundes. Berkeley: University of California Press, 1988.
Smith, Page. *Killing the Spirit*. New York: Viking, 1990.
Smuts, Jan C. *Holism and Evolution*. London: Macmillan, 1926.
Snyder, T. P. *The Biosphere Catalogue*. London: Synergetic Press, 1985.
Solecki, Ralph S. *Shanidar: The First Flower People*. New York: Alfred A. Knopf, 1971.
Somerville, Mary F. *Mechanism of the Heavens*. London: John Murray, 1831.
Sorokin, Pitirim A. *The Sociology of Revolution*. Philadelphia: J. B. Lippincott, 1925.
———. *Society and Culture*. New York: Bedminster, 1937, 1962.
———. *Social and Cultural Dynamics: A Study of Change in Major Systems of Art, Truth, Ethics, Law and Social Relationships,* rev. and abridged. Boston: Porter Sargent, 1957.
Sparks, John B. *Histomap of World History*. New York: Rand McNally, 1931.
Spencer, Herbert and Robert L. Carnero, eds. *The Evolution of Society*. Chicago: University of Chicago Press, 1967.
Spender, Dale. *Feminist Theorists: Three Centuries of Key Women Thinkers*. New York: Pantheon Books, 1983.
Spengler, Oswald. *The Decline of the West,* translated by C. F. Atkinson. New York: Alfred A. Knopf, 1926a.
———. *The Decline of the West,* abridged ed., translated by C. F. Atkinson, edited by Helmut Werner and Arthur Helps. New York: Alfred A. Knopf, 1926b.
Spretnak, Charlene. *Lost Goddesses of Early Greece: A Collection of Pre-Hellenic Myths*. Boston: Beacon Press, 1978, 1984.

Starhawk. *The Spiral Dance: A Rebirth of the Ancient Religion of the Great Goddess.* San Francisco: Harper & Row, 1979.

Stecchini, Livio C. "The Inconstant Heavens: Velikovsky in Relation to Some Past Cosmic Perplexities." *Behav. Sci.* 7, no. 1 (1973): 19–32.

Stewart, Ian. *Does God Plays Dice?* Oxford: Basil Blackwell, 1989.

Stocking, George W. *Malinowski, Rivers, Benedict and Others, Essays on Culture and Personality.* Madison: University of Wisconsin Press, 1986.

Stone, Merlin. *When God Was a Woman.* New York: Harcourt Brace Jovanovich, 1976.

———. *Ancient Mirrors of Womanhood: Our Goddess and Heroine Heritage,* 2 volumes. New York: New Sibylline Books, 1979.

Stone, Michael Edward. *Scriptures, Sects, and Visions: A Profile of Judaism from Ezra to the Jewish Revolts.* Philadelphia: Fortress Press, 1980.

Strassfeld, Michael. *The Jewish Holidays: A Guide and Commentary.* New York: Harper & Row, 1985.

Strauss, Walter A. *Descent and Return: The Orphic Theme in Modern Literature.* Cambridge, MA: Harvard University Press, 1971.

Strauss, William and Neil Howe. *Generations: The History of America's Future, 1584 to 2069.* New York: William Morrow, 1991.

Taylor, Thomas and Alexander Wilder, eds. *The Eleusinian and Bacchic Mysteries, a Dissertation,* 3d ed. New York: J. W. Bouton, 1791, 1875.

Tetsuro, Watsuji. *Climate and Culture.* New York: Greenwood Press, 1961, 1988.

Thom, René. *Stabilité Structurelle et Morphogenese.* Reading, MA: Benjamin, 1972.

———. *Structural Stability and Morphogenesis,* translated by David Fowler. Reading, MA: Addison-Wesley, 1975.

Thompson, R. Campbell. *A Century of Exploration at Nineveh.* London: Luzac, 1929.

Thompson, William Irwin. *The Imagination of an Insurrection: Dublin, Easter, 1916: A Study of an Ideological Movement.* New York: Harper & Row, 1967, 1972.

———. *At the Edge of History.* New York: Harper & Row, 1971.

———. *Evil and World Order.* New York: Harper & Row, 1976.

———. *Darkness and Scattered Light: Four Talks on the Future.* New York: Anchor Books, 1978.

———. *The Time Falling Bodies Take to Light: Mythology, Sexuality, and the Origins of Culture.* New York: St. Martin's Press, 1981.

———. *Pacific Shift.* San Francisco: Sierra Club Books, 1985.

———. "Gaia and the Politics of Life: A Program for the Nineties." In *Gaia, A Way of Knowing: Political Implications of the New Biology,* edited by William Irwin Thompson. Great Barrington, MA: Lindisfarne Press, 1987, 167–214.

Thomson, George Derwent. *Studies in Ancient Greek Society: The Prehistoric Aegean,* volume 1. New York: The Citadel Press, 1949, 1965.

Tickell, Crispin. *Climate Change and World Affairs.* Lanham, MD: University Press of America, 1977, 1986.

Tillich, Paul. *The Construction of the History of Religion in Schelling's Positive Philosophy.* Lewisburg: Bucknell University Press, 1910, 1974.

———. *Systematic Theology.* Chicago: University of Chicago Press, 1951, 1957, 1963.

———. *How Has Science in the Last Century Changed Man's View of Himself?* Preprint. Cambridge: MIT, 1961.

———. *A History of Christian Thought.* New York: Simon and Schuster, 1968, 1972.

———. *Political Expectation.* New York: Harper & Row, 1971.

Tolman, E. C. "Cognitive Maps in Rats and Men." *Psychol. Rev.* 55 (1948): 189–208.

Toynbee, Arnold. *The World and the West.* New York: Meridian, 1953, 1960.

———. *A Study of History.* New York: Oxford University Press, 1956–63.

———. *Civilization on Trial.* New York: Meridian Books, 1958.

Toynbee, Arnold and Jane Caplan. *A Study of History.* London: Thames and Hudson, 1972.

Trigger, B. G., B. J. Kemp, D. O'Conner, and A. B. Lloyd. *Ancient Egypt, a Social History.* Cambridge: Cambridge University Press, 1983.

Turner, Frederick. *Beyond Geography.* New York: Viking, 1980.

Turner, Victor. *The Ritual Process.* Ithaca: Cornell University Press, 1977.

Tylor, E. B. *The Origins of Culture.* New York: Harper & Row, 1958.

Ueda, Yoshisuke. *The Road to Chaos.* Santa Cruz, CA: Aerial Press, 1992.

Ulansey, David. *The Origins of the Mythraic Mysteries: Cosmology and Salvation in the Ancient World.* Oxford: Oxford University Press, 1989.

Varene, Donald Philip. *Vico and Joyce.* Albany, NY: State University of New York Press, 1987.

Velikovsky, Immanuel. *Worlds in Collision.* Garden City, NY: Doubleday, 1950.

———. *Ages in Chaos,* 4 volumes. Garden City, NY: Doubleday, 1952–77.

———. *Earth in Upheaval*. Garden City, NY: Doubleday, 1955.

———. *Oedipus and Akhnaton*. Garden City, NY: Doubleday, 1960.

———. *Worlds in Collision*. New York: Pocket Books, 1977.

Vernadsky, Vladimir Ivanovich. *Problems of Biogeochemistry*. New Haven: Connecticut Academy of Arts and Sciences, 1944.

———. "The Biosphere and the Noosphere," *American Scientist* 33:1 (January 1945): 1–12.

Vico, Giambattista. *Autobiography*. Translated by Max Harold Fisch and Thomas Goddard Bergin. Ithaca, NY: Cornell University Press, 1944.

Virgil. *Georgics*. Oxford: Oxford University Press, 1990.

Voegelin, Eric. *Order and History,* 3 volumes. Baton Rouge: Louisiana State University Press, 1956–57.

Wade, Ira O. *The Intellectual Origins of the French Enlightenment*. Princeton: Princeton University Press, 1971.

Wainwright, Goeffrey. *The Henge Monuments: Ceremony and Society in Prehistoric Britain*. London: Thames and Hudson, 1989.

Wakeman, Mary K. *God's Battle with the Monster*. Leiden: E. J. Brill, 1973.

Walker, Barbara G. *The Woman's Dictionary of Symbols and Sacred Objects*. San Francisco: Harper & Row, 1985(a).

———. *The Crone: Woman of Age, Wisdom, and Power*. San Francisco: Harper & Row, 1985(b).

Wallace, Anthony F. C. *Culture and Personality,* 2d. ed. New York: Random House, 1961, 1970.

Wallace, William A. *Galileo's Early Notebooks: The Physical Questions*. Notre Dame: University of Notre Dame Press, 1977.

Warden, John. *Orpheus. The Metamorphosis of a Myth*. Toronto: University of Toronto Press, 1982.

Wasson, R. Gordon, Carl A. P. Ruck, and Albert Hoffmann. *The Road to Eleusis, Unveiling the Secret of the Mysteries*. New York: Harcourt Brace Jovanovich, 1978.

Waterbury, John. *Hydropolitics of the Nile Valley*. New York: Syracuse University Press, 1979.

Waterfield, Gordon. *Layard of Nineveh*. New York: Praeger, 1963, 1968.

Wertheimer, Max. "The General Theoretical Situation (1922)." In *Source Book of Gestalt Psychology,* edited by Willis D. Ellis. London: Routledge & Kegan Paul, 1938, 12–16.

———. "Laws of Organization in Perceptual Forms (1923)." In *Source Book of Gestalt Psychology,* edited by Willis D. Ellis. London: Routledge & Kegan Paul, 1938, 71–88.

———. "Gestalt Theory (1924)." In *Source Book of Gestalt Psychology,* edited by Willis D. Ellis. London: Routledge & Kegan Paul, 1938, 1–11.

———. *Productive Thinking*. Chicago: University of Chicago Press, 1945, 1982.

West, Delno C. *Joachim of Fiore in Christian Thought: Essays on the Influence of the Calabrian Prophet,* 2 vols. New York: Burt Franklin, 1975.

West, M. L. *Hesiod, Works and Days*. Oxford: Clarendon Press, 1978.

———. *The Orphic Poems*. Oxford: Clarendon Press, 1983.

Westfall, Richard S. "Newton and the Hermetic Tradition." In *Science, Medicine and Society in the Renaissance,* edited by Allen G. Debus, vol. 2. New York: Science History Publications, 1972, 183–98 .

———. *Never at Rest: A Biography of Isaac Newton*. Cambridge: Cambridge University Press, 1980.

Wheeler, Mortimer. *The Indus Civilization*. Cambridge: Cambridge University Press, 1969.

Wheelwright, Philip. *Heraclitus*. Princeton: Princeton University Press, 1959.

Whiston, William. *An Account of the Convocation's Proceedings with Relation to Mr. Whiston, with a Postscript Containing a Reply to the Considerations on the Heretical Preface, and the Premonition to the Reader, to which is added, A Supplement to the foregoing Account of the Convocation's Proceedings*. London: A. Baldwin, 1711.

———. *An Account of the Author's Prosecution at, and Banishment from the University of Cambridge, with an Appendix; Containing Mr. Whiston's Farther Account (Petition), I.* London, 1711, 1718.

———. *Memoirs of the Life and Writings of Mr. William Whiston. Containing, Memoires of Several of Friends also.* London: Mr. Bishop, 1749.

White, Hayden. *Topics of Discourse: Essays in Cultural Criticism*. Baltimore: Johns Hopkins, 1978, 1985.

White, Lynn. "The Historical Roots of Our Ecological Crisis." *Science* 155 (10 March 1967): 1203–7.

Whitehead, Alfred North and Bertrand Russell. *Principia Mathematica,* 2d ed., vol. 1. Cambridge: Cambridge University Press, 1927/1960.

Whitehouse, Ruth and John Wilkins. *The Making of Civilization: History Discovered through Archaeology*. New York: Knopf, 1986.

Wiener, Norbert. *Mechanism and Vitalism*. In Collected Works, vol. 4. Cambridge: MIT Press, 1985, 968–69.

Wiener, Philip P. *Selections/Leibniz*. New York: Scribner, 1951.

Wilber, Ken. *Up from Eden*. Boulder: Shambhala, 1981.

Willetts, R. F. *Cretan Cults and Festivals*. New York: Barnes & Noble, 1962.

———. *The Civilization of Ancient Crete*. Berkeley: University of California Press, 1977.

Wind, Edgar. *Pagan Mysteries in the Renaissance*. New Haven: Yale University Press, 1958, 1968.

Winstanley, Gerrard. *Works*. New York: Russell and Russell, 1941, 1965.

Wittkower, Rudolf. *Architectural Principles in the Age of Humanism*. London: Academy, 1949, 1988.

Wolff, Werner. *Changing Concepts of the Bible: A Psychological Analysis of Its Words, Symbols, and Beliefs*. New York: Hermitage House, 1951.

Wolkstein, Diane and Samuel Noah Kramer. *Inanna, Queen of Heaven and Earth: Her Stories and Hymns from Sumer*. New York: Harper & Row, 1983.

Wright, G. Ernest. *Biblical Archaeology*. London: Duckworth, 1957.

Yarwood, Doreen. *The Architecture of Europe*. London: Chancellor Press, 1974.

Yates, F. Eugene. *Self-Organizing Systems: The Emergence of Order*. New York: Plenum, 1989.

Yates, Francis A. *The Valois Tapestries*. London: Routledge & Kegan Paul, 1959, 1975.

———. *Giordano Bruno and the Hermetic Tradition*. London: Routledge and Kegan Paul, 1964.

———. *The Art of Memory*. Chicago: University of Chicago Press, 1966, 1974.

———. *Theatre of the World*. Chicago: University of Chicago Press, 1969.

———. *The Rosicrucian Enlightenment*. London: Ark, 1972, 1986.

———. *Astrea: The Imperial Theme in the Sixteenth Century*. London: Routledge & Kegan Paul, 1975(a).

———. *Shakespeare's Last Plays*. London: Routledge & Kegan Paul, 1975(b).

———. *The Occult Philosophy in the Elizabethan Age*. London: Routledge & Kegan Paul, 1979.

———. "The Occult Philosophy in the Elizabethan Age." *Humanities in Review*, vol. I. Edited by R. Dworkin, K. Miller, and R. Sennett. New York: New York Institute for the Humanities, 1982a, 201–17.

———. "Lull and Bruno." In *Collected Essays*, vol. 1. London: Routledge & Kegan Paul, 1982(b).

———. *Collected Essays*. London: Routledge & Kegan Paul, 1982(c).

———. "Renaissance and Reform: The Italian Contribution." In *Collected Essays*, vol. 2. London: Routledge & Kegan Paul, 1983.

———. "Ideas and Ideals in the North European Renaissance." In *Collected Essays*, vol. 3. London: Routledge & Kegan Paul, 1984.

Young, Michael W. *The Ethnography of Malinowski: The Trobriand Islands, 1915–18*. Boston: Routledge & Kegan Paul, 1979.

Zeeman, E. Christopher. "Catastrophe Theory." *Scientific American* 234 (1976): 65–83.

———. "Differential Equations for the Heartbeat and Nerve Impulse." In *Catastrophe Theory*, edited by E. C. Zeeman. New York: Addison-Wesley, 1977, 81–140.

INDEX

Clocks, development of, 158, 166
Clock time, 28
Cognitive maps, 8, 20–28, 44, 82, 222; celestial, 158; collective/cultural (CCM), 27–28, 175, 222; double cycle in dream time, 27; individual (ICM), 27–28; wheel, 166–67
Cognitive resonance, 17
Cometophiles, 178
Comets, 58, 179–83, 197
Complex dynamical models, 67, 68–70, 211–18
Complex dynamical systems (CDS) theory, 25–26, 206, 209
Complex systems, 59
Computer: chaos models, 63, 124; graphics, 219; revolution, 124, 219
Comte, Auguste, 38, 39–40
Consciousness: bifurcations of, 49–72; emergence of, 158; evolution of, 14, 21, 27–28, 66–71, 108–9; history of/noogenesis, 14–17, 18, 67, 68, 69–70; patterns in, 17–19; unfolding of, 45
Constellations: polar, 158, 159, 160, 164; zodiacal, 160–62, 230
Coon, Carlton, 234
Cooperation: dynamical model, 214–15; international, 70. See also Partnership
Copernicus, 178–79
Cosmogonies, 114–15, 124, 125–44; Babylonian, 54, 125–30; Ovid's, 117, 174; principles, 34, 126, 145–46. See also Enuma Elish
Cosmogonification, 125
Cosmos, 125, 155–86, 230; vs. Chaos, 65, 137–44, 150, 231; as patriarchal order, 115. See also Order
Creation: as alpha point, 69; morphogenesis and, 1; in theogonies, 86
Creation myths, 65, 97, 114–15, 116, 123–36; aetiological tale, 146; Big Bang, 54; Egyptian, 130; Hesiod's Theogony as, 2; scientific, 177. See also Cosmogonies; Genesis; Theogonies
Creativity, from chaos, 73, 150, 220
Crete, 74, 89–90, 111; caves, 89, 90, 93, 111, 147; cosmogony, 131; Dionysian cult, 89, 90, 109, 111, 113, 114; goddesses/gods, 89–90, 111, 138; language, 89, 228; New Year festivals, 106; wheels, 165
Croce, Benedetto, 38
Croll, James, 204
Cro-Magnon people, 15, 62, 160–62, 199
Cross, Frank, 86, 114–15, 230
Csanyi, Vilmos, 221
Cult patterns, New Year festivals, 106–7, 133–34, 142–43
Cultural anthropology, 23–24, 41, 125, 222
Cultural cognitive maps (CCM), 27–28, 175, 222
Cultural evolution, 8–9, 32–48, 208–9, 223; Artigiani and, 25–26; autopoetic, 17; chronology, 161; in

general evolution theory, 68; schismogenesis and, 24. See also Ages; Social bifurcations
Cultural transformations. See Social transformations
Culture, concept of, 23–26
Cuneiform, 101, 164; Babylonian, 98, 126; Behiston, 101, 164; library of Assurbanipal, 103; Sumerian, 98, 126, 163
Cusanus, Nicholas, 35–36, 178–79
Cybernetics, 24–25, 67, 209
Cycles, 3, 7, 157–67; Babylonian, 52–53; business, 38; celestial, 160–63; climate, 200; double, 27; dynastic, 35; Hindu, 52; historical, 3, 8, 9, 32, 33, 35, 44, 46; mathematical concept of, 62; in Periodic Age, 62–63; terrestrial, 162–63. See also Circles

Daly, Mary, 92
Damascius, 129–30
Daniélou, Alain, 112, 116, 135, 228
Darwin, Charles, 40, 54, 97, 224
Day, Richard, 213–14
Daytime, length of, 162
Deep data, 233
Deep time, 31, 54, 55
Delphi, oracles, 147
Demeter, 90, 93, 94, 99, 116–17, 148, 229
Dendrochronology, 200–201
Dendroclimatology, 200–201, 206; proxies, 206; varves, 206
Derrida, Jacques, 232
Descartes, René, 15, 182
Desertification, Near East, 200
Determinism, Laplacian, 60, 61
Dialectical thesis-antithesis pattern, 14, 39
Diggers, 181
Dilthey, Wilhelm, 13, 16–17, 22, 38, 42, 211, 222
Diodorus Siculus, 27, 32–33, 113, 234
Dionysos/Dionysism, 92, 99–100, 111–14, 148, 228; and animal sacrifice, 112, 114, 171; as Bacchus, 117–18, 148; Crete, 89, 90, 109, 111, 113, 114; culture of, 24; mysteries, 112–14, 117, 229; New Year festival, 106
Dirichlet, Peter, 192
Disorder, chaos as, 2, 81–82, 125, 131–32, 137
Dogma, of stability, 178, 180, 194, 195, 219
Dominator society, 74, 76–77, 87, 141, 220. See also Patriarchy
Dragons: in cosmogonies, 125–26, 127, 131, 134–35, 139, 140, 231. See also Serpents
Dravidians, 89, 110, 116, 228
Dream time, 27, 28
Driesch, Hans, 67
Druids, 110
Dyads, 83; Cretan, 89–90; Egyptian, 87; Gaia/Ouranos, 147; good/evil, 139

Dynamical epochs. *See* Epochs
Dynamical historiography, 7–9, 14, 29–48, 208
Dynamical models, 1, 2, 7, 59–60, 209–18; cusp, 212; double-cusp, 212–13, 214; encyclopedia of bifurcations, 66–67; holarchic/complex, 67, 68–70, 211–18; linear, 210; nonlinear, 211; solar system, 162
Dynamical schemes, 66
Dynamical systems theory, 1–9 passim, 25, 59; bifurcations, 82, 110; cellular, 66; complex, 25–26, 206, 209; extension of, 67; gylanic resurgence waves, 142; Poincaré and, 1, 25, 58, 59, 193; sixties and, 76. *See also* Chaos theory
Dynamics, 59; celestial, 5, 158, 162–63; fluid, 124; of history, 7–9; history of, 58; origin of, 162; population, 124; systems, 209–10; terrestrial, 162–63. *See also* Dynamical systems theory; Erodynamics
Dynastic cycle, 35
Dystopian, 36

Earth, 5; dynamics, 162–63; love of, 125; orbital variations, 204–5, 206. *See also* Climate; Creation; Gaia
Econometrics, 210
Economics, dynamical models, 209, 210, 213–14
Egypt, 74, 163, 221; ages of the world, 42, 53, 223; archaeology, 42; calendar, 166, 232; chaos, 82, 88; clocks, 166; creation myths, 130; disks/tops, 164; dyads, 87; enneads, 87, 88, 130; goddesses/gods, 87–88, 118; hermetics, 221; hieroglyphs, 163–64; history of, 32; Memphis, 88, 95, 234; New Year festivals, 106, 166; Nile flooding, 166, 200; ogdoads, 87; priestly cult, 111; solar temples, 166; triads, 87–88, 95, 130; wheels, 165. *See also* Alexandria
Eisler, Riane, 20, 73–76, 141–42, 164, 169, 174, 225
Eleusis: Orphic Mysteries, 94, 113–14, 116–17, 148; trinity of, 90
Eliade, Mircea, 46
Empedokles, 54
England. *See* British Isles
Enki, 84–85, 86, 115–16, 125, 127, 137
Enneads, Egyptian, 87, 88, 130
Enuma Elish, 103–6, 116, 127–30, 137–39, 145–46, 224, 231
Epochs, 58–65, 157–58; Chaotic, 4–5, 63–64, 154, 157–58, 219; Periodic/Eros, 4, 5, 62–65, 141, 154, 219; Static/Gaian, 4, 62, 64. *See also* Ages
Erodynamics, 3, 5, 24–25, 43–44, 59, 68–70, 208–16; goal, 17; Rashevsky and, 47, 209, 211; Richardson and, 24, 43–44, 47, 209–13. *See also* Dynamical models
Eros, 2, 3, 69, 76, 92, 151; Epoch, 4, 5, 62–65, 141, 154, 219; Gaia and, 145–50; after Hesiod, 147–48; of Hesiod, 132, 146–47, 148; unification by, 174
Eternal descent and return, 99, 100–101, 116, 143, 169–71

Ethos, 24
Etiology, 146
Euridice, 112, 143, 169–74
European culture, 74, 89; Celtic, 94–95; ice ages and, 202; Old, 15, 89–90, 164; Orphic tradition, 74; periods, 42; prehistoric, 158–63, 199; wars, 45. *See also* Crete; France; Greece; Indo-Europeans; Romans
Evil, chaos as, 5, 139, 141
Evolution, 40; biological, 54, 192; of consciousness, 14, 21, 27–28, 66–71, 108–9; Gaian, 56; grok, 21; holarchic, 70; human, 57; mathematics and, 61–64; of myth, 4–5, 169, 175; universal, 40. *See also* Cultural evolution; General evolution theory
Evolutionism, 54

Fairbridge, Rhodes, 200
Feminism, 219; and Cosmos, 115; on goddess religions, 83; of male hero (Orpheus), 170–71; and matriarchal past, 4; of women historiographers, 41–42, 45
Finkelstein, David, 123, 133
Fire, domestication of, 158, 159
Flood: Babylonian story, 87, 103; biblical, 103, 185, 203; Nile, 166, 200
Florentine Renaissance, 149, 173
Four, 38, 95–96
Fourier, Charles, 36
Fowden, Garth, 112
Fractals, 48, 60
France: caves, 160; Institute for Ecotechnics, 66; Terra Amata (Nice), 64, 158–59; troubadour renaissance, 75, 142, 173
Frankfort, Mrs. H. A. Groenewegen, 128
Freud, Sigmund, 22, 194
Future, 8, 175, 206–7

Gage, Matilda Joslyn, 41–42, 45
Gaia, 2–3, 4, 69, 76, 151; and Chaos, 206; Epoch, 4, 62, 64; and Eros, 145–50; evolution, 56; after Hesiod, 147–48; of Hesiod, 132, 146–47; physiology, 206. *See also* Earth
Gaia Hypothesis, 2–3, 4, 5, 205
Gaian fevers, 64, 203, 206
Galileo, 157, 181, 194, 232
Gebser, Jean, 45
Gender, 219; partnership, 171; transformation, 89–90, 98, 109–12, 115, 127–28, 137, 173. *See also* Goddesses; Gods; Patriarchy; Women
General Evolution Research Group (GERG), 20–21, 29, 66, 225
General evolution theory, 2, 16, 25–26, 67–68; encyclopedia of bifurcations, 66–67; Spencer's, 40–41, 192. *See also* Mythogenesis
General systems theory, 16, 17, 24–25, 47, 67, 209, 222
Genesis, 116, 224; and Enuma Elish, 138–39, 224; flood story, 103, 185; Hebrew cosmogony, 132–33;

INDEX

Marriage, sacred, 99, 100, 116
Marshack, Alexander, 160
Marx, Karl, 40
Mary, 88, 96, 118, 147
Mathematical biology, 211, 222
Mathematical sociology, 209, 211
Mathematicians: chronology, 190; raconteurs, 208
Mathematics, 6, 14, 158, 220; classical analysis, 190; dawn of, 62; dynamics in, 59, 61, 68–69, 209; and evolution, 61–64; of metapatterns, 69; nonlinear oscillation theory, 61; ordinary differential equations, 61; in prehistory, 160–63; Pythagoras founding Greek, 113; and stability of solar system, 181; structuralism, 70. *See also* Chaos theory; Dynamics
Matriarchy, 4, 89, 148, 229. *See also* Partnership societies
May, Rollo, 149
Mayans: calendar, 166; toy carts, 164, 232
McKenna, Dennis, 47–48
McKenna, Terence, 2, 47–48, 168
Mechanics, 59, 70
Megalithic, stone circles, 165–66
Mellaart, James, 76, 164
Memphis, 88, 95, 234
Mesolithic, 199–200
Mesopotamia, 74, 111; chronology, 86; clocks, 166; excavations, 97–98, 101–7; Halafian, 87, 89; history, 84–87, 98–107; New Year festivals, 97–107; wheels, 82, 165. *See also* Babylonia; Sumer
Metahistory, 4
Metapatterns, 68–70
Metzner, Ralph, 69–70
Middle Ages, 15; biblical cosmogony, 54; mysteries, 118; Orpheus myth in, 173; Trivium/Quadrivium, 226
Middle East: fertile/desertification, 200; triple goddess, 92; Urban Revolution, 82. *See also* Egypt; Iran; Iraq; Mesopotamia
Migrations, seasonal, 163
Milankovitch, Milutan, 204–5
Milky Way, 127, 158, 229
Mimesis, 18
Minoans. *See* Crete
Models, 18–19, 25, 59–60; chaotic, 59, 63, 124, 195–96; climate, 205; computer-graphic, 219; concept of, 18; solar system heliocentric, 178–79; stability of solar system, 181, 195. *See also* Dynamical models
Moon: Cro-Magnon phase calculations, 62, 160; lunar theory, 190–91; lunar zodiac, 164
Moran, Hugh, 164
Moriarty, Gene, 13
Morphic resonance, 17
Morphogenesis, 1, 17–18, 41
Mummu, 86, 104, 127–30, 133, 137

Music: opera/operettas, 173–74; Orpheus and, 112
Mycenae/Mycenaeans, 74, 89, 90, 92, 165
Mysteries, 74, 116–19, 148–49; Dionysiac, 112–14, 117, 229; Eleusinian Orphic, 94, 113–14, 116–17, 148; Isis, 88, 118; Osiris, 88, 106, 113–14; Phlya, 148
Myth, 21, 26–27; ages of the world, 51–54; complex, 169, 173, 175; defined, 4, 21, 169; diffusion, 113; evolution of, 4–5, 169, 175; Orphic trinity in, 4–5, 73–151; themes, 136. *See also* Creation myths
Mythogenesis, 5, 8–9, 20–28, 169, 173–75
Mythography, 26
Mythology, 76, 82

Natura, 117, 147, 174
Nature/Natural philosophy, 14–15, 141
Neanderthal people, 158, 160
Nebular hypothesis, 192
Needham, Joseph, 67
Neem Karoli Baba, 51
Neolithic, 73–74; Agricultural Revolution, 4, 7, 62, 64, 163, 199–200; Anatolia, 89, 111, 114; creation myths, 65; Crete, 89; early, 83; goddess religion, 109, 111–12, 125, 138; migrations, 163; patriarchal vs. partnership societies, 73, 74, 164; Zagros religions, 89, 109
Neoplatonism, 75, 94; Alexandrian, 94, 95, 178; and Babylonian trinity, 129–30; and Eros, 149; trinity, 94, 95; writings, 15, 112–13
Neumann, John von, 209, 210, 229
Newton, Isaac, 5, 15, 180–81; calculus, 58, 181; and celestial stability, 60, 124, 180–85, 195; *Chronology of Ancient Kingdoms Amended*, 33, 184; dynamical systems theory created by, 1, 7; as grok hermeticist, 19; *Opticks*, 184; and ordinary differential equations, 61; and primitive sphere, 232; *Principia Mathematica*, 181, 182, 184; Vico and, 38; and Whiston, 180–85
New Year festivals, 97–107, 124, 137; Babylonian/Akitu, 100–101, 104–6, 114, 117, 129; cult patterns, 106–7, 133–34, 142–43; Egyptian, 106, 166; Indo-European, 14; Sukkot, 106, 133–34, 228
Nietzsche, F., 24, 174
Nilometers, 200
Nilsson, Martin, 115, 145–46
Nine, Egyptian, 87, 88, 130
Noogenesis, 14–17, 18, 67, 68, 69–70
Noosphere, 67, 69, 125

Observatories, astronomical, 165–66
Old Testament. *See* Bible
Omega point, 69–70
Omophagia (animal sacrifice), 112, 114, 171
One, 82–83, 139; definition, 97; God, 83, 109, 138–39, 181–82; India, 92; Neoplatonic, 94
Opera/Operettas, 173–74

Women: in historiography, 41–42, 45; misogyny toward, 171; university exclusion/inclusion, 192–93. *See also* Feminism; Goddesses; Matriarchy

World: international cooperation, 70; mundane/consensual reality, 118; mystique, 69–70; problematique, 69. *See also* Ages; Underworld

World Futures: The Journal of General Evolution, 20

Writing: alphabets, 15, 164; development of, 90, 98, 111, 158, 163–64; hieroglyphs, 97, 163–64; petroglyphs, 164. *See also* Cuneiform

Y (*upsilon*), Pythagorean, 84

Yeats, William Butler, 28

Yugas, 52

Zagreus, 89, 92, 111, 114, 117

Zagros mountains, religions, 89, 109

Zeeman, Christopher, 58, 209, 211–12

Zeus, 54, 89–94 passim, 111, 131, 147, 148

Zodiac, 160–62, 230; lunar, 164; solar, 52, 96, 164